A South-Asian History of Britain

A South-Asian History of Britain

Four Centuries of Peoples from the Indian Sub-Continent

Michael H. Fisher

Shompa Lahiri

Shinder S. Thandi

Greenwood World Publishing
Oxford / Westport, Connecticut
2007

First published by Greenwood World Publishing 2007

1 2 3 4 5 6 7 8 9 10

Greenwood World Publishing
Wilkinson House
Jordan Hill
Oxford OX2 8EJ
An imprint of Greenwood Publishing Group, Inc
www.greenwood.com

British Library Cataloguing-in-Publication Data: a catalogue record for this book is available from the British Library

Library of Congress Cataloging-in-Publication Data

Fisher, Michael Herbert, 1950–

A South-Asian History of Britain/Michael Fisher, Shompa Lahiri, and Shinder Thandi.
p. cm.
Includes bibliographical references and index.
ISBN 1-84645-008-X (alk. paper) 1. South Asians – Great Britain – History.
2. South Asians – Great Britain – Social conditions.
I. Lahiri, Shompa, 1969– II. Thandi, Shinder S. III. Title.

DA125.S57F576 2007
941′.004914 – dc22

2006039651

ISBN 978-1-84645-008-2

Designed by Fraser Muggeridge studio
Picture researched by Zooid
Typeset by TexTech
Printed and bound by Bath Press

To the many settlers from the Indian subcontinent who have made their home in Britain, including the anonymous family that graces our book cover.

Contents

Acknowledgements

We remain grateful to all the individuals and institutions that have enabled us to complete the researching and writing of this book, particularly our editor Simon Mason, who has generously provided sage and effective guidance. Considering the lives of the many South Asians who settled in Britain over four centuries has truly been a daunting task.

Many of the primary sources we have drawn upon have been carefully preserved in archives and libraries across the world: the British Library; the National Archives of India; the Maharashtra and West Bengal State Archives; National Archives, Kew; Moving Here project; Theatre Museum, London; BBC Written Archives, Caversham and in oral and visual history projects in cities such as Liverpool, Birmingham, Leicester and Coventry. We sincerely thank all the archivists and librarians at these institutions who assisted us.

Generous financial support for this research was offered by the American Council of Learned Societies, the American Institute of Indian Studies, Oberlin College and the University of Michigan. None of these organisations, however, is responsible for the contents of this book.

Introduction

From There to Here

People of South-Asian descent collectively comprise the largest ethnic minority here in Britain today. Further, the earliest arrivals of South-Asian settlers and visitors date back to about 1600, when conditions differed considerably from the present. Over four centuries, these individuals and communities have created new places for themselves in British society even as they faced and used shifting British attitudes towards them. We begin this book with the first people to reach England from the lands that are today India, Pakistan and Bangladesh. Over each subsequent chapter, we recount succeeding phases in the lives of these enterprising people and diverse, newly arriving groups, concluding with the current situation in 'multicultural Britain'.

Throughout this 400-year period, the fascinating lives of these men and women reflected and affected the larger social, cultural, political and economic conditions present in both Britain and South Asia, indeed globally. The continuing associations of these people with South Asia made them – to differing degrees – distinct from other Britons. Their status, struggles and scope for advancement resulted, at least in part, from the dramatically changing relationships between their lands of origin and their new homeland. Over the advent, expansion and end of colonialism, South Asians living here moved from being rare and exotic outsiders to integral components of British society. Some of the earliest arriving people came from the most powerful empire in the world of its day, that of the Mughals, to a relatively poor and divided island. Over the late eighteenth and nineteenth centuries, colonialism gradually reversed this relationship as Britain conquered and ruled South Asia. Over the twentieth and early twenty-first centuries, Britain's colonial empire has given way to the Commonwealth, even as the new nations of South Asia have developed their post-colonial places in the world during a period of enhanced globalisation. This book considers the histories of South Asians in Britain not as an off-shoot of race relations or defined by white racist definitions of them, but rather in their own terms, from their own perspectives.

Categories of Definition

Issues of identity, which remain a continuing theme, are central to this book: the identities chosen by the (diverse) South Asians themselves and those imposed on them, legally and popularly, by white British society. In order to develop a continuous narrative, we have used the idea that there was a general 'South-Asian' identity throughout these four centuries, for both individuals and communities. Yet, that concept has not in practice been consistently defined and applied over time. In the early seventeenth century, for example, neither 'South Asia' nor 'Britain' existed as we think of them today in the twenty-first century. Many early settlers and visitors never considered themselves part of a single South-Asian community. Rather, they identified with their home region, religious community, class or gender. The terms 'South-Asian', 'Asian', 'Asian-British', 'Indian', 'Pakistani' and 'Bangladeshi' only gradually and relatively recently came into common currency. Indeed, who exactly should be included in each of these categories, and what that inclusion actually means, remains disputed even today. Nonetheless, for clarity and simplicity, we have projected the term 'South-Asian' back in time, aware of the strategic choice this entails.

While we have concentrated on people from the lands that are today the nations of India, Pakistan and Bangladesh, we have occasionally found that people from Sri Lanka and Nepal need to be included as well. The boundaries of today's nation states hardly contain the diversity of real peoples' experiences, especially those who travelled over great distances and settled in new lands. In the later chapters, people of South-Asian descent who had settled in Africa – sometimes for generations prior to coming to Britain – appear as integral parts of this history. Yet, we have consistently excluded from our study people of entirely European descent, even if their families had long settled in South Asia before returning to Britain. Nor do we include people of part-South-Asian descent who have largely left behind the South-Asian origins of their ancestors and merged into the majority community in Britain. Thus the boundaries we have used have a cultural rather than a biological basis.

We also understand how the roles and experiences in Britain of South-Asian men and women of various social and economic classes have differed from each other over these four centuries. Settlers, for instance, interacted with Britons somewhat differently from short-term visitors.

Particularly in the early period, when people from South Asia were relatively rare in Britain, most Britons had little knowledge of South Asians which provided more scope for self-representation than in later periods when British stereotypes about them had developed.

Overall, the structures of both South-Asian and British societies tended to empower men over women, at least those within the same or lower economic class. A woman from South Asia who married a British man often took on the status of her husband, depending on how he regarded and treated her. A further consequence of these gender disparities has been that Indian men often had power over British women of their own class or lower, either as wife or servant. Finally, the historical record often highlights men rather than women, although we have made special efforts to include women's life histories where surviving evidence allows.

In addition, the strong class divisions that have existed historically in Britain and South Asia have meant that South Asians of different economic status have met with varying degrees of acceptance and social empowerment here. South-Asian seamen, servants, manual labourers and other members of the working classes who came to Britain lived here quite differently than princes, diplomats, scholars, businessmen and professionals who made the same journey. Indian working-class seamen and servants both merged into, and conflicted with, working-class Britons and other immigrants like Irish and African-Caribbean peoples. Moreover, all these working-class people were classed together by the British elites. By contrast, wealthy and aristocratic people from South Asia often found acceptance by their British peers and hired British servants to attend to their wants. Several South Asians have entered Parliament representing British voters and have entered or married into the British aristocracy.

Religious affiliation also affected the relationships between South Asians and Britons: until the late nineteenth century, sizable numbers of South-Asian settlers converted to Anglican Christianity, at least nominally. Only, much later, after substantial and ongoing South-Asian communities had developed in Britain did South Asians find they could practice their own religious traditions with relative degrees of acceptance. Yet, even today, one's apparent religious affiliation shapes how other people in Britain, both white and South-Asian Britons, respond.

Nonetheless, South Asians shared with other non-whites in Britain many aspects of the treatment meted out by (some) white Britons to immigrants. These are highlighted in some of the later chapters of this book though they are woven into larger themes that have persisted over the longer period. Thus, while this book presents a South-Asian History of Britain, it really contains many different histories which we intertwine.

Different Histories of South Asians in Britain

This book comes at a dynamic moment in the ongoing history of South Asians in Britain. Developments in the post-Second World War period of decolonisation and aspects of new forms of globalisation have deeply affected their lives and the ways in which their histories have been written. Attitudes among white Britons have never been uniform and have changed over time. Yet, especially since the 1960s, nativist white British hostility to the markedly larger number of South-Asian immigrants has at times increased. Part of that nativist agenda has been to portray a historically insular all-white England under threat from newly arriving non-white aliens. Enoch Powell's famous 'rivers of blood' speech, the National Front and the British National Party have all argued a right-wing, racist British view virulently opposed to all non-white immigrants.

In response, many committed community activists and scholars have opposed white racism by working to bring together in solidarity all 'black' Britons and to reconstruct 'British History' so that it reflects the presence and contributions, as well as the struggles, of all black people in Britain. A growing number of commentators have tried to recuperate the hitherto unrecognised accomplishments and contributions of a distinctive black community in Britain, historically shared by all non-whites. Their goal was a unified front of South Asians and Africans against white racial prejudices; as Ron Ramdin argued in 1999, black is 'a "political colour"'.[1] In this contest, all sides have tried to rewrite British history in light of their own political commitments, often mapping contemporary concepts onto the past.

Such categorisations, however, presuppose that the concept of 'race' has always separated people on the basis of biological inheritance. This concept of fixed and physical race, however, only gradually came into British society. It originated with the perceived need by British colonial officials to distinguish themselves, and all Europeans, from the vastly larger number of South Asians over whom they wanted to rule. Thus, in Britain, at various moments in the last two centuries, people from South Asia, Africa and the Caribbean (and occasionally Irish and Jewish people) have been collectively called 'black' by some Britons, both 'white' and 'black'. Indeed, there have been times and places where working-class or indigent Africans and Indians especially came together due to shared experiences. While we recognise how some white Britons have held prejudices against non-whites living here, we also recognise the variety of the experiences of settlers from Asia, Africa, and the Caribbean. The quite dissimilar dimensions of the European slave trade in Africa and Asia and their separate colonial histories have meant that most Indians and Africans had varying experiences in Britain. Based on their words and actions throughout history, most Indians and Africans and their descendants in Britain have regarded their histories and situations as distinct. Hence, given the book's already vast scope, Africans and other non-white settlers appear primarily for comparison when closely identified with Indians.

Many of the people we are studying have either rejected, ignored or embraced any single classification, preferring rather to highlight one or more of their identities by religion, regional-origin, economic class, and/or gender. Though some community activists have sought to enhance the solidarity of all 'black' peoples in Britain, others have deliberately sought to prevent the distinctive identity of their particular community from being lumped with all other non-whites.

Among recent scholars, Rozina Visram has compiled the most extensive documentation about South Asians in Britain. Through painstaking archival research and interviews with descendants of Indian settlers, she has assembled an extensive narrative of '400 Years of History' up through the 1950s, stressing the contributions of Indians living in Britain and tracing the development of their communities from the mid-nineteenth century onwards. We have all learned much from her pioneering work in this field, which has not been as widely recognised as it should have been. Building on her writings, this book develops a more chronological analysis, studying how class, race and gender affected the lives of diverse Indian peoples from the earliest times up to the present.

In recent decades, religion-based community identities have become ever more salient. In the later chapters of this book, we see how current international and global conflicts, which many have tried to couch in terms of religion, variously affect the lives of people identified (or self-identified) as Sikhs, Hindus or Muslims in Britain. The Sikh, Khalistan and Hindutva movements of the 1980s and 1990s resonated in both India and Britain, as politicians tried to mobilise and unify their own religious communities over and against the others. Especially in the last decade, a Muslim's faith has seemed more important than his or her regional, class or gender identity. Furthermore, there are clear differences of prosperity among the different South-Asian communities in today's Britain and different degrees of cooperation with the majority population. By taking a long historical perspective, this book shows how ideas about community identity developed and changed over time – trends which reveal they to be recent and constructed rather than eternal or fixed, however, when seen in the larger historical trajectory of four centuries.

From the Earliest Arrivals to the British Empire

People from South Asia have been coming to England for about as long as Britons have been sailing to India at the start of the seventeenth century. Indian sailors, male and female servants and the wives of Englishmen comprised the first people to sail here. They found that few in the host society had much knowledge about India or what someone from India was actually like. This unfamiliarity provided these early visitors and settlers with opportunities to explain themselves in creative ways. Furthermore, the developing class, religions and other divisions within Britain often enabled these incoming people to relate themselves in advantageous ways to the local society. Many of the South-Asian seamen and servants who settled here married British people of their own working class. South-Asian merchants hired British servants and also interacted socially – and in the law-courts – with British elites.

Living in Britain, however, required South Asians to adapt. Most people in Britain in the seventeenth and early eighteenth centuries regarded religion as a crucial part of a person's identity: people from India who appeared to be Christian, even nominally so, were accepted more readily than Muslims, Hindus or Parsis. Similarly, those who adopted British fashions appeared more approachable, if less exotic. And, since much of English socialising took place around shared dining and drinking, South Asians who adapted to British cuisine mixed more easily than those who retained their distinct customs. It remained a fact that although the colonial conquests of South Asia had not yet commenced, the early Indians were mainly dependents – travelling to Britain on East India Company ships, often as employees of Britons. The small numbers of South Asians who settled in Britain mixed into the local society rather than forming their own communities.

After the 1750s, the East India Company began a century of dramatic conquests in South Asia. The resulting shifts in military, political and economic power broadened the classes of South-Asian people wishing to travel to Britain. These changes also affected South-Asian attitudes towards Britons once they arrived here as well as their reception. Indian royalty, including the Mughal Emperor himself, began to send diplomatic delegations to London to negotiate with their new British colonial rivals and rulers. Expanding trade between South Asia and Britain attracted Indian merchants, both for profit and also to reverse injustices perpetrated against them by British colonial officials. Indian scholars, students, officials and tourists ventured to Britain to educate, advance or amuse themselves in the land that had come to rule theirs. Some stayed on, marrying and settling in British society; most remained only temporarily. But some educated South Asians began to write books about their experiences in Britain, either writing in English for a British audience or in Persian for educated readers back in India.

By the early nineteenth century, British colonial expansion across South Asia was transforming relations between South Asians and Britons, in Britain as well as in South Asia. By then, Britons thought they knew what being an Indian meant, and this shaped the lives of South Asians here, limiting their scope for self-representation.

Nonetheless, some proved able to profit from these British images of South Asia. At least one Indian restaurant – the 'Hindostanee Coffee House', established in 1810 by Dean Mahomed – purveyed South-Asian cuisine to Britons seeking a taste of 'the East'. Later, Mahomed became a famous surgeon by providing what Britons believed to be exotic South-Asian medical therapies. In London's East End, near the docks where East India ships discharged South-Asian seamen, a transient South-Asian community began to develop, drawing on the increased numbers of South-Asian seamen – nearly a thousand a year – arriving in London. Indian servants in Britain seeking companionship and familiar Indian-style foods also joined the community.

By the mid-nineteenth century, virtually all Indians lived under British 'high colonialism', either under direct British rule or indirect, in India's remaining princely states. Consequently, ever larger numbers of South-Asian men and women made places for themselves in British society and, though they did so now in the light of the colonial subjugation of their homelands, many of them adjusted themselves to British expectations and prospered. Indian aristocrats, including pensioned princes, found that their status and wealth brought them freedom and pleasure among their peers in Britain. Indian scholars, students and businessmen made places for themselves among Britons of their own class. And the closing of the East India Company's barracks led to the opening of the 'Oriental Quarter' further east in London's docklands, an unofficial but distinctly South-Asian community largely run by entrepreneurs, often assisted by their British women partners. Yet, South Asians of all classes felt deepening white-British prejudice against them and their homelands, a hostility peaking during the bloody conflict of 1857 which pitted Britons against many north Indians, with brutalities on both sides. The subsequent closure of the East India Company marked the termination of the first 250-year-long period of relations between South-Asians and Britons and led to the new era of the British Raj in India, with all its attendant effects on the lives of South-Asians in Britain.

Strangers, Sojourners, Settlers

The year 1857 was significant in Indo-British relations, both on the subcontinent and in Britain. Not only did the 1857 Indian uprising form the prelude to the transfer of India from Company to Crown rule in 1858 and the subsequent hardening of British attitudes towards India and Indians, 1857 was also the year the Strangers Home opened in Limehouse, London, to meet the welfare and perceived spiritual needs of Indian seamen and other non-Europeans. Despite sustained missionary activity among working-class South Asian men and women, however, many – but not all – South Asians resisted conversion. The construction of the Suez Canal in 1869, which reduced journey time from India to Britain, and the easing of Hindu restrictions on sea-voyages encouraged more South Asians to travel to Britain in the late nineteenth century. Among those able to take advantage of these developments were colonial India's western-educated urban elite, comprising students, social reformers, royalty and tourists. The published accounts of these men and women expressed both admiration for, and stinging criticism of, British society and politics.

By the end of the Victorian era, Indians had become increasingly visible in Britain's streets, homes, docks, courts, parks, buses, trains, workhouses, Inns of courts, medical institutions, universities and

Parliament. As both sojourners and settlers, South Asians inhabited all walks of British life, continuing to shape the social, economic and political landscape of both imperial Britain and colonial India. To describe Britain's South-Asian population in the period prior to the early twentieth century as 'miniscule',[2] comprising a handful of princes and a couple of hundred Ayahs and lascars (as one commentator has), misrepresents the diversity and significance of the Victorian Indian presence which ranged from ayahs to appellants, paupers to princes, seamen to social reformers and performers to politicians. The absence of reliable statistical data makes attempts to determine the exact size of imperial Britain's South-Asian presence very difficult, but its variety is beyond doubt.

The early twentieth century was a period of particular state interest in the activities of South Asians, both as groups and individuals. In the First World War, the British government sent Indian soldiers to the South Coast to receive medical treatment. In the inter-war period, Indian seamen in Britain had to fight to maintain their rights as imperial subjects when their citizenship was challenged through the Coloured Alien Seamen's Order. Indian peddlers, who were coming to Britain in increasing numbers, suffered from measures taken by the government to restrict their employment and travel rights. Indian women activists joined women's suffrage and feminist politics in Britain in order to claim citizenship rights and gender equality. At the same time, other South Asians sought to relinquish imperial citizenship in favour of Indian nationality, through political organisations such as the India League, which campaigned for Indian Independence. Passports granted to Indians travelling to Britain in the 1930s reveal a wide array of occupations, reflected in the proliferation of British, South-Asian journals and social, political and religious associations.

The Second World War further exposed the conflicting loyalties of some South Asians in Britain. While many were keen to join the war effort, others rejected participation in an 'imperialist war'. The campaign for decolonisation on the Indian subcontinent, in which many South Asians in Britain had participated, finally culminated in Indian and Pakistani Independence in 1947. But though the majority of South Asians in Britain returned to the subcontinent in this period, some chose to take up permanent residence. Indeed, links can be made between pioneering Sylheti seamen, Punjabi peddlers and factory workers, who settled in Britain before 1947, and some of the key communities that make up Britain's contemporary South-Asian population.

Decolonisation and Post-War Migration

Although India and Pakistan won their independence in 1947, there was a heavy price: the Indian subcontinent witnessed the bloodiest period in its history, as the two most strategic states of the British-Indian Empire, Bengal and the Punjab, were partitioned. In addition to the communal killings – estimated to be between 200,000 and 1 million – and the abduction of thousands of women and children, millions were uprooted and dislocated, creating the biggest refugee movement of the twentieth century. In Punjab alone, 5.5 million Hindus and Sikhs moved eastwards into India, and 6 million Muslims moved westward into Pakistan, all in a matter of few months. This colossal event provided the context for the start of the last phase of migration of South Asians to Britain covered in this book, with many refugees migrating to Britain, from East and West Punjab, Kashmir, East Pakistan (after 1971, Bangladesh) and Sri Lanka. Obviously there was some continuity with the earlier types of migrants, but the new mass migration, especially in its early phase, was dominated by Punjabis, not least because of the imperial connection through the army.

As in previous periods, these new 'ready-made' subcontinental migrants faced great racial hostility as 'unwelcome guests'. The pattern of their settlement was shaped by a number of factors: their limited means, meagre skills and family and village connections, and by the 1970s, that pattern is clearly visible, with rapidly developing South-Asian communities in metropolitan areas and towns where unskilled jobs, mainly in manufacturing, were more readily available. At this point, a political reaction set in. Limits were placed on further fresh migration by successive British governments influenced by continuing public hostility – though, subsequently, political events in East Africa were to force the British government to (grudgingly) allow thousands of East African Asians to enter the UK. This not only enlarged the size of the British-Asian community but, importantly, also changed its composition, as these latter arrivals came with considerable personal resources, skills and experiences. The most dramatic effect of this was the emergence of a significant South-Asian middle class, which counter-balanced the migrants of the 1950s and 1960s, who had come mainly from rural backgrounds. As their communities grew in size and confidence, these South-Asian settlers transplanted their roots in British soil more firmly and began a process of political and civic engagement – at first not always successful – to win cultural and religious rights. This process accelerated with the emergence of a British-born, second generation of South Asians, particularly in education and the workplace. For many individuals and communities, however, the relative economic success was abruptly shattered by the Thatcherite free-market policies of the early 1980s, which accelerated the decline in British manufacturing, on which so many South Asians depended for their livelihoods. Depressingly, economic decline and restructuring caused further racial tensions, especially in socially deprived areas with immigrant settlement, but the early 1980s was also the period when a more politicised South-Asian youth mobilised themselves against racist and fascist organisations such as the National Front.

Towards the end of the decade, as the ideology of multiculturalism prevailed, South-Asian achievement began to be acknowledged, with increasing numbers of South Asians excelling in business, politics, education, music, media and – famously – the culinary industry. Currently, South Asians are relatively well represented in Parliament and other civic institutions. However, as clearly demonstrated by the 1991 and 2001 census data, South-Asian communities have not shared equally in this success. Inequalities in education, housing and health and discrepancies in occupational patterns and unemployment rates were clearly apparent, not just between British and Muslim communities, but also between Muslim and non-Muslim communities. Academics have identified a significant Muslim 'underclass', especially after the racial disturbances and rioting in the summer of 2001. Many observers have pointed to a disconnection between white British society and Muslims, suggesting that the latter live 'parallel lives', but nothing tangible has so far been proposed to address such structural inequalities. The emergence of 'home-grown', Muslim suicide-bombers in July 2005, so shocking to the British public, at least in part, need to be related back to the inequalities, alienation and powerlessness which many young Muslims experience and the allure of radical Islam as a potential remedy.

The growth in radicalism among South-Asian youth, focused now on religious identity politics, and a general backlash against the British brand of multiculturalism, has led to a furious debate about British identity. Is the increased importance of religious identity (a development promoted, and indeed, often funded, by multicultural policies) a reaction to the perceived exclusivist nature of British identity or a deliberate move towards separateness influenced by global identity politics? This is a complex question and Britain is currently struggling hard to find workable solutions to it. After 400 years of South-Asian presence in Britain, it represents the greatest challenge facing both the British State and British-South Asians.

Authorship

Although this book stands as an integrated narrative, the distinctive interests of the three authors inevitably emerge. The first four chapters were primarily composed by Michael H. Fisher who was trained as an historian of South Asia and has studied the early history of relations between South Asians and Britons in Britain and South Asia. The two chapters on the ninety years between 1857 and 1947 are the work of Shompa Lahiri. She was trained in British imperial and Indian colonial history and has researched colonial travel and migration from South Asia to the West. The final two chapters, covering the period after the Second World War, are the work of Shinder S. Thandi. He was trained in development economics and international political economy and has also examined different dimensions of the lives of Indians, particularly Punjabi, diaspora communities.

Note: We respect the spellings of people's names that they themselves used, although they did not all do so consistently, especially for the earlier period.

Chapter 1

Earliest South-Asian Visitors and Settlers during the Pre-colonial Period, *c.*1600–1750s

Michael H. Fisher

Questions of Identity and Location in the Early Period

People from South Asia have been venturing to the British Isles since at least the early seventeenth century, about as long as people from England have sailed to India. Some Asians came as seamen or skilled artisans, others as wives travelling with their husbands, some as servants or slaves, still others as merchants seeking profits and justice. They made this long and dangerous sea voyage for a range of reasons, and met with receptions that varied over time which also depended on how they presented themselves and how they were perceived by Britons. A few married and settled down in England, but most only visited – for months or for years at a time – before returning home. At first, few Britons understood what being Asian really meant; this gave these earliest Indians the opportunity to explain themselves and their homeland in their own terms. While their numbers remained modest during this period, their lives in Britain reflected their diversity and the exchanges that preceded colonialism.

During the 150 years addressed in this chapter, both India and England changed radically. In 1600, the Mughal Empire (founded 1526) was rapidly conquering most of South Asia. Its fabled wealth and luxury goods attracted merchants and adventurers from Europe as well as from elsewhere in Asia. Yet, tensions and conflicts continued among regional rulers and various communities across India, leading various groups and individuals to seek new opportunities, even by working with or for the relatively few and exotic Europeans among them.

The England of Queen Elizabeth was internally conflicted with Protestants versus Catholics, merchants versus aristocrats, urban versus rural, workers versus employers/landlords, among many other divides. Yet, England was beginning to strive outward across the globe dispatching ships, to trade as well as to plunder, to Asia as well as the Americas and Africa. One of Queen Elizabeth's more consequential acts

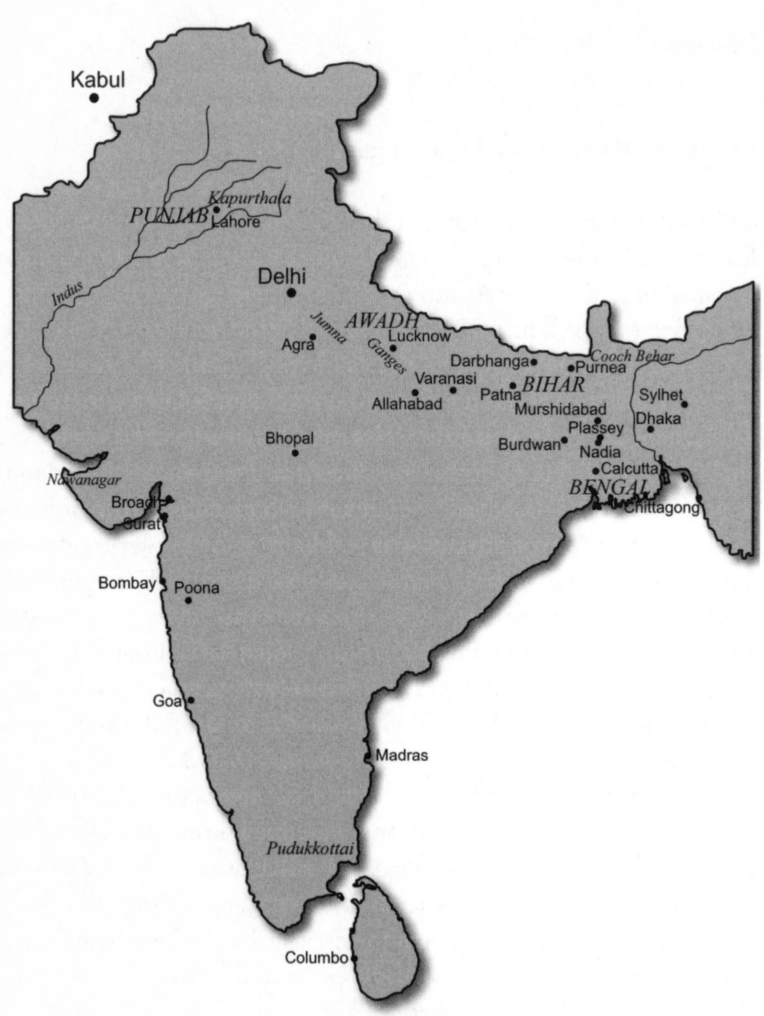

Map 1: Origins of Visitors to Britain from the Indian Sub-Continent, pre-1947.

Map 2: South-Asian Presence in Britain, pre-1947.

was that of chartering the East India Company in 1600, giving this body of merchants a monopoly over all English trade in the lands from southern Africa to the Philippines. She thus empowered the stockholders of this corporation to pool resources and collectively rent ships, hire men and create the organisation that would begin to explore commercial opportunities in Asia. While the East India Company had its own complex history of challenges, re-organisations and internal divisions, for 250 years it remained the main employer of Indians coming to Britain, its ships provided the main means of their transport and its head-quarters represented one of the main authorities with whom most Indians dealt during their lives here.

By the 1750s, conditions within both Britain and South Asia and the relations between them had shifted drastically. England and Scotland had ended their bloody fight and had united. The British commercial middle classes were rising towards economic and political power, based in part on profitable international trade and on 'gentlemanly capitalism'. The East India Company embodied the premier example of these economic, political and social processes. In contrast, the Mughal Empire had long been fragmenting as regional states broke off and new groups arose to pursue their own interests. Among the most dynamic forces in India were those of the English East India Company and its growing number of allies and rivals – Indian and European. For many Indians, these shifts meant new prospects and incentives for travel and employment in Britain, but also changing receptions and roles in society once they arrived here.

Over this period, particular patterns arose in the ways South Asians participated in the British society. Not all people were equally willing to make the long and dangerous journey from India to this distant, relatively small, and not yet particularly prosperous island. Communities with traditions of long-distance travel – including Muslims, Parsis and people of mixed Asian and Portuguese and other European ancestry – proved more willing to travel than high-born Hindus, especially given the Brahminic avoidance of pollution that one inevitably encountered across the 'Black Waters'.

British society, wracked by sectarian conflicts at home and wars on the continent, from the beginning weighed heavily the religious identity of the Indians among them. The English had long been battling, and often losing to, Ottoman Muslims in the Mediterranean; thus, popular and official attitudes towards Muslims in Britain were mixed. On one hand,

Britons valued and assimilated many commodities associated with Muslims, including coffee, muslin and other exotic cloth. On the other, Muslims represented a dangerous, and often triumphant, enemy in the East. In contrast, India's other religious communities remained largely unknown – curious, attractive, and yet alien and heretical. Thus, those Indians in Britain who remained by name and habit visibly Muslim, Parsi or Hindu necessarily distanced themselves from the local population, a distance that some Indians may have sought, but others found an unwanted distraction from their worldly pursuits. Indeed, most Indian men and women who settled here during this time took European names, married Britons and converted (at least nominally) to one or another form of Christianity. Once Christian, these settlers customarily found acceptance as full members of local Anglican or Catholic congregations, deserving of welfare as needed and worthy of all the sacraments including baptism for their children and burial among other parishioners.

In Britain, socio-economic class has always had powerful effects in defining a person's identity, with subtle and not so subtle identifying markers for each class. Since people coming from India did not have easily decipherable class markers, they had some scope for mobility, although their occupations and incomes revealed their class to some extent. The largest number of arriving Asians were working class men and women, particularly seamen and servants, including domestic slaves. Like almost all working class people of their age in Europe or Asia, few of these people were noticed as individuals or documented for history. Nonetheless, some drew official attention by appealing for work or assistance or by allegedly committing crimes. Some entered the households of the British elite; a few of these appeared as 'trophy servants' who brought distinction to those households, memorialised in valuable portraits. Life for most Indian working-class people remained a constant struggle, however, as it was for most Europeans of that class during that age. Some Indians who reached Britain had been enslaved in India and occasionally gained freedom after their arrival. Slavery in India or for Indians in Britain, however, rarely reached the level of brutality of chattel slavery as imposed by Europeans on people of African descent in the Americas. Further, the East India Company sought to constrain all working class Indians in Britain through various means including a system of bonds.

In part because of popular ignorance, in part because the East India Company's territorial monopoly stretched from southern Africa to the

Philippines, people from India and people from Africa appeared largely the same to some Britons. The East India Company's own records identify some people brought from Africa and also people of European descent who had settled in India as 'Indian'. Other Britons recognised distinctions among these peoples, particularly those of the middle and upper classes.

Women and men in this period held quite unequal positions in British society, legally and culturally; they did in somewhat different ways in South Asia as well. Some classes of Indians in Britain, particularly seamen, were all male; those who settled in Britain almost always married British women. Other classes, including Asian servants, comprised about the same numbers of men and women; some married each other, others with native Britons. Some of the Indian merchants and other elites who travelled to Britain brought their families and servants with them, and met socially with Britons of their own status. Since fewer European women went to Asia than men, various Indian women came back to Britain with their European husbands or lovers, and often with their children. Once in Britain, these men and women had to negotiate the cultural norms and conventions of their own class and gender as practiced by Britons.

First Encounters in London

While for centuries much of the history of South Asians in Britain remained intertwined with that of the East India Company, some people from India made their way to England independently of it. Early in 1607, when word spread in London that the Company was sending its first ships to India, four Indian men who were already in England sought work on these ships and so journey home. Unfortunately, we cannot know exactly when or how these four arrived in England or the ways they lived here. These men may have come via Portugal, which a century earlier had established enclaves along India's coasts and occasionally brought back Indian seamen or workers. All four men used European-style names. Perhaps they chose names they felt would be more familiar to Europeans, or else they had these names imposed on them by their European employers; they might also have been converts, even nominally, to Christianity; or they might have been people of part or all Portuguese descent who had settled in India. Each of them had found life in London difficult, and as working-class men, they received only mixed receptions from the Company.

One of these men, who called himself 'Marcus the Indian', was hired to join the crew on one of these first Company ships bound for India. Since he claimed to lack the proper clothing to undertake the journey, the Company ordered that he be provided with a 'gown and other necessities' – the cost of which they probably docked from his pay. The Company, however, regarded him in an inferior light, specifying that the clothing should only be of a quality 'fit for such a dissolute person as he is'.[1] Whatever nautical skills that he possessed, and whatever knowledge of India that he could pass on to the Company's ship captains, apparently were not highly valued.

At about the same time, 'John Mendis the Indian' and 'John Rodrigoe the Indian' separately wrote to the Company seeking relief from their hardships in London. In the tragic case of Rodrigoe, the Company could not come to a decision whether to grant his request and appoint him to a place on this first fleet bound for India until after it was too late: the ships departed at the end of March 1607 without him. In June that year, Rodrigoe wrote from prison, seeking aid from the Company in securing his release; his letter does not state what he had allegedly done to run afoul of the law, but he may have been imprisoned for debt. His subsequent appeals expressed his hope that the Company would intervene to free him as well as provide him a passage home to India with the next fleet. Yet another of his fruitless petitions followed in August. The Company felt responsible enough to him that his letters received its consideration, but not so responsible that it actually provided any aid. Indeed, before the Company had decided what to do about him, he died in December, only days before the next fleet was due to depart for India. The Company thereupon felt obliged enough to him that it sold some of its lumber to pay his debts and, evidently, his minimal burial expenses.

Yet another man, 'John Taro the Indian', had earlier found work with the Company in London. In February 1607, the Company ordered that £5 out of his wages were to be garnished to pay his debt to an Englishwoman, Katherine Gibson. Since this was a substantial amount of money for a working-class man at that time (with the purchasing power of over £600 today), he may have been a skilled artisan. Similarly, in 1609, the Company approved a petition from 'John, the Indian', who 'having by some mishap lost his thumb, and not being able to work at his trade as a weaver, to be employed about the ships as he requests'.

Thus, we have tantalising but fragmentary evidence about various working-class people from India who had travelled to London on their own and then struggled to make places for themselves here, even before the East India Company launched its first ships towards India.

First Encounters in India

In addition to 'Marcus the Indian', these first East India Company ships to reach India in 1608 carried on board an ambassador, William Hawkins, a man only in his twenties but already well travelled, designated to represent both the East India Company and King James jointly before Mughal Emperor Jahangir (*r.* 1605–1627).[2] After these ships arrived at Surat on India's west coast, much depleted of manpower through the deaths of many in their crews, they recruited Asian seamen to sail home. Thus began an ever-expanding flow of Indian seamen who sailed British ships to London. As we will see, the English government and the East India Company soon instituted laws and policies that controlled the numbers and careers of these Asian seamen.

When these first East India Company's ships sailed away from Surat, Hawkins proceeded with a small party to the Mughal imperial court at Agra. His mission was to beg permission from Emperor Jahangir for a permanent English outpost (a 'factory') where East India Company factors could begin to purchase the fine cloth, spices and other luxury goods produced in such abundance by Indian artisans. During his tumultuous years at the Mughal imperial court, Hawkins married an Indian noblewoman, Mariam, the orphaned Armenian Christian ward of the Mughal imperial family. Since no Christian priest was available, Hawkins' servant, Nicholas Ufflet, presided; as soon as they encountered a priest later during their travel, they remarried. When Hawkins sailed back to England in 1612 on board a later fleet of East India Company ships, Mariam accompanied him, leaving behind her disapproving mother and brothers. This voyage via South Africa, however, proved typically deadly. Most of the ship's company and passengers died, including Hawkins. Further, contrary winds drove the ships to Waterford, Ireland, in September 1613, where widowed Mariam buried Hawkins.

Mariam finally reached London early in 1614, but not alone. She travelled with Gabriel Towerson, an English merchant and captain of the ship *Hector*, which had sailed in their fleet. Soon after Mariam and Towerson reached London, they married in Saint Nicholas Acons Parish Church. Mariam's new husband, Towerson, had spent years in south-east Asia but his interactions with Asians and Africans were far less sympathetic than Hawkins' had been. This included his relations with his new wife, Mariam. Their first years in London, however, apparently went successfully.

In London, Mariam and Towerson took their complex financial affairs before the Company. In particular, her late husband, Hawkins, had borrowed £300 from his brother, Charles, who now wanted this money back from his widow, Mariam. They all agreed that the Company would arbitrate this dispute and also settle accounts among Hawkins, Mariam, Towerson and the Company itself. In these negotiations, Mariam made a good impression. The governing committee of the Company, 'being charitably affected towards' her, forgave her the debts of her late husband, and gave her £250 'as a token of their love' and in exchange for her 'general release' of the Company for all remaining monies due to Hawkins. Less than a week later, however, Hawkins' servant Nicholas Ufflet (who had presided at her first wedding to Hawkins in Agra) revealed that Mariam was not destitute as the Company had supposed, but rather possessed diamonds and other precious stones worth some £6,000. Nevertheless, the Company reconfirmed its agreement and paid her the £250 it had promised. Under English law, a married woman's money came under the control of her husband, in her case Towerson.

During Mariam's stay in London, other people also labelled 'Indian' also lived here. In 1614, three Indian sailors petitioned the Company that they could take their English wives on board with them on the voyage back to India. The Company, however, replied that it was unfitting 'for such women to go among so many unruly sailors', arranging instead that some of the Indians' wages be paid in London to their wives here.

Further, from this time onwards, young Indian men began to come to London for their education. Mariam may have personally known a young man from Surat who reached London on 19 August 1614, soon after her. He studied English and Latin, proving particularly noteworthy to the English for his desire for conversion to Christianity. The Company allowed him £13 annually for expenses and expected him to return to India as 'an instrument in converting some of his nation'. After consultation with the Archbishop of Canterbury, the Lord Mayor and King James, this boy was baptised 'Peter' in St Dionis Backchurch,

Fenchurch Street (near the Company's headquarters) on 22 December 1616.[3] This man later returned to India to evangelise, reporting in Latin to his spiritual mentors. Mariam, as a Christian from birth and an elite Englishman's wife, apparently entered London society differently than Indian converts and students.

In 1616, Mariam's second husband, Towerson, received a commission from the Company to return to India. With him went Mariam in style, served by English attendants: a 'gentle waiting woman', Mrs Frances Webb, a female companion, Mrs Hudson, and several servants. Towerson hoped his wife's connections would gain him political influence and wealth in India. Their financial hopes and marriage, however, both deteriorated. By 1618, tensions between Towerson and Mariam had worsened. He departed to seek his fortune elsewhere. Unwilling or unable to leave with him, Mariam remained in Agra, attended by her mother and only one of her servants, a young English boy. Towerson left her merely Rs 200, which she soon expended. Towerson failed to send her more, despite pleas from other Company officials that he provide Mariam with alimony. We do not know Mariam's final fate but Towerson went out as the Company's principal merchant in Amboyna, where the Dutch executed him in 1623. Learning of this massacre, the Company paid the money owing to the late Towerson to his brother, rather than to Mariam. Mariam's two English marriages, which might be considered 'inter-racial', did not to our knowledge evoke any adverse comment in London at that time. Indeed, John Dryden made her the noble heroine of his patriotic play, *Amboyna (c.*1673).[4] Like Mariam, Indian wives of British men would return with them to Britain over subsequent centuries. Most Britons of their day regarded these women's personal identities as subordinated to those of their husband. Hence, formal history has often failed to note them as individuals or their (or their children's) participation in the British society.

Indian Seamen Work the Passage to Britain

Throughout most of the period covered in this book, the largest number of Asians who came to Britain were seamen. Particularly on the return voyage to Britain, many British ships recruited Indian seamen to replace European seamen who had died, deserted or been conscripted by the

Royal Navy. After their arrival in Britain, some Indian seamen married and settled; their work patterns meant, however, that many more remained for only the few cold winter months between sailing seasons.

Most Indian seamen did not work their way to Britain alone. Instead, they served in maritime labour gangs: men who worked together as lascars (from *lashkar*, or *khalasi*, 'a group of armed men, an army'). They took employment as a group, and worked under their own petty officers: a *serang* ('headman') and his assistant, *tindal* ('head of a work-gang'). Lascar referred to their terms of employment, rather than their ethnicity; so men with very diverse religious, regional and caste backgrounds often worked in a single maritime labour-gang. Despite their diversity, lascars on a voyage seem generally to have bonded with each other. Consequently, in Britain, most did not seek to integrate themselves into local society and, as a group, often stood in adversarial relationships with the British establishment.

Lascars and their petty officers generally had salaries quite comparable with other Indians and Britons of their class. Lascar salaries ranged considerably over time and specific conditions, but in the early seventeenth century were roughly 15–22s. monthly (equivalent to £56–£83 in today's purchasing power) plus provisions, considerably above British sailors at that time. Indeed, Company officials in India complained about what they considered these excessively high demands. For example, during 1637–1638, an English official in South India wrote of the need to hire 'these country people at extraordinary great wages to sayle in our ships', due to the shortage of European seamen.[5] Further, captains and Company officials perceived Indian lascars as generally less productive: physically weaker and less willing to fight an enemy than Britons. Yet, the rising demand for lascars further lifted their wages to 23–30s. during the mid-eighteenth century. Indian petty officers got appropriately higher wages: 28–40s. monthly for serangs (in the mid-eighteenth century), plus fees collected from their lascars. The wages paid to British sailors on these same Asia-bound ships rose from 8–9s. monthly in the early seventeenth century (less than lascars) to 30–45s. by the mid-eighteenth century (more than lascars).[6] This marked shift in respective wage levels between lascars and British seamen came, at least in part, because the labour market for Asian seamen in Britain was legally suppressed by Parliament through the Navigation Acts.

The British mercantilist Navigation Acts, particularly those passed from 1660 onwards, privileged those ships defined in law as British.[7]

Non-British ships were excluded entirely from certain kinds of trade with Britain and suffered higher tariffs on other designated commodities. For most of this period, the Acts defined as British only those ships with a crew at least three-quarters British – as well as being British-built, British-owned and British-captained.

Through their constructions of ethnic categories, these Acts profoundly and particularly affected Asian seamen by defining them as 'non-British'. In contrast, African and Caribbean seamen could be classified as British. The Royal Navy justified this as necessary to produce a pool of experienced and trustworthy merchant seamen ready for conscription – men the Navy considered worthy fighters. The Navy generally regarded Asian seamen as lacking sufficient bodily and moral strength to plunge themselves into battle; in contrast, African-descended sailors reputedly embodied these qualities, as did British seamen, of course. In practice, the Navy impressed and hired substantial numbers of Indians, although this reflected its frequent desperation for manpower rather than its preference. Thus, for example, in 1749 at the end of the War of Austrian Succession, the Navy discharged and consigned to the Company for repatriation fifty-six Indian seamen who had survived its service.[8]

The Navigation Acts thus created an unintended surplus of unemployable Indian seamen in Britain. Ships arriving from Asia were excused from the requirement of three-quarters British crew, since the Government recognised the necessity of hiring Asian seamen there for the voyage home. Yet, on leaving Britain, these Acts precluded ships which wished to be classed as British from employing Asians above one-quarter of the crew. Indeed, the Company periodically instructed its outgoing ships to have all-British crews, thereby minimising dependence on lascars.

Not surprisingly, labour relations between lascars and British captains frequently proved acrimonious. Storms and contrary winds, inadequate and unhealthy food, inevitable shortages and spoilage of water and rampant diseases in confined quarters all combined with hostile naval and pirate ships made life on board these relatively tiny and fragile vessels hellish for all. During the Company's first twenty years, less than half its ships ever returned from Asia; between 1700 and 1818, 160 Company ships either sank or were captured.[9] While officers and passengers suffered much, the rigid discipline and inevitable class and personal conflicts during long voyages made life for all seamen extremely brutal. In the case of Indian seamen, linguistic and other cultural differences between them and their British officers often exacerbated these confrontations.

Under such conditions, the serang also served as shop steward, representing the lascars against the captain. Given the inherently conflicted relationship between captains and their crews, labour disputes frequently oppressed the lascars and troubled the Company. The time of disembarkation and final 'paying off' in Britain, when the contradictory expectations of the crew and owners culminated, often proved a particular time of confrontation. Many serangs and their lascars turned successfully to the Company, British law courts or other British authorities for redress of grievances inflicted by their British captains.

On their part, the Company and other British authorities struggled with the perennial problem of growing numbers of stranded and unwanted lascars in their midst. While some owners made provision for their lascars, others did not, simply discharging them into British society. Well into the nineteenth century, reports repeatedly reached the Company about Indian seamen 'daily strowling about [London's] Streets, and begging'.[10] In what was described by British authorities an act of lunacy, but might have been a desecration of symbols of British world-power, an armed lascar entered St Paul's cathedral in 1679. He broke away the orb and sceptre from a statue of Queen Anne and defaced the symbols of the four quarters of the globe over which Britain ruled, before he was subdued.[11] Most lascar resistance was less overt.

The Company largely accepted paternalistic responsibility for these men, motivated only in part by a sense of humane justice due to them. The Company also feared harm to its image in British official and public opinion, which regarded such indigent Indians as their moral obligation. Thus, the Company intervened to repatriate lascars, on occasions having to bail them out of British jails first. Nevertheless, out of deference to the Company's profits, it sought the lowest reasonable expense in discharging this burden. Generally, in accord with the Navigation Acts, the Company arranged for lascars to travel back to India free as passengers – at the cheapest cost. Nevertheless, in practice many captains evidently forced lascars to work – despite officially being passengers with their passages prepaid.[12]

Over time, the financial obligations of the Company towards these lascars proved considerable. At the end of the seventeenth century, for example, the Company allotted 6 pence daily per man, plus return passage of £4–6 for each lascar and £10 for each serang. Since this was roughly equivalent to the wages already paid to them for the voyage here, it doubled the cost of employing a lascar. The Company regularly charged these expenses to the owners of the ships which had brought those particular lascars, when they could be identified. Since owners of arriving ships were liable for this fixed cost, they had no financial incentive to give the lascars they discharged any clothing or food, or even their wages. Until the end of the eighteenth century, no regular system existed for housing or feeding these Asians awaiting passage home.

Serangs learned how to put political and moral pressure on the Company. On at least four occasions early in the eighteenth century, serangs sent petitions not only to the Company, but also to the British royal family. These included: the serang of the *Montague* who petitioned Queen Anne's husband, Prince George of Denmark, in 1706; the serangs of the *Mermaid* and the *St George* who petitioned Queen Anne in 1713; and the serang of the *Torerie* who petitioned King George I in 1721.[13] Their faith in the authority of the Crown over the Company seems indeed to have helped draw attention to their cases, since in each instance officials in the royal establishment wrote to the Company demanding an explanation. On the other hand, so 'clamourous' was Ghulam Mahmud, serang of the *St George* who petitioned Queen Anne in 1713, that, although he succeeded in his case in Britain, the Company blacklisted him and his tindals, ordering Company's officials in India never to employ them again.[14]

During this period, the frequent lack of an explicit contract between the serang and the captain often led to strong differences between them as to the terms of employment. After a particularly bitter disagreement in 1706, the Company ordered each of its port officials in India to require a written labour contract before a ship could leave. The captain and the lascars were all to appear in person and sign an 'equitable' agreement, countersigned by the local Company's agent, copies of which were kept by the serang, the captain and the local Company official, with yet another copy sent to Britain.

In practice, the contracted amount due to lascars shrank at the time of payout due to various deductions. Even before the voyage began, the Indian recruiter who assembled the labour gang customarily took a quarter of the lascar's entire salary, plus any loans or provisions he had advanced. During the voyage, ship serangs appear to have regularly charged lascars under them customary and occasional fees, including fines for alleged violations of discipline. Likewise, Captains levied fees for sundry alleged infractions and also charged highly for required or optional clothing and supplies from the ship's store. Further, the official

British tariffs on all seamen included fees to Greenwich Hospital (a home for disabled seamen); by the late eighteenth century, lascars had 1s. monthly deducted by the Merchant Shipping Office in London and another fee taken by the Navy Agent.[15] In all, of the contracted salary due on disembarkation in Britain, lascars often received less than half. Nevertheless, what they received could be a substantial sum for a working-class man at that time. For example, account books from 1693 show some serangs receiving in London £15 and lascars £4 each.[16]

Once in Britain, most Indian seamen were determined to seek entertainment and opportunities. Like many seamen around the world, many lascars often quickly spent their pay and fell into destitution. Others, however, found employment, married, and/or settled here. Marriages in Britain between Indian men and British women would continue as a frequent occurrence and Indian sailors became a visible feature of British working-class society, particularly, but not exclusively, in the dock areas of east London. Indian seamen who failed or simply wished to return home increasingly relied on the Company to provide them basic maintenance and free passage back to India.

Indian seamen sailing to Britain thus endured not only the hardships common to the working-classes in their age but also the ever present dangers from the sea. Yet, they commanded relatively high wages, retained much of their customary form of recruitment and collective service and occasionally secured their rights in the face of hostile British authorities. A few saved or earned enough to pay their own passage home. Many evidently returned to India with little materially to show for their long labours, although they had learned much about Britain. Thus they knew better what to expect when they were approached by recruiters for future voyages bound here. Nevertheless, many of the economic and legal forces and constraints on them and other Indians in Britain were beyond their control; during this period, most working-class people, Indian and British, needed to struggle to survive.

Indian Servants

In addition to Indian seamen to sail their ships home, Europeans also hired Indian servants and purchased Indian slaves. Indian servants and slaves were unusual enough in the seventeenth century Britain that they often provided a particular cachet as trophy servants. In 1630, for example, William Feilding, Earl of Denbigh (1582–1643), went to India representing King Charles I. Returning in 1633, Denbigh brought with him at least one Indian.[17] He then commissioned Anthony Van Dyck to paint a joint portrait. The painting highlights Denbigh's oriental experiences, but in complex ways. Although Van Dyck painted the figures from life in England, he created an Indian setting (not botanically or topographically accurate). Denbigh's own jacket and pyjamas vaguely imitate an Indian gentleman's clothing. Yet, Denbigh, according to his family's oral tradition, had become totally lost in an Indian jungle until this youth rescued him by directing his safe return. This portrait thus not only shows Denbigh as semi-orientalised in dress but also disoriented in location, needing an Indian's knowledge in order to reorient him. While Van Dyck highlighted the patron, he also painted the young Indian with personality and status, wearing an elaborate turban and robe, incongruous for a servant. This young Indian, after about two years living in Britain and adding lustre to the Earl's household and status, sailed home with much to recount to his friends and family about his life in Britain.

Other British aristocrats likewise used Indians to distinguish themselves, sometimes with only limited references to the 'orient'. Around 1674, Lady Charlotte Fitzroy, the king's illegitimate daughter, was painted by Peter Lely as being served by an Indian, evidently done from life. Yet, in the vaguely Greek or Roman classical setting, neither the servant's costume nor the frieze in the background marks him as Indian, although his physiognomy does. Lady Charlotte was apparently not claiming any 'oriental' accomplishments for herself but rather displaying her possession of a rare and valuable attendant who was Indian by birth if not for the dress. Further, Lely's careful delineation of the Indian's face reveals him as having character, rather than as an abstract stereotype, even if he remained in a serving role and also unnamed in the caption.

In contrast, English use of Indians took a more crude form when, in 1683, King Charles II sought to add distinction to his court through combining the oriental and the grotesque. He commanded the East India Company to provide him with 'one Male, and two Female Blacks, but they must be Dwarfs, and of the least size that you can procure'.[18] Thus, in this period, some English aristocrats and gentry evidently recognised Indian attendants as individuals who informed them or added to their status, while others regarded them as simply rare and costly objects indicative of English possession of the exotic personified.

Becoming Christian might emancipate slaves here, but emancipation could expose them to hardships all too common to the poor. A 10-year-old Indian came to London from Bengal around 1741 as the slave of Mr Suthern Davies, who passed her on to a relative, Mrs Ann Suthern. This young Indian converted into the Church of England: christened 'Catherine Bengall' at St James, Westminster, London on 26 November 1745.[19] Emancipated by this, she left Mrs Suthern's household (either voluntarily or perforce) and lodged at the Ship tavern. An ongoing relationship with William Lloyd, however, left her pregnant and destitute. When her pregnancy became evident in July 1746, she had to appear before the local magistrate who admitted her to the workhouse of the Parish of St Martin in the Fields where she resided. There, she gave birth to a son, christened with the father's name William, on 22 September 1746. Like so many women of her class, Indian and British, she and her son then disappeared from surviving British records, either due to death or due to merger into British society.

Even in the seventeenth century, a small market for Indian labour had emerged here. Some Indian workers clearly adapted themselves by taking English names and converting (at least nominally) to Anglican Christianity. Indication of their Indian origins by name or complexion only occasionally appeared in parish, other legal records or newspaper job-wanted advertisements, often through the qualifier 'the Indian' or 'the East Indian'. Thus, James, 'the Indian' who worked for James Duppa, a beer brewer in London, died in September 1618 and was buried in the parish church of St Botolph Without Aldgate. His Indian origin and continuing identity did not prevent him from being accepted as a member of the Church of England and was buried with honour.

Nonetheless, quite apart from any exotic appeal, their Indian identity occasionally marked them as different from other working-people here, for better or worse. They could turn to the Company which accepted special responsibility to provide them succour and relief, much as an English church would for any established parishioner. Yet, in 1657, the Company inadvertently made it more difficult for Indians who had reached England to return home. To reinforce the Company's shaky monopoly over trade with India, the Company decreed that henceforth all people leaving England for India must purchase a license or 'permission' from the Company – for the substantial sum of £12 (worth £1,235 today). This regulation intended to block European commercial rivals but it also unintentionally encompassed all Indians, including servants seeking to sail to India.

When Indian slaves or servants left their masters or employers, their Indian identity made it more difficult for them to escape. Returning home independently required the purchase of a £12 'permission' from the Company in addition to the £4–9 passage fare, both very difficult for a runaway servant or slave to manage. Furthermore from the seventeenth century onwards, English newspapers began to carry advertisements calling for the return of self-liberated Indian slaves or servants. Such descriptions typically identified them as Indian, but their clothing tended to be European in style, suggesting their Anglicisation. For example, in July 1702, an employer in London sought the return of an

> Indian Black Servant: Went away from his master's house in Drury-Lane upon Monday ... and has been since seen at Hampstead, Highgate, and Tottenham-Court, an Indian black boy with long hair, about 15 years of age, speaks very good English; he went away in a brown fustian frock, a blue waistcoat, and scarlet shag breeches, and is called by the name of Morat: Whoever brings him to, or gives notice of him, so as he may be brought to Mr. Pain's House in Prince's Court, Westminster, shall have a guinea reward, and the boy shall be kindly received.[20]

Such advertisements were also common for British runaways as well, suggesting that class conflict (not necessarily ethnicity) impelled them to flee, but their Indian identity made them stand out once they had done so.

Thus, servants from India held many roles in Britain. Given the cost of their transportation to and from Britain, they were by no means inexpensive labour. Some found that their Indian identity enhanced their value to their masters by distinguishing them from British servants, albeit at the cost of occasionally being treated as 'oriental' ornaments. For a few, particularly Indian slaves, there were possibilities for upward mobility if they were willing to adapt to British culture and religion. Nor were their roles fixed. Sometimes a man might work as a sailor or lascar on the voyage in, and then as a servant once here or on the return voyage. The growth of British colonialism in India from the mid-eighteenth century onwards, the concomitant shifts in British concepts of race and the changes over time in class relations within Britain, all affected the lives of Indian servants and slaves here.

Indian Merchants Make Their Way to Britain

As British merchants extended their commercial intercourse with India, they needed Indian brokers to deal with both the producing artisans and also the many layers of Mughal and other Indian officialdom. For decades, men of the Rustamji family of Parsis had served as Chief Broker to the Company in Surat. In 1716, however, this family confronted the Company's newly appointed Governor of Bombay, William Philips.[21] The family had delivered extensive goods, which the Company's Bombay officials later claimed were of inferior quality, refusing to honour the bonds it had given to them. During this long commercial dispute, in 1721, the Governor had two Rustamji brothers arrested.

When petitions to Britain did not help, the third brother, Nowroji Rustamji, sailed to London to appeal directly to the Company about the legal and moral injustices of the Bombay Government. With Nowroji came his wife and children, plus a dozen Parsi servants. Soon after his arrival early in 1724, he personally presented his case to the Company, which they agreed to consider. The English climate proved unhealthy for Nowroji, however. Further, London was far more expensive than he had anticipated. After considerable negotiations the Company agreed to loan Nowroji £2,000 and also ordered his brothers released.

By November 1724, the Company's directors proposed their solution: four arbitrators from among their own number would decide the case. Nowroji was to select two, the Company the others. Nowroji agreed. Early in 1725, these arbitrators recognised the legally binding force of contracts and thus found in favour of Nowroji: the Company had accepted the goods and, regardless of their quality, it must honour its bonds given in payment. The Company therefore paid the money due his family, £57,753 (today worth over £6,000,000) plus 10 percent interest. Further, the Company ordered the award of robes of honour (*saropa*, literally 'head to foot') and a horse to the Rustamji brothers, plus tax exemption for Nowroji's houses in Bombay. Additionally, the directors promised to help him sell the Indian goods he had brought with him. Nowroji received one instalment of £14,625 in London. With this money he purchased local merchandise that he knew would sell in India: weapons (16 brass cannon, 10 lead sheets for bullets, 720 knives and 100 sword blades) plus mechanical equipment (11 clocks) and distilling equipment (10 copper pots, 12 pewter distilling worms, 3 small stills), in addition to personal clothing, liquor and other provisions.

Meanwhile, both the Bombay Governor's agents and Commodore Thomas Matthews, the Royal Navy commander who had conveyed Nowroji to London, brought lawsuits against him here. Threatened with arrest, Nowroji appealed to the Company to guarantee bail, which it did and further recommended its lawyer to him. Nowroji won these lawsuits and returned to Bombay in triumph, having successfully overridden the Bombay Governor through his negotiations in London. While the family was not restored to its position as the Company's Broker, Nowroji rose up to be a prominent member of the Parsi community.

Despite his religious and ethnic differences from the British, Nowroji obtained a fair hearing and justice in London, both from the Company and from British law-courts. Nowroji thus set the pattern that dozens of other Indian merchants, rulers and employees would attempt to emulate over succeeding centuries. For example, in 1769, two Armenians of Bengal, Khwaja Gregore Cojamaul and Khwaja Johannes Padre Rafael, brought lawsuits in London against former Governor of Bengal, Harry Verelst, accusing him of false imprisonment and confiscation of their goods.[22] After seven years of trials, these merchants won judgements totalling £9,000, plus full costs (reduced on appeal to £7,200) against Verelst (although the East India Company reimbursed him). Not all Indian plaintiffs proved as successful, however. Further, over time, the growth of British colonialism made it harder for Indians to gain redress in London. Yet, British ideological assertions that their administration guaranteed the rule of law to Indians under its authority continued to convince many Indians over the centuries that if they, like Nowroji, could only reach London, injustices suffered at the hands of Company officials in India would be rectified.

South Asians in the British Isles before Colonialism

During the 150 years considered in this chapter, South-Asian people of various social classes came to England as workers, wives or plaintiffs. Although these islands were not large or rich, particularly compared with the extensive and wealthy Mughal Empire, they nonetheless began to attract Indians seeking opportunities not available in India. The largest number were seamen and servants, numbering in the hundreds, but dozens of middle-class Indians also made the journey in. Since neither Indian ships arrived nor Indian communities existed here, the relatively few Indians who had settled here had to merge into British society, often as part of British households or parishes.

Thus, these early visitors and settlers came on English ships as employees or dependents of Britons. Once here, they had to conform to English customs and laws. In contrast, most Europeans in South Asia lived in their own enclaves, apart from Indian society, and few worked for Indians. Hence, even in the centuries prior to British colonialism in South-Asia, the relationships between Indians and Britons in Britain tended to be asymmetrical.

This does not mean that Indians here were without scope for upward mobility or self-representation. Since few of the English knew much about Asia or Asians, there was room for Indians to shape the attitudes of local people. Further, if Indians were willing to conform to British expectations, including by using English-style names, professing Christianity and submitting to the judgements of British courts and authorities, they could sometimes find justice and acceptance, especially by people of their own class. The rapid expansion of East India Company's colonial rule over vast numbers of South Asians from 1757 onwards would raise the number of Indians coming to Britain, diversify the reasons why they came and deeply affect their roles once they arrived here.

Chapter 2

South-Asian Arrivals during Early Colonialism, 1750s–1790s

Michael H. Fisher

Connecting Histories

Over the late eighteenth century, British colonialism began to spread rapidly across South Asia, expanding and altering interactions between Britons and Indians in India and Britain. Earlier, the British presence in India had been largely confined to small coastal enclaves, primarily the ports of Bombay, Madras and Calcutta. After the crucial battle in 1757 at Plassey in Bengal, however, the East India Company ousted the ruler of that rich province, gaining effective control over an area of around 390,000 square kilometres (three times the size of England) with a population of around thirty million. By the 1790s, the East India Company's Indian sepoy armies had defeated various Indian regional rulers and the Mughal Emperor, extending British power over a total of 650,000 square kilometres. While the actual number of Britons who went out to India to govern or trade remained remarkably small, hundreds of thousands of Indians began to work directly for the Company or for individual Britons; tens of millions of Indians began to pay taxes to the Company or produce goods that it purchased. Many Indians were beginning to understand the cultural, economic and political impacts on their lives resulting from these ongoing British conquests.

This new and increasing British dominance meant that thousands of Indian men and women of all social classes decided to travel to Britain, many to visit, some to settle. The very process of coming to Britain, however, tended to subordinate Indians of all classes. Most Indians who came sailed on East India Company ships as employees or dependents of Britons. Indian men and women servants attended on their British masters, labouring for them here. Indian seamen worked on British vessels and some sought jobs once in Britain. Indian wives and their children were brought by their European husbands and had to depend on them once here. Indian scholars, diplomats and merchants, frustrated by British colonial officials in India, began to arrive to try to educate Britons about India, to advise and influence British politicians about how to rule India and also to obtain justice in British courts denied in Asia. Yet, even elite Indians sometimes felt overwhelmed by the strangeness of Britain, and how alien they appeared here. Nonetheless, some men among them took comfort in their power over British women and the evident superiority of their religion over Christianity. As many more Indians began to see Britain as dominating their lives in the late eighteenth century, half a dozen people from India wrote books based on their experiences here, explaining India to Britons or Britain to Indians.

Over this period, global and domestic conflicts were transforming Britain. Long British wars against the French and other continental powers in Europe, the Americas, and Asia affected attitudes towards foreigners and redefined what it was to be a Briton. Particularly after Britain lost most of its North American colonies, India and Indians emerged as ever more central to British life and global commerce. While most Britons did not yet know much about India, some were starting to take interest, particularly as they encountered Indian people and products in their daily lives.

British attitudes towards the Indian visitors and settlers in their midst proved mixed. Many Britons prided themselves on their expanding power over Indian lands, wealth and people. Indian servants and wives brought exotic distinction to British households that could afford them. Indian seamen made British imports from India possible but proved expensive. Britons thrilled to see Indian 'princes' (or people they took to be royalty) and diplomats in British cities and towns, particularly enhancing London into an imperial capital.

Some Britons, however, saw the influx of Indian people and cultures into Britain as threatening. The easy riches, oriental despotism and immorality that many Britons associated with India seemed to arrive with wealthy British 'nabobs' and their Indian servants, wives and mistresses. The parliamentary investigation against Governor of Bengal, Robert Clive, for corruption just before his suicide in 1774 and the parliamentary impeachment and 7-year trial (1787–1795) of Governor General Warren Hastings for even more oriental abuses reflected widespread British resentment against Asian-based corruption. Edmund Burke, who demonstrated in Parliament how Britons had become morally corrupted by exploiting Indians, had personally hosted several Indian friends in Britain. In 1784, the India Act regulated the Company and created a Parliamentary Board of Control to oversee the Company's directors with regard to political activities.

In this context, Indian envoys, scholars and merchants testified to and lobbied Parliament and appealed in London law courts, challenging the East India Company's illegal or merely embarrassing policies in India. Among the masses of poor Britons thronging the streets of London and elsewhere, indigent Indians appeared to stand out as a special social problem. Most Indians did not find life in Britain attractive enough to settle here; but a substantial number of Indians did decide to remain here permanently. Further, Indians who had personally experienced the pleasures and vicissitudes of life in Britain wrote or spoke about these to people back in India. Thus, in many complex ways, the histories of Indians and Britons were becoming ever more connected over the late eighteenth century.[1]

Indian Servants In and Out of British Households

The thousands of Indian servants, seamen and other working class people who reached Britain during this period had to have something special about them. The long, dangerous and expensive voyage from India meant that they were not 'cheap labour' once they arrived. The East India Company made repeated efforts to keep such Indians out of Britain and also to ensure the departure of those who nonetheless came. Yet, many had skills that no Briton could match. The receptions they received varied, however. Sometimes Indians clearly earned respect for their accomplishments, often distinct from what Britons of their class could offer, and therefore valued by employers and fellow workers. Other times, they met puzzlement since many Britons did not know much about Asia or Asians. In some cases, they met hostility as some Britons had already begun to develop stereotypes against them.

Among these working-class Indians, many of the dozens of servants who came to Britain annually did so in the households of nabobs. In India, newly enriched British officials, officers and merchants hired large numbers of Indian servants and attendants. Many of these nabobs brought these servants back to Britain with them, seeking to continue their comfortable lifestyle and also to impress their neighbours. The cost of bringing an Indian servant to Britain, and paying eventually to return her or him back to India meant that they were more expensive than British servants, even if the actual wages paid were similar. As we saw in Chapter 1, these Indians often seem to have received more regard and attention from their British masters than did mere British servants since their very presence added distinction to the employer's household. On their part, these Indian servants had to adapt to the expectations of their masters and mistresses.

Living isolated from their Indian homeland, these Indian servants, however, had few options should they be abused except appealing to British authorities for justice and to the East India Company for passage home. Their very distinctiveness in Britain meant that liberating themselves by fleeing their employer was more difficult than for British servants. Thus, Indian male and female servants lived in British society, but also occasionally apart from it.

Illustrating the intricate roles that Indian servants played in such households, we have the case of a Bengali nursemaid (*ayah*) called Bolah. In the early 1760s, she came from India in the household of the newly wealthy George Clive (cousin of Robert Clive). As a mark of his family's regard for Bolah, in 1765 Clive paid the famous and expensive artist Sir Joshua Reynolds to paint her as a central figure in the family portrait. She appears with a distinct personality adorned with gold and ivory jewellery, including a necklace indicating her married status. She has a supporting role, looking down modestly, yet clearly central to the social space of the family. Her clothing could be Indian but it is not highlighted as such. While various British paintings of Indians in Britain similarly did not feature them in Indian-style clothing, the many British paintings of Indians that were painted in India at this time virtually invariably depict them wearing Indian-style clothes. In contrast to Bolah, Clive's daughter wears Indian costume for the painting, explicitly alluding to his career and source of wealth. None of the three women is named in the caption. This and similar artistic representations suggest the positions in British households held by Indian domestic servants there. Bolah returned to Bengal in 1766 with much to say about her life in Britain, leaving her features immortalised in the canon of British fine art.

Many of the servants who came from India to Britain succeeded in making comfortable places for themselves in British society but others encountered abuse or abandonment by their British employers. As indigent Indians began to appear on Britain's streets, many Britons expected the East India Company to take care of them, and especially to send them home to India as quickly as possible. The Company's directors recognised this responsibility, as they explained in 1769:

> It has happened of late years amongst the many Natives of India, who have been sent to England as Servants to Gentlemen or their Families returning home, that several have been forsaken entirely by the Persons in whose Service they engaged, and these poor Creatures from their destitute Circumstance in this distant Land, have Petitioned us for going back at the Company's Expence ... which not only from the distress of these Indigents, but to prevent reflections on us in this respect from the People of India, we have been induced to grant.[2]

Nonetheless, while recognising this responsibility, the directors also resented these expenses. For the Company to maintain each Indian in Britain, it cost about 2s per day, plus at least £15 for the cheapest passage back to India.

In order to make the employers of Indian servants financially responsible for them, the directors in 1769 ordered that every employer post a £50 bond (equivalent of £5,300 today) for each Indian servant they took from India. This considerable bond made the wages that the servant actually received only a small fraction of the cost to an employer of bringing him or her to Britain. Nonetheless, many employers evaded giving these bonds and significant numbers of destitute Indians continued to appear unbonded on Britain's streets, in its prisons and poorhouses; many of these indigent Indians appeared on the Company's doorstep and received clothing, housing and passage home at the Company's expense. When further orders from the directors to Company officials in India failed to reduce the number of servants coming to Britain, the directors in 1807 doubled the bond to £100 – five or six times a servant's annual wage. Further, an employer wishing to send his servant home from Britain still had to pay the £12 'permission' required (until 1813) by the Company, plus passage fare back.

Despite these elaborate Company efforts, many unbonded servants continued to enter Britain undetected. Employers found the £50 or £100 bond a significant amount of money to deposit; it was also cumbersome to recover. Hence, departing India, some employers simply hid Indian servants, boarded them once out of port or used influence or bribed ship captains and Company officials to overlook them. Approaching the

British coast, many Britons and their Indian servants went ashore via local fishing vessels or professional smugglers, thus evading government customs. Once in Britain, Indian servants faced virtually no official monitoring.

As the number of abandoned servants in Britain increased, so too did public protests which lamented such inhumane treatment. For example, in one 1786 newspaper (seventeen years after the bond system began), a Briton publicly chastised irresponsible British female and male employers for the prevalent abuse of Indian women servants in particular:

> SIR,
> When a family return from India, they generally bring over with them one or more female blacks to take care of the children, under a promise to send them back to their native country free of expense. – Many, no doubt, have honesty or humanity enough to keep their word; but the number of those poor wretches who are daily begging for a passage back, proves the generality of those that bring them over leave them to shift for themselves the moment they have no further occasion for their services. Many of them, I am informed, have been in England two or three years; and some of them must for ever remain here, unless the Company will generously give them a passage to India ...
>
> I am not such a fool ... as to expect much humanity from a *female adventurer to Bengal*; but the nation has a right to demand common justice from their husbands. – TRUTH.[3]

In reply, another Briton disputed these assertions of inhumanity towards Indian servants, retorting that most of the destitute were 'only' African or Caribbean people, therefore not the Company's concern.[4] Significantly, from 1797 onwards, the directors equated lower-class British women with Indians by requiring a bond 'to the same amount as that which is deposited respecting Black servants' for European women (often the wives of soldiers) coming from India as servants.[5]

In terms of their conditions of service, whether or not a bond existed undoubtedly affected the relationship between Indian servant and British employer. Such substantial bonds encouraged masters to retain restrictive supervision over their servants. Almost all of the thousands of bonds were eventually redeemed, meaning employers satisfied the Company that the servant had either returned home or died. These controls by masters would allow servants less opportunity for mobility or finding alternative employment in Britain. The lack of a bond, however, did not make a servant more vulnerable to deportation. The British Government in this period did not have comprehensive checks on immigration, nor any system of official identity papers, nor an effective expulsion mechanism. Masters thus could not use such undocumented status coercively to threaten their servants. Indeed, when unbonded Indians left their masters, the absence of a bond made it more expensive for the Company to deport them to India. Nor did the bonding procedure succeed in protecting all Indian servants from abandonment or maltreatment. A substantial number of bonded but abandoned Indians applied for succour from the directors. Although the Company deducted its expenses from the bond posted for that servant, this usually did not improve the servant's situation.

This bonding requirement did discourage some Britons from bringing servants to India. Britons complained how the bond created a severe financial obstacle for junior officers and other relatively impecunious Britons who nonetheless required an Indian attendant on the voyage home, due to illness for example. Nevertheless, the numbers of Indian servants entering Britain continued to increase. Once here, some faced abuses but others found justice and opportunities, depending on their personal situation and adaptability to British conventions.

The Specially Skilled

One particular niche that only highly expert Indians could fill was that of trainer of rare Indian beasts being transported to Britain as valuable gifts. Both Indian rulers and British officials in India made such costly gifts of wild cats, elephants, rhinoceroses and birds. Their Indian keepers sometimes made multiple trips between India and England. One such trainer, Abdullah, evidently came at least three times.

In 1759, Abdullah arrived in London with several rare animals, the most notable being a syagush (from the Persian *siayah gosh*, 'black ear') or caracal from central Asia. This fierce and yet delicate feline had been a present from Nawab Mir Jafar to Robert Clive, who had recently enthroned him as nominal ruler of Bengal. Clive sent this beast and its keeper to London as a gift for William Pitt, the King's Secretary of State, who then presented them to King George II.[6] The caracal became the latest addition to the royal menagerie in the Tower of London.

Abdullah, a Muslim member of Mir Jafar's own household staff, received an honourable welcome in London. The British press celebrated him and the caracal. After being escorted around London by the Royal Keeper of the Beasts in the Tower, Abdullah received a comfortable passage home to Bengal (costing 30 guineas) and Secretary Pitt, who 'very strenuously interested himself in favour of' Abdullah, added another £52 10s. as gratuity. A skilled attendant, Abdullah gained much materially and in terms of knowledge about London from his stay there. Similarly, in both 1763 and 1764, King George III received elephants from British sea-officers, each accompanied by two Indian keepers.[7]

In 1764, Abdullah (apparently using the name of John Morgan, which was easier for Britons to pronounce) returned to London with yet another rare beast – a cheetah. Sir George Pigot, recently Governor of Madras, had hired him to deliver the feline as a gift to King George III. Indeed, Pigot brought back an assistant for Abdullah, as well as four other Indian servants. Once again, the feline and his Indian attendant made a major impression on London society.

Very soon after their arrival, King George entrusted the cheetah to his brother, the Duke of Cumberland, Ranger of Windsor Forest. At noon on Saturday, 30 June 1764, the Duke staged an experiment in Windsor Great Park: setting the cheetah on an English stag. After three attacks failed, the cheetah broke away and killed a fallow deer. Newspapers reported: 'While it was devouring its prey, the Indian attendants caught it, covered its head with a hood, put on its collar and secured it'.[8] The prominent English painter George Stubbs recorded the event, including also the portraits of Abdullah and his assistant. Here, their oriental clothing reiterates the exoticism of the cheetah but their stature also suggest their own proud bearing and professional accomplishments.

On his visit to Britain, Abdullah described how he lived in Pigot's mansion on Soho Square but often used to attend the cheetah at Kew Gardens, south-west of London. Once, in late October 1764, he and his assistant groomed the cheetah until the early English evening, too late in to return easily to Pigot's place in central London. Instead, they took rooms in a lodging house off nearby Rosemary Lane. Later that night, Mary Ryan, the housewife, entered Abdullah's room and robbed everything except the shirt and trowsers he wore in bed. He listed all that she stole:

> a pair of silver shoe-buckles, value 10s. a pair of cotton stockings, value 1s. one silk purse [sash], value 2d. one linen purse, value 1d.

> one piece of silver coin, called a rupee, value 2s. two pieces of coin called Fernams [Fanam], value 1d. [plus] five guineas, and fourteen shillings

(worth £600 today). His considerable cash around had been wrapped in his waist sash. When he dashed downstairs and complained to John Ryan, the husband and proprietor, Abdullah reported:

> he took and held a poker to my head, and threatned to knock me down; and bid me go out at the door, and not dispute with him. I said but little, fearing he would break my head: he bid me go along, and called me Black D[evil]l. I staid till morning at the door ...[9]

Determined to have his rights, next morning Abdullah summoned a passing constable. They tracked down the Ryans in the local Ship tavern, drinking a morning draught of hot beer with gin, ginger and sugar. Arrested, the Ryans denied the entire incident but their conspiring together in Irish language raised the constable's suspicions, which were confirmed when the Ryans clumsily tried to toss away Abdullah's distinctive clothing and had his uniquely Indian money in their pockets. The other Muslim, Abdullah's assistant, slept through this entire incident and never appeared in court.

The trial at the Old Bailey delayed for two months, until the end of February 1765, while the judges decided how to get a sworn statement from a Muslim. Finally, the presiding judge asked Abdullah what was customary as a legally binding oath for Muslims in India. He replied 'I touch the book, the Alcoran, with one hand, and put the other hand to my forehead; then I look upon it I am bound to speak the truth'. This the judge accepted. He and the jury also believed the truth of Abdullah's testimony. Despite their continuing denials, the Ryans were found guilty and sentenced to be transported to Australia. Later that spring, Pigot sent Abdullah and his assistant home, along with several other of his Indian servants; the cheetah ended up in the Tower.

Indian trainers therefore served a specialist role in conveying valuable animals from India and instructing British zookeepers in their care and feeding. Like their exotic beasts, these Indians found the British public and elite curious about them. Despite some clear prejudice against all foreigners and non-Britons, particularly among the British lower classes,

British authorities – including British courts of law – seem to have respected their customs and taken their word. Further, these Indian trainers returned with personal accounts of Britain to convey to their peers in India. We do not know how many additional times Abdullah returned to Britain, but others like him continued to arrive and participated in the British society in distinctive ways.

Indian Lascars Arrive in Britain

The rapidly expanding trade between India and Britain during a period of shortage of European seamen meant a rising demand for Indian seamen to work on ships on the return passage. As we have seen, most lascars sailed as part of maritime labour gangs, hired collectively by the captain to replace European seamen who either died or otherwise left the ship on the passage to or in India. During the Anglo-Napoleonic wars that killed or conscripted so many British seamen, lascar wages rose by almost half and about a thousand lascars arrived annually in Britain.

British ship captains and owners, as well as British seamen, however, tended to resent the necessary employment of lascars. The intensity of life aboard during the long and dangerous wind-dependent passage around the tip of south Africa and the frequent brutality routinely practiced by British officers towards their crews seemed to bond lascars to each other and to divide them from Britons. Many Britons believed that lascars were physically and morally inferior to British seamen, so a lascar's work (and wages) was deemed only two-thirds as valuable as a Briton's. These tensions between lascars and Britons often continued after they landed in Britain, where their legal status further discriminated between them.

As we have seen, the Navigation Acts distorted the labour market for lascars by preventing most Indian seamen in Britain from being hired for the voyage out to India. This legislation thus simultaneously reduced a lascar's employment opportunity while it raised the employer's cost for hiring him, since the East India Company or their ship owners had to pay for his food, shelter and clothing in Britain and then passage back to India as a passenger. In addition to lower wages, lascars who wanted to return to India had to endure long periods without wages (indeed, in defiance of the law, some captains forced the lascars returning to India to work without pay).

Although lascars often received harsh and exploitative treatment in Britain, they had some recourse to British authorities for redress, even against Britons. In various cases, serangs, lascars or official or self-appointed British advocates went to court in order to extract wages due to lascars from defaulting ship owners. In 1785, for example, a London jury awarded four lascars each £20 10s. in wages from their ship-owners.[10] British law courts also sometimes punished individual Britons who abused them. That same year, Sawney Clough, a lascar, claimed that a Royal Navy seaman, Patrick Coffield, had assaulted and robbed him of four shillings and some clothing. The lascar also claimed that Coffield had called him a 'black bugger', combining racial and sexual slurs. The Old Bailey court found for the lascar, sentencing the Royal Navy seaman to be hanged.[11]

The East India Company's directors also recognised their general moral and legal responsibility to maintain and return lascars to India. The Company, however, repeatedly struggled to offload these expenses, which cost it about £500 annually by the 1780s.[12] Nonetheless, Company officials rejected responsibility for some indigent Indian seamen because of their alleged misbehaviour or inability to prove that they were really Indian. Further, until the end of the eighteenth century, the directors made no systematic provision for the reception, maintenance or transportation home of lascars.

As we have seen for abandoned Indian servants, the growing presence of homeless lascars on the streets of London and other British cities produced a range of responses from Britons. Some were offended. Others responded with sympathy, leading British social activists to create charities.[13] For example, the 'Committee for the Relief of the Black Poor' established in 1786 'a plan for public donations to relieve the distress of many Asiatic Blacks ... some of whom have absolutely expired in the streets'.[14] Charities paid bakers to provide a loaf of bread per day to each indigent lascar. Yet, lascars comprised only about 10 percent of the people assisted; most of the rest were of African descent. Further, the ill-fated Sierra Leone scheme to remove blacks from London's streets and send them off to west Africa included Indian lascars among its doomed colonists.[15] Overall, charities did little to improve the lives of most Indian seamen or servants in Britain. Nonetheless, individual Indians who came to Britain as seamen, servants or other workers sometimes succeeded in raising their status here based on good fortune and their ability to shape British attitudes towards them.

From Camp Follower to Subaltern to Author

Many people in British society during this period had little knowledge of what being 'Asian' actually meant. This enabled entrepreneurial people from India to shape, at least in part, how they were perceived. Some Indians began to write books designed to instruct their British readers about the author and his culture. Those creative and fortunate enough to catch the attention of British patrons through their deeds and words could sometimes rise in British society.

The life and writings of Dean Mahomet (1759–1851) reflect the variety of the lives of Indian settlers in Britain and also his own creativity throughout his several careers here.[16] Orphaned at age eleven when his army officer father died trying to force Indian landholders to pay their taxes to an agent of the East India Company, Dean Mahomet left his home at Patna in Bihar to attach himself to the Company's Bengal Army as a camp follower. Under the patronage of a teenaged Anglo-Irish officer, Ensign Godfrey Evan Baker, Dean Mahomet rose over the next fifteen years to the rank of *subedar* (lieutenant), the highest post open to an Indian in the Bengal Army at the time. In 1782, however, Dean Mahomet resigned from the army and the next year emigrated to Cork, Ireland, where Baker's father had been mayor and his family owned large estates. Settled in Cork, Dean Mahomet worked for the Bakers, perhaps as the major-domo of their mansion. He also continued his education, converted to Anglican Christianity and in 1786, eloped with a young Anglo-Irish fellow student, Jane Daly, whom he married nearby.

After a decade living in Cork, Dean Mahomet publicly announced in March 1793 that he would publish his autobiographical travel narrative, *The Travels of Dean Mahomet*. In response, 320 of the local nobility, gentry and clergy entrusted him with half a crown (2s. 6d.) each, long in advance of the book's completion and over a year before its delivery. Their trust was justified when he published his two volume book in 1794. This book, written as a series of letters to 'a Friend', described his military career in India and the cultures of its peoples, including his own Shi'ite Muslim community. Dean Mahomet thus explained to the Britons around him about India, and in the process, demonstrated his own stature as an author. This book was only one of Dean Mahomet's many accomplishments during his seven decades of living in Britain (see Chapter 3).

Dean Mahomet met other Indians in Cork. On 7 December 1799, Mirza Abu Talib Khan (1752–1806) chatted with him there. Abu Talib's Persian account of this chance meeting reads:

> Mention of a Muslim named Din Muhammad
> Another person in the [Baker] house ... is named Din Muhammad ... [Godfrey] Baker raised him from childhood as a member of the family. He brought him to Cork and sent him to a school where he learned to read and write English well. Din Muhammad, after studying, ran off to another city with the daughter, known to be fair and beautiful, of a family of rank of Cork who was studying in the school. He then married her and returned to Cork. He now has several beautiful children with her. He has a separate house and wealth and he wrote a book containing some account of himself and some about the customs of India.[17]

Thus, not only were the histories of Britain and India becoming more connected, Indians in Britain were connecting with each other, not yet as ongoing communities, but as diverse individuals.

Indian Scholars Come to Teach and Explore

Abu Talib, like a number of other Indian scholars, had come to Britain in order to teach Britons about India and its cultures. Indeed, Abu Talib intended to establish a British government-sponsored Persian language training institute in Oxford or London under his own direction to prepare Britons to govern India properly. Born in Lucknow, the capital of the nominally independent north Indian kingdom of Awadh, he had received an excellent education in Persian language, culture and administration – traditions central to the Mughal Empire and its successor states.[18] The East India Company itself used Persian as its official language of rule until 1837. Hence, there developed in Britain a recognised need for professors of Persian. Britons who had themselves studied Persian began to teach that language in Britain, but a growing number of Indian scholar-officials with generations of expertise came in order to offer superior training. Some found pupils by advertising in British newspapers; others, like Abu Talib, had widespread reputations that attracted private pupils.

Abu Talib and three other visiting Muslim Indian scholars of the late eighteenth century wrote books in Persian or Arabic about their experiences in Britain. Unlike their contemporary Dean Mahomet, who published in English for British readers, these authors wrote books for the edification of Indian readers, making largely consistent moral judgements about British faults as well as accomplishments. They generally admired and wished to emulate British technological advances. Yet, during this early period of colonialism, these Muslim men found Christianity unpersuasive and British morals questionable. Some found the freedom with which British women of all classes interacted with them attractive but not something to be emulated by Indian women. Of them, Abu Talib's account circulated most widely in India and (through an edited English translation) in Britain.[19]

After his chance meeting with Dean Mahomet in Cork, Abu Talib went on to Dublin. Abu Talib, like many other Indians in Britain, found that most Britons were extremely naïve about Indians and other foreigners. Abu Talib described his experience:

> For some time after my arrival in Dublin, I was greatly incommoded by the common people crowding round me, whenever I went out. They were all very curious to see me, but had no intention of offending me. Some said I must be the Russian General, who had been for some time expected; others affirmed that I was either a German or Spanish nobleman; but the greater part agreed that I was a Persian *Prince*.[20]

Accepting this misleading title, as 'the Persian Prince', Abu Talib went on to a distinguished stay in England.

Abu Talib wrote about how he revelled in British society, particularly in its women (and they in him). Soon after his arrival in London, his letters of introduction gained him a presentation to King George III and Queen Charlotte, who received and conversed with him; they continued to welcome him periodically to court. Following his first royal presentation, many other elite Britons vied for his company, lavishing hospitality and gifts on him. Abu Talib proved the toast of three London seasons and he repeatedly recorded his twin intoxications from the European female beauty and wine in which he indulged (citing the Persian poet Hafiz for justification).

Abu Talib engaged in extensive banter with a wide range of European women including aristocrats, gentry women, shopkeepers and streetwalkers. Overall, he alleged that elite European women essentially possessed 'beauty and elegance', by which he meant sensual attractiveness to men and skills displayed in public spaces respectively. He celebrated the physical features of many of these women. For example, he lauded Miss Ann Cockrell's 'beauty of form and countenance', and he graphically depicted her 'beauteous lips, fair complexion, and black eyes' that inspired him to poetry.[21] Such female characterisations were highly conventional for the abstract, unnamed 'beloved' in Persian literature; Abu Talib's descriptions did not vary much from European woman to woman. What was highly unconventional in Persian literature was his explicit descriptions of specific named women, either married or unmarried, with whom he socialised. Abu Talib even presented descriptive verses celebrating their bodily charms to the women themselves and their families. Rather than appearing insulting to the woman's or her family's honour, these graphic depictions made him ever more popular among his European hosts because they were flattered in exotic ways.

Among others, the King's brother, the Duke of Gloucester, teased aristocratic women about their falling in love with Abu Talib. In British high society at the time, Abu Talib found, a nubile woman's skill in flirtation added to her social prowess, rather than stigmatising her as immoral. Since Abu Talib was at this time married with a family, in his late forties, and exotically outside the conventional marriage considerations of the women with whom he jested, his relationships with most of them were apparently not taken as serious by either side.

At least one London 'beauty' attracted Abu Talib to the extent of 'love'. Abu Talib abruptly ended one of his convivial visits to the country home of former Governor General, Warren Hastings, on 26 September 1801 with a dash back to London, writing: 'my desire was aroused by a fair beloved in London, so I could not be detained.'[22] While no permanent attachment eventuated, Abu Talib's interest in British women was apparently not always purely sociological.

Beneath this apparently comfortable heterosexual banter, however, Abu Talib perceived an immorality which he would never expect nor tolerate from Asiatic women of his own class. While Abu Talib never wrote about the sordid morals of some aristocrats among whom he moved, many were notorious in their own society, not for mere flirtation, but for adultery. For example, the Duke and Duchess of Devonshire stood out as among his most socially prominent and most frequent hosts. The Duchess Georgiana gambled to the point of crushing debt and engaged to an infamous degree in public affairs, including election campaigning on behalf of Charles Fox, allegedly providing kisses to commoners in exchange for their votes. At parties, she entrusted Abu Talib to her husband's current mistress and his future wife (already the mother of three of the Duke's illegitimate children), Lady Elizabeth Foster, who had abandoned her own abusive husband. Abu Talib described strolling one evening with Lady Foster 'according to the custom of the women of London, arm linked in arm' through the flowering gardens of the Devonshires' estate.[23] Abu Talib reported that even the Prince of Wales (later King George IV) deferred to her beauty by stepping back to allow Abu Talib and Lady Foster to precede before him. Abu Talib regarded such incidents as indicative of the priority English royalty paid to their women's physical beauty, rather than to their morality.

Abu Talib also expiated extensively on the pervasive licentiousness among the English generally. He described the many unmarried but cohabiting couples. He repeatedly noted the large number of European prostitutes whom he encountered, but apparently did not employ; just in the parish of London where he lived, Marylebone, he reported 60,000 prostitutes. Thus, Abu Talib evidently regarded the life styles and status of European women as often overly associated with sexuality which, while personally attractive to him as a male, indicated the moral inferiority of British culture.

Comparing Wives in Indian and British Society

In addition to describing British women, Abu Talib also described the Indian wives of Europeans whom he met while in Britain, a few of the growing number of such women here. Many Britons believed that the local climate affected a person's very nature and that women took on the social status of their husbands. Further, given the patrilineal nature of British society, the European father, more than their Indian mother, affected the position in society of their children. In one later example, Amelia Jenkinson, granddaughter of an Indian woman, came to Britain and married in 1769 the Earl of Liverpool. She then died giving birth to his son, Robert Banks Jenkinson (1770–1828), eighth Baronet

Hawkesbury, second Earl of Liverpool, who entered Parliament as a Tory in 1790, rising to be Prime Minister (1812–1827, the longest term in that office during the nineteenth century).[24] His peers knew of his part-Indian ancestry, but his father's wealth and social position made it relatively immaterial. Most people with mixed Indian-British parentage did not rise as high (but another, Dyce Sombre, would be elected to Parliament in 1841).

Abu Talib, in contrast to his often bantering and sexually suggestive encounters with British women, consistently stressed the domestic virtues and command over European culture of the Indian women whom he met here. He explained that they had come to England out of 'affection for their children' and not out of desire for their European husbands.[25] He also recognised how anglicised they had become by living here as wives.

Two of the women whom Abu Talib described meeting had married anglicised Frenchmen. One was widely believed to have been a widow, converted to Christianity, and married around 1780 by Gerard Gustavus Ducarel (1745–1800). The Ducarel family claimed she was a daughter of the Maharaja of Purnea in Bengal.[26] From her decades of living in Britain, she had Anglicised, including appearing to Abu Talib's unpractised eye as virtually English: very fair in complexion, fully Anglophone and displaying British-style dress and deportment. Her teenage children impressed Abu Talib as fully English.

Another woman whom Abu Talib admired was Nur Begam (or Halime Begum, 1770–1853), although her treatment at the hands of her husband left her less privileged than Mrs Ducarel. Nur Begum had been born into a prominent Muslim family of Lucknow. Her sister had already married William Palmer, an affluent banker of mixed British-Indian ancestry. When the French mercenary, General Benoit de Boigne (1751–1830), moved to Lucknow, Nur Begam agreed to become his wife (through Islamic rites). Although de Boigne had other Indian wives and mistresses, when he retired as a wealthy man to London in 1797, he brought with him Nur Begum and their two children, Banu (*c.*1789– 1804) and Ali Bakhsh (*c.*1790–1853). De Boigne renamed her Hélène Bennett and himself received British denisation.[27] They socialised with distinguished members of the British society, including Edmund Burke and his wife.

De Boigne's ambitions, however, drove him to seek higher social status. De Boigne moved Nur Begum out of London, first to Enfield and later to Lower Beeding, Sussex, giving her a modest £300 annual allowance.[28] He contracted a Catholic marriage with Charlotte d'Osmonde (1781–1866), daughter of exiled and impoverished French nobility. They baptised Nur Begum's children as Catholic and christened them Anna and Charles Alexander. Many prominent members of the British society supported Nur Begum, offering to use British law to enforce her rights to de Boigne's wealth. She, however, humbly refused their offers and accepted a quiet retirement. The local villagers and her English maidservant showed her respect, although they thought her exotic, as a mysterious 'dark' lady. De Boigne and his new wife eventually established themselves in 1803 at Chambery, in Savoy. While de Boigne's and Nur Begum's daughter, Anna, died tragically young in 1804, their son, Charles, succeeded his father as Count de Boigne in 1830.

Just before leaving Britain in 1801, Abu Talib wrote an essay entitled 'Vindication of the Liberties of Asiatic Women' which demonstrated that women in Indian society received more respect and had more freedom than did British women.[29] Abu Talib published this essay in London and then, after he had returned to India, European editors republished this essay in at least ten English, Dutch, German and French journals and books between 1801 and 1819. Well into the 1840s, his 'Vindication' remained the benchmark used by European editors to judge Asian critiques of European society. His words echoed the sentiments of other Indian male visitors of his age, before British colonialism had asserted British ascendancy over the colonised.

Indian Ambassadors and Royalty Adorn and Challenge London

From the mid-eighteenth century onwards, a small but growing number of Indian royalty, frustrated by Company officials in India, sought to supersede them by influencing London directly. Various Indian rulers hired Britons as representatives, but few of these proved satisfactory. Instead, rulers sent Indian intermediaries or trusted courtiers, or came themselves. The earliest of these diplomatic missions tended to be relatively small and uninformed about what they would find in Britain. During this early period, British authorities in London also had few precedents dealing with such embassies or even knowledge of the identities of the diplomats (or the rulers they represented).

Once here, these Indian diplomats began slowly to learn about the British society and its complex political processes. They sought to shape

British colonial policies by communicating with the King, testifying before Parliament, negotiating with the directors and lobbying influential Britons. They also struggled against growing colonialism supported by and supporting 'Orientalism' – constructions of 'the Orient' by Europeans. The effects of these interventions, however, were modest since British colonial policies persisted.

The first such embassy came from Mughal Emperor Shah Alam (*r.*1759–1806). After his capture by the Company's Bengal Army in 1764, he decided to send a diplomatic mission to request that King George III send a British army to restore his imperial power.[30] Although the Emperor hired a former officer in the East India Company's army, Captain Archibald Swinton, to lead the mission, he also appointed Sayid Shaikh I'tisam al-Din (1730–1800) as the mission's expert in Persian diplomacy. I'tisam al-Din (born in Nadia, Bengal), initially trained as a scholar-official under the Nawabs of Bengal, had long experience serving and teaching Britons. To elevate I'tisam al-Din's status, the Emperor granted him the title Mirza ('prince') and Rs 4,000.

Governor Robert Clive made every effort to frustrate this imperial mission to London. Clive forced Swinton and I'tisam al-Din to delay their departure for England for a year; they finally sailed from Calcutta on a French ship in 1766. Clive then further delayed for another year the imperial letter to King George. Additionally, the Emperor's gift of Rs 100,000 never reached the English King and was never satisfactorily accounted for by Clive, despite frequent queries from the Emperor and the Company's directors. I'tisam al-Din claimed that Clive personally presented the imperial gifts to the King in his own name.

I'tisam al-Din, like all Indians in Britain, made choices about his deportment. Like Abu Talib, he decided to retain his customary turban, shawl and Hindustani robe, which attracted admiring attention. The British public regarded him as a nobleman, particularly, he reported, compared to the many lascars with whom they were more familiar. Unlike Abu Talib, I'tisam al-Din observed Muslim halal dietary practices, eating only food prepared by his servant, Muhammad Muqim. Since Swinton ridiculed these restrictions as superstitious and allegedly arranged to frustrate them, I'tisam al-Din often suffered privation. Also, he did not know English which kept him particularly dependent on Swinton.

I'tisam al-Din grew increasingly frustrated at his own inability to advance the Emperor's cause. As with many other British agents hired by Indian rulers, Swinton showed little loyalty. Rather, Swinton settled into prosperous retirement in Scotland, coming to London mainly to join attacks on Robert Clive. Thus, this mission failed in its overly-ambitious goal: inducing King George to send a British army to restore the Emperor and overrule the Company's Bengal government.

Finally, I'tisam al-Din returned to Calcutta in 1769 with little to show in political terms but with much information about Britain, its people and its politics. In addition to his oral accounts of Britain that he passed on to his peers, he wrote in 1784/1785 an extensive Persian language book about his trip: *Shigrif-namah-i Wilayat* ['Wonder-book of Europe'].[31] Like Abu Talib and other contemporary authors of Persian language books about life in Britain, I'tisam al-Din described the weaknesses of British morals and Christianity, even as he was impressed by British technology. Unlike Abu Talib, I'tisam al-Din apparently kept his distance from British women.

I'tisam al-Din apparently inspired the former and would-be Peshwa of the Maratha confederacy, Raghunathrao (1734–1784), to send his own Indian ambassador to Britain. Like the Mughal Emperor, Raghunathrao sought to appeal to King George III to overrule Company authorities in India and restore him to power. Like the Emperor's request, Raghunathrao's was unrealistic given politics in both Britain and India.

Raghunathrao selected as his ambassador a loyal fellow Chitpavan Brahmin, Hanumantrao. Hanumantrao, however, did not know English or apparently have much experience with Britons. As Hanumantrao's assistant, therefore, Raghunathrao appointed Maniar Ratanji – accompanied by his son, Cursetji Maniar – from the Parsi community which had long dealt with Britons.

Throughout their stay in Britain, Hanumantrao faced difficulties, both because the directors refused to act and also because of his own Brahminic purity. Hanumantrao often starved rather than eat impure food. Generously, Edmund Burke provided his greenhouse at Beaconsfield for Hanumantrao to live in, and thus prepare his food and bathe in the pure isolation that he required.

While negotiating with the unresponsive Company directors, Hanumantrao came to the attention of Parliament to represent India and its people directly. Other Indians had earlier testified before Parliament about Islamic and Hindu legal practices, including in 1773 a Bengali Hindu by birth, Goneshamdass.[32] In 1781, the Parliamentary Committee investigating Warren Hastings invited Hanumantrao as an expert witness, calling him 'the most authentic Source of Information, concerning the Usages and Religion of the Hindoos'.[33] Accompanied by his Parsi companions, Hanumantrao testified about the system of 'cast', describing the religiously, socially and judicially privileged position of Brahmins, including himself. His testimony particularly condemned Warren Hastings for the public hanging of a Brahmin, Nandakumar. During the subsequent impeachment and trial of Hastings by Parliament, Hanumantrao's patron, Burke, took a leading role.

Despite Hanumantrao's appeals, the directors refused to commit themselves to make his master the Peshwa. They finally gave Hanumantrao £1,200 to cover his expenses, but simultaneously demanded his delegation leave London. Burke, however, interested King George III personally in these ambassadors. That monarch ordered his Government to write a letter of appreciation about Hanumantrao and to give presents worth £267 15s., declaring 'Nothing can be more shameful than the conduct of the East India Directors toward the Agents ...'.[34] Burke also wrote graciously to Raghunathrao, seeking to compensate for the cold reception these agents had received and promising to make better arrangements for any future Brahmin emissaries:

> The sufferings this Gentleman underwent at first was owing to the ignorance not to the unkindness of this Nation. Hunment Row is a faithful and able Servant of yours. And Manuar Parsi and his Son used every exertion to second him. If your affairs have not succeeded to your wishes it is no fault of theirs.[35]

Indeed, the mission and Raghunathrao's political career both failed to live up to his expectations. Nonetheless, his son, Baji Rao II, succeeded as Peshwa in 1795. Even a century later, the precedent of Hanumantrao's visit still served as justification for other Brahmins making the voyage to Europe without automatic excommunication.[36] Further, it gained Indian rulers in the region valuable information about Britain, especially highlighting the divisions within British politics.

In addition to Indian diplomats, Indian royalty also began to come to Britain. In 1794, Mirza Odudeen Khan (*d.*1814) reached London (accompanied by a secretary, Mustapha Khan, and a servant, Adun Mahomet) representing himself and five brothers, sons of the late Nawab of Broach – whom the Company had deposed in 1772.[37] In violation of treaties, the Government of Bombay had reduced their pensions to a few rupees monthly. Mirza Odudeen convinced the directors, after much struggle, that he and his brothers should each receive Rs 2,400 monthly and a house in Surat. Thus, after receiving only rebuffs from Company officials in India, this family gained much financially in Britain.

Over this period, various other Indian missions reached London. As a result of these experiences, the directors became wary of all Indian dignitaries who reached London unannounced and unknown to them. As Abu Talib noted around 1800:

> When I first arrived in England, several of the Directors imagined that I had been sent as an agent by some of the Princes of India, to complain against their servants. They were therefore, for some time very distrustful, and reserved in their conduct; but after they were convinced of their error, they received me kindly, and paid me much attention.[38]

Yet, in British high society, Abu Talib himself passed as 'the Persian Prince'.

By the mid-nineteenth century, at least thirty diplomatic missions by Indians had reached London. While these comprised a growing and continuous presence in London, they came from only a small fraction of the hundreds of Indian rulers whom the East India Company negotiated with or deposed. Hence the Company was relatively successful in preventing Indian princes from dealing directly with higher authorities in London. Nonetheless, many of the missions that managed to reach London affected British attitudes towards India, and several obtained substantial financial gains here. Further, being Indian 'royalty' continued to hold a cachet in the British society. Overall, however, Indian diplomats in London faced British authorities with growing experience in identifying and managing them and a British public ever more familiar with Indians as the colonised.

Indians as the Colonised

The establishment of East India Company rule over ever larger numbers of people in India fundamentally altered the connections between Britons and Indians. We can never know exactly for this period how many Indians of all social classes came to Britain as a place to work, to obtain justice or to settle. Well over 1,000 Indian servants officially purchased 'permissions' from the East India Company to depart from Britain and return to India. The number of lascars arriving in Britain rose from about forty to several hundreds annually. Further, a dozen or so Indian scholars came to educate Britons. By the end of the eighteenth century, six Asians wrote books explaining India and themselves for British readers or explaining Britain for Indian readers.

These Indian settlers and visitors did not come as conquerors or rulers as did Britons to India. Indeed, most came to Britain on British ships and as dependents or employees of Britons. While some scope remained for Indians to shape British attitudes, they faced the growing sense in the British society that Indians were the colonised. Over the early nineteenth century, many of these patterns would intensify along with British colonialism in India.

Chapter 3

Widening and Deepening of the South-Asian Presence in Britain, 1790s–1830s

Michael H. Fisher

Colonial Relations Shape Indian Lives in Britain

Most Indians came under British rule during the period covered in this chapter. By the 1830s, the East India Company had annexed and directly governed about half of South Asia, some 1,700,000 square kilometres (thirteen times England's size), while it indirectly controlled much of the rest. Britons employed hundreds of thousands of Indians in India and growing numbers in Britain. Hundreds of Indian servants entered British households here. Indian entrepreneurs used the allure of Asia to create new careers. Indian scholars in Britain taught Persian and other Indian languages at Company colleges and privately. In order to overrule Company officials in India, Indian diplomats politicked in London. Tens of thousands of lascars sailed Company ships here. While Indians of various classes connected with each other, those who settled tended to merge into British society.

By travelling to Britain, Indians removed themselves from the authority of the Company and immediately became subjects of the British monarch. There, the Company discriminated in its employment practices and law-courts between Europeans and various classes of 'natives of India' (depending on their place of birth, place of domicile, type of education, and ancestry). Once in Britain, Indians could call upon the Company for assistance but were not under its jurisdiction but rather that of British crown law. Indeed, they could became citizens, with the right to vote for Parliament (once they met the same standard qualifications of property, religion, and residence as other Britons).

Yet overall, the lives of Indians in Britain came to be dominated by the effects of spreading British colonialism. British attitudes toward Asians generally began to change as more Britons returned home with experience of military and economic triumphs in the colonies and with stereotypes about Indians as subordinated people. This left many Indians with limited scope to shape how Britons regarded them. As Indians became more numerous, especially in London, British authorities increasingly regarded the poorest among them as 'social problems' which the East India Company had legal and moral responsibility to solve. In 1813, the directors ceased demanding for 'natives of India' the £12 'permission' to leave for India (instituted in 1657). This marked a major change in the Company's efforts to control working-class Indians: no longer restricting their departure from Britain (through 'permissions') while continuing to limit their entry into Britain and speeding their departure (through bonds required for Indian servants).

Further, Britain was undergoing the stresses of change domestically. Notable among these were the Industrial Revolution, the emergence of the British working class, the redistribution of wealth and power between landed aristocrats and the rising urban bourgeoisie, and the manifold effects of the Napoleonic wars and the post-war depression. Nonetheless, many Indian men and women prospered here, able to raise their social status from what it had been in India.

People who immigrate often prove highly entrepreneurial, constantly striving to improve themselves. One distinctive asset that Indian settlers had over local competitors was the attractive exoticness that Asia continued to conjure in the minds of many Britons. Cleverly done, this marketing of being Asian could work for a time, although at the cost of having to conform to British stereotypes.

As political, economic, and cultural power continued to shift to Britain from India, however, it became ever more difficult for Indian settlers to maintain their distinctive identity on their own terms. Indeed, some Britons themselves pretended to 'Indian' characteristics. Indian settlers here might distinguish themselves for a time but eventually joined an Anglican parish, married a Briton and merged into British society, or returned to India. We begin this chapter by considering the several careers two entrepreneurial settlers. Both laboured as servants, rose into the middle-classes, and established Anglicised families within British society. Not all Indians here proved so creative or fortunate but the lives of Munnoo and Dean Mahomed suggest the variety of opportunities and limitations for Indians here during this period.

Purchased in Youth, British 'Licenced Victualler' by Death

In India, vast numbers of Indians served Britons as domestic servants or slaves. Even lower-ranked Britons could afford these inexpensive domestic workers; upper-ranked Britons might have dozens or more. As we have seen, however, Indian servants were costly to bring to Britain due to the Company's required bond on their leaving India, the 'permission' necessary to return them, and the passage fares to and fro. Once in Britain, Indian servants stood out depending on their complexion and degree of Anglicisation. For those Indians who wished to do so, and had the support of their employers, settling in Britain could open possibilities for advancement.

From 1804 when he was age nine, a boy called by the affectionate diminutive 'Munnoo' had been working with his mother in the Calcutta household of the notorious Anglo-Irish lawyer William Hickey. Wherever Hickey dined, Munnoo stood behind his chair and served him. Hickey also occasionally caught Munnoo making 'the other servants laugh by his monkey tricks' from behind Hickey's back.[1] As Hickey approached age sixty, he decided to retire to England, but wished to bring Munnoo as a remnant of his extensive Calcutta household. Munnoo's mother long resisted Hickey's desire until he offered her 500 rupees (£50). While this transaction suggested the sale of Munnoo, Hickey seems to have regarded the boy, his sole attendant on the voyage, more as servant than slave.

Munnoo's departure from home proved heart-wrenching. On first sailing, Hickey locked 'the wretched boy' in their cabin: Munnoo 'looking the very image of despair ... in the midst of strangers and in a scene as uncouth as it was novel to him'.[2] While sympathetic with Munnoo, Hickey clearly asserted his control throughout their voyage. Further, Hickey apparently smuggled Munnoo unbonded from India.

Once in England, Munnoo lived as a personal servant with Hickey's family. The aging Hickey treated Munnoo paternalistically, desiring to impress him with London's glory: 'I had anticipated some pleasure from the delight I expected Munnoo would betray upon first beholding the splendid capital of England'.[3] While Hickey may have purchased Munnoo, he came to treat him as a ward, calling him 'my friend', someone who shared Hickey's sense of being an outsider in England due to their mutual domicile in Bengal.

Hickey eventually retired to Beaconsfield; even this small Buckinghamshire village had seen other Indians. Edmund Burke had hosted Hanumantrao there and Burke's relative and close companion, William Burke (*d.*1798), had brought Tombee ('Little Brother') from India in 1793. William Burke's will stated: Tombee

> a native of India [who] did accompany me to this Country thereby losing his Cast privilege and having ever behaved to me with the most dutiful attention, common Justice required I should restore him to his Religion and friends ... the sum of £350 ... should be applied to the purpose of recovering his Cast and of conveying him to his native country ...[4]

Instead, Tombee begged to remain near William's grave rather than return to India, although he later seems to have gone.

In Beaconsfield, Munnoo studied and Anglicised himself. Hickey credits Munnoo with the full initiative in converting to the Church of England in 1809:

> my favourite Munnoo, without the least hint or solicitation on my part upon the subject, expressed an earnest desire to be made a Christian. I had ... put him to school to be taught to read and write; his schoolmaster, having made the Catechism the first object, probably turned his thoughts that way ... as the boy was extremely zealous, he soon entitled himself to receive baptism ...[5]

Hickey determined 'to anglify his name a little, and therefore instead of Munnoo, I had him designated in the parochial register, "William Munnew"'.

While he remained Hickey's servant, Munnew also started his own family. Around 1813, Munnew married an Englishwoman, Anne. They had a daughter, christened Anne in 1814 at the Beaconsfield Parish Church.[6] In 1817, Hickey, with Munnew his family, moved to London, taking rooms in Westminster.[7]

Here, in 1819, Hickey commissioned William Thomas to paint a joint portrait of him, Munnew, and Hickey's dog (it currently hangs in the halls of Parliament).[8] Hickey was a very experienced sitter, having commissioned many portraits of himself. The caption was demeaning for Munnew, as Hickey's 'favourite black servant'. Nevertheless, this joint portrait also reflects the eye of the artist, revealed visually to the elite of London when displayed in the Royal Academy Exhibition. Hickey clearly sits as the proprietor, with books and papers piled around him, suggesting his professional career as a lawyer, and perhaps as a autobiographer – he had just finished writing his memoirs. On the other hand, Hickey (age seventy), appears quite elderly, holding a limp paper in one hand while the other extends empty. His legs are thin and he inattentively looks vaguely in front of him. He is centred in the composition and yet also partly shadowed.

In clear contrast, Munnew (age twenty-four) and the terrier both display youthful vigour and energy. It is Munnew who provides direction, illuminated by the English sun, and pointing levelly outward into the open countryside (or India). Glancing down, he guides Hickey which way to look, although Hickey seems unaware. The terrier devotes his attention to Munnew not Hickey. Munnew's complexion clearly distinguishes him as Indian. Yet, Munnew has dressed not in oriental or servant's garb but rather in the clothes of a British gentleman (or gentleman's gentleman), complete with stylish cravat and waistcoat, plus gold watch-fob and other jewellery. Overall, this painting contrasts sharply with most earlier portrayals of Indian servants as oriental ornaments and/or subordinated by posture to their British masters.

Around 1820, Hickey, Munnew, and Munnew's growing family moved to Richmond, Surrey. Here, Munnew and Anne christened their newborn son, William.[9] Hickey returned to London sometime before his death in 1827.[10] Around then, Munnew rose from servant to 'licenced victualler', before he himself died in the 1830s. His family settled in Westminster. His eldest son, William, became a skilled pianoforte-tuner and maker, marrying Elizabeth Mills (1816–?), the daughter of a Kent horse-dealer, soon after the birth of their son, William, the first of at least ten children. The family had merged into British society, associated neither by name nor deportment with India. This was a long way from Munnoo's life in Calcutta. Like so many other Indian slaves and servants, Munnoo found that Anglicisation and marriage with a British woman proved ways of settling successfully in Britain.

An Indian Entrepreneur's Careers

As the East India Company brought ever more Indian goods and people to Britain through its spreading conquest and trade in Asia, various Britons at home wanted to sample its secrets, medical and sensual. Through creative use of his Indian identity, Dean Mahomet (1759–1851) perhaps more visibly than any other settler in this period, used to his advantage these British desires to experience and taste 'Asia'. In each of his several careers, however, Britons ultimately took control over his creations.

We saw in Chapter 2 how Dean Mahomet left India for Ireland in 1783, married, and published his two-volume autobiography in 1794. Around 1805, he immigrated once again, settling in London with several of his children born in Cork. In 1806, he married for the second time to Jane Jeffreys, an Englishwoman, at St. Marylebone Church where they baptised the first two of their seven children.[11] Adapting to English conventions, he began to spell his name Dean Mahomed (occasionally William Dean Mahomed). He also adopted the honorific 'Sake' (*Shaikh*) meaning 'venerable-one' – an epithet often used by upwardly mobile Muslims in India. He then tried a number of careers, each using his distinctive talents and Indian identity to distinguish him from the many Britons and Irish also seeking work.

For a few years, he worked practicing allegedly Indian medicine for a controversial nobleman, the Honourable Basil Cochrane (1753–1826), sixth son of the Earl of Dundonald. Cochrane had recently returned from India as a wealthy 'nabob', having extracted money from Indian merchants and the Royal Navy through highly suspect means. While in India, Cochrane had discovered a 'vapour cure': applying cooled, medicated steam to the patient's afflicted parts. To improve his own reputation, he hired Dean Mahomed to provide charity vapour cures in Cochrane's mansion in fashionable Portman Square. (The Ottoman Ambassador also maintained an imposing residence on Portman Square and a mosque in its park.) Dean Mahomed apparently added to the vapour bath a practice that he would make famous in England as 'shampooing': full-body therapeutic massage (from the Indian practice *champi*). Cochrane took full credit for these treatments.

In 1810, Dean Mahomed left Cochrane's service and created nearby a new enterprise featuring his distinctly Indian talents, an establishment he named the 'Hindostanee Coffee House' – also famous as the 'Hooka Club' – at the corner of George and Charles Streets (a site recently memorialised with a commemorative 'Green Plaque').[12] Unique among the thousands of coffee-house, taverns, and other eating-houses of London, Dean Mahomed's restaurant provided what he called authentic Indian cuisine and ambiance. He constructed bamboo-cane sofas and chairs on which the patrons would recline or sit. He adorned the walls with paintings including Indian landscapes, social activities, and sporting scenes.[13] He débuted his creation through newspaper advertisements:

> HINDOSTANEE COFFEE-HOUSE, No. 34 George-street, Portman square – MAHOMED, East-Indian, informs the Nobility and Gentry, he has fitted up the above house, neatly and elegantly, for the entertainment of Indian gentlemen, where they may enjoy the Hoakha, with real Chilm tobacco, and Indian dishes, in the highest perfection, and allowed by the greatest epicures to be unequalled to any curries ever made in England with choice wines, and every accommodation ...[14]

He catered not to the numerous other Indians then living scattered across London but rather to Europeans with experience in India, men he called 'Indian gentlemen'. His restaurant received favourable reception and soon expanded. One connoisseur listed Dean Mahomed among the 'Artists who administer to the Wants and Enjoyment of the Table'.[15]

To be economically successful, however, restaurants must either generate a loyal clientele or have a prime location. The elite of Portman Square could easily hire Indian servants or Europeans with experience in India if they wanted Indian-style food. Therefore, the relatively exclusive location of the Hindostanee Coffee House and its novel and specialised cuisine meant that its gestation time proved longer than Dean Mahomed's limited capital could support. After less than a year, he took a partner, John Spencer, fruitlessly trying to infuse more cash into the business. Less than a year later (March 1812), Dean Mahomed (but not Spencer) had to petition for bankruptcy. As an aficionado regretted: 'Mohammed's purse was not strong enough to stand the slow test of public encouragement'.[16] While the Hindostanee Coffee House apparently eventually succeeded, continuing on the same site as late as 1833, Dean Mahomed lost his financial interest in it.

Dean Mahomed's bankruptcy stripped him of his assets and kept him enmeshed in complex legal processes for seventeen months.[17] His bankruptcy was publicised in the *London Gazette* and many other newspapers. In July 1813, he publicly distributed his property among his creditors in front of London's Guildhall.

This bankruptcy left the fifty-four year old Dean Mahomed free to begin yet another career. But it must have been an extremely difficult period for him and his growing family, recent immigrants trying to establish themselves in a distinctly English society which relegated most Indians and Irish to the lower classes. Not surprisingly, Dean Mahomed soon excised all reference to his life in London from his subsequent autobiographical writings.

Meanwhile, Dean Mahomed had to support his family. In fall 1812, he moved his family out of the Hindostanee Coffee House to lodge with one of his former servants.[18] His young son William Mahomed, in his mid-teens, apparently already worked as a postman, an occupation he followed in London until his death. A postman's salary, however, could hardly support the entire family. Further, Dean Mahomed and Jane had a son, Deen Mahomed, Jr, about this time. Hence, he advertised himself as an upper servant: 'MAHOMED, late of HINDOSTANEE Coffee House, WANTS a SITUATION, as BUTLER, in a Gentleman's Family, or as Valet to a Single Gentleman; he is perfectly acquainted with marketing, and is capable of conducting the business of a kitchen; has no objections to town or country ...'.[19] Although he sought a position as a major-domo, based on his experience with the Bakers in Cork, he found employment giving baths and shampoos, based on his experience working for Cochrane. By September 1814, he was established managing a bathhouse in the burgeoning seaside spa of Brighton.

In Brighton, near the Prince Regent's exotic Pavilion, Dean Mahomed's self-promotion of his oriental origins, scientific medical professionalism, and elite patronage led quickly to his most illustrious career as 'The Shampooing Surgeon'. He began by selling a range of 'Indian' services and products, including tooth power and hair blackening paste but soon concentrated on the 'Indian Medicated Vapour Bath' and 'Shampooing'. His success enabled him to move up through a series of bathhouses: 11 Devonshire Place; the Battery-House at East-Street; West Cliff; and then the magnificent Mahomed's Baths on King's Road (which opened in 1822).[20]

To broadcast his expertise, he published many hyperbolic newspaper advertisements and self-promoting books including: *Cases Cured by Sake Deen Mahomed, Shampooing Surgeon, And Inventor of the Indian Medicated Vapour and Sea-Water Baths, Written by the Patients Themselves* (1820) and *Shampooing* (1822, 1826, 1838). In these, he made an escalating series of assertions about his cure-call treatments, the number and quality of his grateful patients, and also his own medical qualifications. He backdated his birth by a decade to 1749 in order to fit in alleged training at the Calcutta Hospital and experience as a surgeon in the Bengal Army.[21] He also omitted his earlier careers in Ireland and London, implying he had come to Brighton as a shampooer in 1784. Increasingly, he claimed to have developed his treatment through scientific experimentation and an innovative use of steam – the miraculous source of power and progress in that age.

Dean Mahomed's developing persona as The Shampooing Surgeon from India resonated with Brighton's own rise as a resort. Publicists who touted Brighton and its growing health care industry featured his treatments in their guidebooks. Kings George IV and William IV submitted their bodies to his ministrations, as did many European aristocrats. Large numbers of Britain's middle classes imitated them in purchasing his services. His royal court costume was visibly modelled on Mughal imperial dress (although modified by his English shoes, neck-cloth, and presumably other English undergarments). He reportedly wore these robes to the horse racing track where he contributed handsomely to the Brighton Race Fund. Some Indians in Britain patronised his 'Indian' treatment.[22] Dean Mahomed made himself and his baths the epitome of fashion in Brighton for nearly two decades. He opened branch bathhouses in London and negotiated with British backers for franchises in other resorts (which never materialised).

As a rising figure in Brighton society, he showed himself a public-spirited citizen. He donated generously to the Sussex County Hospital and General Sea-Bathing Infirmary, regularly appearing as an official Steward for its Annual Charity Ball. He was a registered voter from 1841 (but he did not actually vote in Parliamentary elections until 1847).[23] On every royal visit, birthday, marriage, or birth, his bathhouse featured some of the town's grandest, brightest, and most patriotic gas-light illuminations. He also prominently subscribed for the relief of Brighton's destitute, supplying them with free soup and coal, as well as his own medical treatment, which his advertisements noted. Over his decades of prominence, many witty visitors and grateful patients penned prose and poetic eulogies (and parodies) of his 'Indian' method, his 'Muslim' or 'Hindu' identity (despite his conversion to Anglicanism a half century earlier), and himself as one of the town's most distinctive personalities. Ever the entrepreneur, he incorporated some of these eulogies into his own publicity.

His very success inspired British rivals to imitate his 'Indian' treatment. He repeatedly rejected their appropriation of his identity: 'In consequence of the many IMITATIONS of and the repeated attempts to rival his celebrated Indian Bath, [Dean Mahomed] thinks it necessary to assure the public that the art of SHAMPOOING, as practiced in India, is exclusively confined to himself in Brighton'.[24] Nonetheless, his English competitors continued. For instance, in 1823, the Royal Original Baths (Brighton's oldest bathhouse, founded 1769) renamed its featured treatment: 'Improved Indian Medicated Vapour and Shampooing'. The initial advertisement for this featured the terms 'improved' six times and 'Indian' four times.[25] In the heated public exchanges and competing advertisements that followed such challenges, Dean Mahomed trumpeted his unique authenticity as an actual Indian: 'The herbs and essential oils with which my Baths are impregnated, are brought expressly from India, and undergo a certain process known only to myself ...'.[26] Nonetheless, he had made the terms 'shampooing' and 'Indian bath' widespread, consequently losing proprietary control over their use.

In his eighties, an unfortunate financial blow hit. When the British owner of Mahomed's Baths, Thomas Brown, died in 1841, his executors determined to liquidate. Despite twenty years of flourishing practice, Dean Mahomed himself did not have enough capital to purchase the establishment and had to offer to lease it from whomever made the highest bid. To add to this public humiliation, the first auction failed, since no one met the reserve price. Almost two years later, Brown's executors once again offered Mahomed's Baths at public auction, this time with no bottom price. The new British owners used Mahomed's name and method but did not employ him.

Dean Mahomed and Jane moved to a far more modest rented establishment at 2 Black Lion Street. Dean Mahomed continued to advertise in newspapers, offering 'reduced rates', although their youngest son, Arthur, apparently did the actual shampooing.[27] By the time Jane and Dean Mahomed died (26 December 1850 and 24 February 1851 respectively), they had largely fallen from public attention. British obituaries uniformly lamented that Dean Mahomed, once so important to Brighton's development, had largely been forgotten.[28] After his death, shampooing became mere hair wash and the steam bath became 'Turkish' instead of 'Indian'.

Further, Dean Mahomed had so identified himself as Indian with his method that his British-born children found it quite difficult to sustain his enterprise. In 1830, Dean Mahomed had established a bathhouse for his teenage son Deen, Jr, at 11 St James's Place, among London's numerous gentlemen's clubs. Unfortunately, Deen went bankrupt in 1836 and apparently died soon thereafter.[29] In 1838, Dean Mahomed created a London bathhouse for his next son, Horatio (1816–1873), at 7 Little Ryder Street, St James's. Lacking his father's Indian origins, however, Horatio struggled until his death.[30] The next son, Frederick (1818–1888) developed his own successful, independent career in Brighton teaching European-style dancing, fencing, gymnastics for men, and 'hygeinics' for women. Dean Mahomed and Jane's youngest son, Arthur Ackber Mahomed (1819–1872), carried on the family business but never prospered.[31] In the twentieth century, two branches of the family changed their surname from Mahomed respectively to Deane and Ryder.[32] Thus, as British attitudes toward India shifted, the entrepreneurial opportunities that had made Dean Mahomed so successful as the Indian Shampooing Surgeon lost value and proved beyond his descendants to continue.

Professors in East India Company Colleges

The continuing expansion of East India Company rule over ever more of India during this period meant an increasing demand in Britain for teachers of Indian languages. As we saw, Indians like Abu Talib – trained in the Persian language and technology of rule that had dominated much of India for centuries – possessed a wealth of knowledge they felt British officials and scholars should and would appreciate. Yet, growing colonialism also meant many Britons valued the expertise of Indians less over time. These conflicting factors shaped the careers of Indian teachers, both creating positions for them and also questioning the worth of what they offered. The most salient examples of this class were four Indians appointed to prestigious positions at the East India Company's own civil service college at Haileybury (originally in nearby Hertford) established in 1806 and its military seminary at Addiscombe (south of London) founded in 1809. Until 1823, these Indian professors taught hundreds of Britons preparing for careers ruling India. As appropriate for men of their social standing, they socialised with each other and with other Indians in Britain, and also made respected places for themselves in British society.

Sheth Ghoolam Hyder (1776–1823) of Darbhanga, Bihar had, like Abu Talib, journeyed of his own accord to London, seeking employment teaching Persian. Hearing of the Company's newly-opened civil service college, he applied in August 1806 'as Persian Writing Master'. He enclosed with his unsolicited application a sample of his calligraphy, using Persian verses as his text. Although the College deemed his English barely adequate, he was immediately appointed at an annual salary of £200, equivalent to his European colleagues. After settling, he returned his Indian servant to India and hired British ones. As indicated in a contemporary image, he instructed his students wearing his turban and traditional robes, even as they wore traditional British academic caps and gowns. In his pedagogy, Ghoolam Hyder had Haileybury students copy Persio-Arabic characters which had been 'engraved upon several copper plates' and pronounce 'Select passages'.

Ghoolam Hyder served as assistant to the Professor of Persian, Captain Charles Stewart, newly-appointed at £500 annually. They comprised the first appointees in 'the Muhammadan Division' (which included Persian, Hindustani/Urdu, and Arabic) – as opposed to the 'Hindoo Division' (Sanskrit and Bengali). Such linguistic alignments reflected British colonial sociologies that linked language and religion. While numerous Muslim scholars travelled to Britain, few educated Hindu ones did so the 'Hindoo Division' remained exclusively in British hands.

Even as Hyder joined the faculty, the Company's directors sought to recruit more language teachers directly from India. They first invited Abu Talib to return at a handsome salary of £600. Unfortunately, Abu Talib died only months before this invitation arrived. Eventually, the Company recruited two scholars from the staff of its Fort William College in Calcutta: Moolvey Meer Abdool Alee of Varanasi and Moolvey Mirza Khaleel of Lucknow. Both were persuaded to accept these appointments, but only at the annual salary offered Abu Talib: £600 plus expenses (including free passage to and from England). Indeed, Haileybury authorities complained that this created an 'unpleasant situation' since their salary exceeded by £100 that of the highest paid British professors (including Thomas Malthus and their direct supervisor, Stewart). These two men made their way separately to England in 1807 and 1808 respectively, each attended by a Muslim servant.

On their arrival, they received appointments as Assistant Professors, higher in status and salary than Ghoolam Hyder. They were also his social superiors, in India and Britain. They taught rudimentary Persian, Hindustani, and Arabic to some 130 students annually. They, along with British professors, read out, glossed, and parsed selections, and dictated translations to their students, who memorised their words. Thus, Abdool

Alee and Mirza Khaleel were comparable to the highest British faculty in duties and salary, if not in rank or administrative responsibilities.

The fourth professor, Meer Hassan Ali of Lucknow, a well-born scholar and former official for the Company and the ruler of Awadh, had come on his own to England in September 1809, seeking employment as professor of Persian, Arabic, Hindustani, or Bengali. He applied first to Haileybury but that college believed it had enough Indian professors. Then he successfully applied to newly-opened Addiscombe college, joining that faculty (initially paid £250 annually, raised to £400 in 1811) as Assistant to the Professor of Oriental Literature, John Shakespear.

Of these Indian professors, three married Englishwomen. Two, Moolvey Abdool Alee and Ghoolam Hyder, remained in Britain until they died (in 1812 and 1823 respectively), leaving their widows and children dependent on pensions from the East India Company. Meer Hassan Ali remained six years on the Addiscombe faculty. Complaining of ill health, however, he resigned in 1816, receiving an annual pension of £120 plus £205 for his sea passage home. Just before leaving Britain, he married a British woman, Biddy Tims, in St. James Parish Church, Westminster. In India, they lived a dozen years in his family home before she left him and returned to England. She then published a two volume book about her life as his wife: Mrs Meer Hassan Ali, *Observations on the Mussulmauns of India* (London: Parbury, Allen, 1832).[33] Hassan Ali subsequently married women of his own class and had descendants who served the Company. Only Mirza Khaleel never married in England. In 1819, he resigned with a pension of £360 annually for life. Although he originally intended a journey home via the Islamic holy lands, he apparently remained in England until 1826. He evidently earned enough to live on (probably by teaching Indian languages) and returned to his wife and family in Lucknow with £2,500 cash.

After 1823, both Haileybury and Addiscombe decided that they desired no more Indian faculty. Although the language teaching given by their British instructors was notoriously weak, the social and cultural cost of having Indian professors appeared too high. Company directors and college administrators disliked having future British rulers of India learn from Indian professors with English wives. Haileybury College did appoint an Iranian, Mirza Muhammed Ibrahim (*c.*1800–1857) to the faculty for eighteen years (1826–1844), although he spoke a different form of Persian and no Indian languages. Thus, the force of Anglicisation and colonial racial distancing were such that the Company rejected Indian experts in Indian languages, preferring less linguistically competent Britons. Nonetheless, Indian teachers of various Indian languages continued to offer private tuitions in Britain throughout this period.

Indian Diplomats and Royalty Enter Britain

Among the scores of Indian rulers deposed and pensioned by the Company during this period, a relatively small but growing number decided to come or send envoys to London in order to overrule authorities in India. Part of the Company's policy in India was to project a unified British front while simultaneously isolating Indian rulers from each other and from London. However, those Indian diplomats who overcame the Company's obstacles and made the slow and dangerous voyage to London discovered the deep divisions among various contending factions within the Company's directors and Parliament and between those and Company officials in India. Various claimants to Indian thrones or pensions continued to appear in London whom the uninformed directors were afraid to offend but also feared to support least they disrupt the Company's political alliances in distant India. Gradually the directors developed archives and tactics to identify and try to constrain these envoys and princes. Only the most assiduous among them achieved even partial success in London.

The exceptional Rammohun Roy (1772–1833) proved more insightful and prepared than most envoys of his time, but even he was not fully satisfied. Roy, born into a landholding Brahmin family, had prosperously served the Company in his youth. Extensively educated in Sanskrit, Bengali, Persian, Arabic, and English, he also studied Latin and Greek in order to read older Christian texts. A founder of the 'Bengal Renaissance', his debates in Calcutta with both Hindu and Christian religious leaders and his many publications had long made him famous even in Britain.[34] In 1828, Mughal Emperor Muhammad Akbar II (*r.*1806–1837) bestowed on Roy the titles *Raja* and *ilchi* ('ambassador'), giving him 'full and unlimited powers' to negotiate a restoration of the Emperor's pension up to the level specified by treaty but for decades denied by his British guardians in Delhi. The Emperor also contracted to pay Roy in perpetuity a percentage of whatever increase in the pension he achieved.

While the Company still nominally recognised the sovereignty of the Emperor, the Governor-General rejected Roy's credentials as imperial envoy and strove to prevent him from leaving India. He pressurised the Emperor to repudiate Roy, succeeding in exciting the imperial Heir Apparent's jealousy against him. Nevertheless, the Governor-General recognised he could not legally forbid Roy from coming here.

Roy sailed from Calcutta (November 1830). His suite included: his adopted son, Rajaram Roy; a long-time associate, Ramrotun Muherjah; servants, Ramhurry Dass and Shaikh Baxoo (for the last three Roy posted £100 servant bonds); Robert Montgomery Martin, an editor of one of Roy's multilingual newspapers, the *Bengal Herald*, who was being deported from India for a critical editorial; plus cows to provide fresh milk for Roy. During the passage, Roy ate apart from the British passengers, having his servant cook in his private cabin. However, he reportedly joined the other passengers after dinner for wine.

After reaching Britain (April 1831), Roy's charisma, tremendous intellect, and powerful reform programme – expressed through well-received speeches, sermons, and publications – expanded his strong British following. Sympathetic Britons regarded him as a savant from 'the East' yet one sympathetic to progressive Christianity, a man from whom they could derive 'Oriental wisdom' but also someone who could spread the message of European-style modernity among the Indian people. Unitarians particularly welcomed him, believing his religious views resonated with theirs.

More than most people of his day, Roy understood how lack of Indian 'patriotism' had enabled the British conquest.[35] Thus, while Roy accepted the Emperor's authority, he regarded himself as representing all Indians: 'I am here [in London] so situated as to be responsible not only to the King of Delhi but to the whole body of my Countrymen for my exertions on his behalf and for their welfare'.[36]

Roy experimented with different life-styles to find one appropriate to his status. He retained his customary clothing. But he also hired a fashionable coach, with liveried coachman and footman, as proper for a 'gentleman of moderate fortune'.[37] Roy hired Stanford Arnot (former assistant editor of the newspaper *Calcutta Journal*) as his secretary. Arnot apparently convinced Roy to rent for a time extravagant apartments in Cumberland Terrace, Regent's Park. Roy received more invitations from distinguished people than he could possibly accommodate. Roy attended the coronation of King William IV, seated among the Foreign

Ambassadors in Westminster Abbey. Among his conversation partners were James Mill and Jeremy Bentham; Bentham proposed nominating Roy for Parliament.[38]

Roy further enhanced his understanding of British politics and ideology. He researched earlier Indian diplomatic missions – learning tactics and assessing results. In contrast, his contemporary Indian envoys usually arrived (and departed) ill-informed about British politics. Roy intended to publish a book informing Indians of his discoveries concerning 'the intelligence, riches and power, manners, customs, and especially the female virtue and excellence existing in' Britain.[39] While several others before and after him did write such accounts, Roy's untimely death prevented him from doing so.

Roy did not confine himself to exploring Britain. In preparation for his trip to France, he corresponded with Tallyrand (1754–1838), protesting the need for a visa to enter such a free land. In Paris, he was very well received, including by scholars and King Louis Philippe (*r.* 1830–1846). He also planned trips to Austria and Italy.

Nevertheless, many Britons, particularly those with experience in India, refused to recognise Roy as a gentleman. For example, Captain Manleverer, observing Roy at a London soirée, exclaimed angrily: 'What is that *black fellow* doing here?'[40] William Thackeray (who was born in India) later in his fiction ridiculed both Roy (as the character 'Rummun Loll', a petty merchant claiming royalty) and the British hostesses who fawned on him.[41] Some of this hostility emerged during Roy's ultimately frustrating role as imperial envoy.

The directors attempted initially to deal with Roy's mission as they had learned to do with others: refuse to recognise his accreditation, demand the Emperor communicate only through local authorities in India, and deny Roy knowledge of its deliberations until he ran out of money and departed. Roy had prepared for their stonewalling even before he left India. He held impeccable credentials from the Emperor and documented his spurned attempts to correspond through British officials there.

Once in London, Roy negotiated shrewdly, strengthening his hand through his evidence, argumentation, and personal connections among influential Britons. When first writing to the directors, Roy submitted his printed pamphlet detailing and documenting the Emperor's case: *Treaty with the King of Delhi* (London: John Nichols, 1831). But he cannily promised that he had not yet distributed copies, intimating that he could do so to gain public support: 'I mention this fact because I am anxious to bring the whole matter quickly and unostentatiously before the Honourable Court of Directors'.[42] Roy cited specific Government of India Regulations proving his case, marking each by hand in a printed manual. Roy insightfully cast his argument in terms of the sanctity of contracts and of private property, bedrocks of British legal and social thinking: '[If the Emperor's legal treaty] be not valid and obligatory, then no contract can be considered binding, no man's property is secure …'.[43] Further, he appealed to the British 'love of justice which breathes through the Acts of Parliament'.

Roy cultivated his friends, especially those in Parliament. He was already admired among reformers for his advocacy of the abolition of *sati* among other measures. Indeed, a Parliamentary Select Committee requested that he, 'as a native' of India, advise them on the upcoming 1833 Company Charter Renewal Bill. Roy published a book compiling his extended advice on colonial policy: *Exposition of the Practical Operation of the Judicial and Revenue Systems of India and of the General Character and Condition of Its Native Inhabitants* (London: Smith, Elder, 1832). When the 1832 Reform Bill passed Parliament, Roy wrote: 'Thank heaven I can now feel proud of being one of your fellow subjects'.[44] The directors therefore decided to make an exception in his case, concluding it would be politic to deal with him rather than have him negotiate directly with Parliament.

Yet, even as the directors opposed his official purpose, they recognised his personal prestige. They hosted an eighty person 'family dinner' for him, avoiding officially recognising him as imperial envoy but showing their respect for him unofficially. The Chairman toasted that he hoped other 'able and influential' Hindus would emulate Roy by coming to London. Roy ate in their presence, but only rice and water prepared by his own cook.

Despite Roy's social and intellectual advantages, he experienced frustrations that plagued other Indian diplomats and envoys. The directors, after deliberating nearly two years, conceded (February 1833) only a partial increment in the Emperor's pension, from its current Rupees 1,200,000 annually to Rupees 1,500,000. Yet, since the 1805 Treaty explicitly promised the Emperor the revenues of the Delhi territories, which had risen to Rupees 3,000,000, this was an increase only from 40 percent to 50 percent of the amount legally due. Further, to accept this modest increase, the Emperor had to relinquish any claim on the rest.

Roy wrote how compromised he felt by his need to plead before the directors, not only on behalf of his imperial master but also in terms of his own self-respect. The directors tried to maintain even in his case their custom of not informing Indian envoys of the outcome of their appeals. Only Roy's warm personal relationship with Charles Grant, President of the Board of Control, convinced the directors to notify him as a 'personal courtesy to himself ... [since] it is not usual for the Court [of Directors] to enter into any explanation of their decisions'.[45] When he learned how little he had gained, Roy advised the Emperor to reject this offer, promising to increase it through further negotiations with Parliament. Nevertheless, Roy's modest success inspired various Indian rulers to try to employ him, send their own Indian representatives, or travel to Britain themselves in emulation. Ultimately, the British never paid even this increase, due to Roy's early death and subsequent disputes between the Emperor and Governor-General over the money.

Further, Roy faced additional embarrassments. The British banking-house in Calcutta which managed his money failed, leaving him without funds. He repeatedly appealed to the directors for a £2,000 loan. They demanded a 'respectable' person as his guarantor. When he offered only his own personal guarantee, they refused the loan. Roy proudly refrained from asking for money from his admiring British supporters, but had to depend upon them for hospitality. Thus, despite his social prominence, publications, and successful public lectures, sermons, and private dialogues, he fell into despondency and illness over his slighted treatment by the directors and his financial difficulties. Additionally, his secretary, Arnot, demanded large sums from him and later claimed authorship of publications that Roy had dictated to him. On a trip to Bristol, Roy died (27 September 1833). He was much mourned among his British and Indian supporters.[46]

His suite consequently received the sympathies of the British public, Government, and even the directors. Ramrotun Muherjah was an envoy in his own right, presenting a petition from Indian owners of tax free lands who felt threatened by the Bengal Government's Regulation III of 1828 that empowered local British officials to dispossess them.[47] After Roy's death, Mukerjah received an appointment in the unconvenanted civil service, and became Native Deputy Collector of Murshidabad. Roy's servant Ramhurry Doss returned to India, where the Maharaja of Burdwan appointed him Head Gardener. Shaikh Baxoo had apparently returned earlier. Roy's young adopted son, Rajaram Roy remained in Britain for eight years, adapting himself to British society, working for the Board of Control, but then returning to Calcutta and a minor post in the British administration. Thus, while Rammohun Roy functioned far more effectively than many other Indian envoys, even for him, the power inequities inherent in colonialism brought much frustration.

The Collective Lascar Presence in British Ports

Indian seamen who accepted employment on the long voyage to Britain voluntarily entered a world of severe hardships and expected rewards. Over half of some lascar crews died on aboard or in Britain.[48] Yet, many men made multiple trips, so they were well experienced in what they would encounter here. During the Napoleonic wars that consumed so many British seamen, ever more lascars found work: the years 1803–1813 saw 10,050 lascar arrivals in Britain, peaking at 1,336 in 1813 alone.[49] Further, in 1813, Parliament ended the Company's monopoly over trade with India which created jobs for lascars on British private merchant ships now able to import Indian goods. The end of the Anglo-French wars, however, released many British seamen from the Royal Navy during a worldwide depression, temporarily reducing the number of lascars who could find work sailing here. Thereafter, with recovered trade, their numbers rose significantly again; during the 1820–1821 season, 509 lascars arrived, many more followed in subsequent years.

For many Britons, a major benefit of colonialism in Asia was the growing importation of Indian goods but this had the undesired cost of tens of thousands of Indian lascars coming to Britain. Unlike Indian servants, scholars, wives, and diplomats who brought some distinction, lascars presented what British authorities increasingly regarded as problems. Many respectable Britons were offended by their alleged begging, petty-theft, street-peddling, or their very presence in Britain. Yet, many British evangelicals and other social reformers worked to convert or 'improve' the lascars living among them.

While most Indian seamen remained together in London's docklands, a significant number appeared in other cities, towns, and villages. Sometimes they succeeded in establishing themselves: finding work, joining the local congregation, and marrying. When less successful, however, they generated unfavourable public or official notice as 'infesting the streets in the metropolis and wandering about the Country'.[50] Magistrates and poor house administrators wrote the Company's directors from all over Britain, seeking reimbursement for maintaining indigent Indians and requesting instructions for their disposal. For 1804–1814 alone, impoverished Indian seamen appeared in Alnwick (Northumberland), Chelmsford (Essex), Cork (Ireland), Dartford (Kent), Durham (Durham), Exeter (Devon), Leicester (Leicestershire), Lewes (Sussex), Lincoln (Lincolnshire), Liverpool (Merseyside), Maidenhead (Windsor), Maidstone (Kent), Plymouth (Devon), Portsmouth (Hampshire), St Albans (Hertfordshire), Shepperton (Surrey), Symington (Ayrshire), and Winchester (Hampshire).[51] Further, various 'riots' broke out where lascars congregated, as when armed Indian and Chinese seamen fought a 'desperate affray' at Stepney (London) in 1785.[52]

Until 1797, the lascar's ship-owner was supposed to maintain him between his arrival and passage back to India, but often did not. An informal array of lodgings arose to house lascars who could pay, but an increasing number of evidently penurious Indians appeared throughout Britain. The Company's directors, Parliament, law courts, the Navy Agent, Christian missionaries, and other British authorities recognised the need – and the Company's responsibility – to protect lascars, particularly against predatory British sex workers, tavern keepers, and swindlers. Consequently, from 1797, the Company contracted with a series of lodging-house keepers in London's Shoreditch and Shadwell to provide lascar housing.

One of these contractors, Abraham Gole, in 1804 obtained sole rights from the Company to provide shelter and food for lascars in his purpose-built depot off Ratcliffe Highway, Shadwell. Gole (until his death in 1819) and then his son, Abraham Gole, Junior, retained this exclusive contract until 1834, housing and feeding tens of thousands of lascars as well as other indigent Indians (including impoverished women and men servants and diplomats). Over the 1803–1813 period alone, the Company paid Gole £117,958 and other contractors £51,837 more for medicine and clothing (plus £200,692 for lascar passage home).[53] No one, however, had authority to force lascars to go to Gole's depot or remain in it; the directors rather relied on the shelter's free food, lodging, clothing, medicine, and camaraderie to attract and hold lascars. Indians who approached the directors (or were sent by local authorities), even after a decade in Britain, received maintenance and free passage home. Overall, Gole's depot centred a collective but transient Indian community for three decades, with an entire service industry around it.

Behind the tall compound wall that separated Gole's barracks from the surrounding British society, lascars largely organised themselves. Indians, Chinese, Arabs, and Malays tended to live in separate areas. Each serang exercised authority (including corporal punishment like whipping and close confinement) over of his lascar crew, who lived together in a room equipped with its own stove. Within a single crew, ethnicities (including Muslims, Christians, Parsis and Hindus of several castes or regions) may have cooked and eaten separately. Gole's staff issued clothing ('[a] Blue Jacket lined throughout with Flannel, Blue Trowsers lined throughout with Flannel, Guernsey Frock, Shoes, Stocking and Cap') and raw food ('Each man one pound of rice with sugar, tea, pepper, salt and onions also an unlimited allowance of vegetables and potatoes, every day; every second day, three quarters of a pound of mutton; and each intervening day, two or three red herrings according to the size') plus candles and fuel.[54] Nonetheless, the poor food, living conditions, and diseases in the often over-crowded barracks meant that many died; in the peak 1813–1814 season, ninety-one Indian lascars died (plus thirty-one Chinese), five died on one particularly cold day (14 March 1814) alone.[55]

Around Gole's depot grew up an array of pawnbrokers, clothing shops, taverns, and houses of prostitution which thrived on separating these lascars from their money and possessions. The Company blamed lascars for patronising these places which impoverished and diseased them, allegedly leading to their shockingly high death rates. Indian lascars occasionally openly confronted such purveyors and rival groups. For example, in 1803, three lascars armed with cutlasses broke into the City of Carlisle public-house in Whitechapel, seeking to recover the substantial sum of £150 they claimed that local sex workers had stolen from them. The landlord had them arrested. The directors bailed them out, paid the damages, and put them aboard an outgoing ship: 'for their better protection from the women of the town'.[56] Elite British fears about the predations by the British poor, especially British poor women, on Asian seamen would recur. Just two years later, lascars took over the streets of Shadwell in a large-scale tumult in which fifteen people were hospitalised and nineteen arrested. Only a month after that, lascars seised the streets east of the Tower of London one Friday night, claiming a sex worker had robbed one of their members. In 1806 near Gole's barracks, 150 Indians fought 300 Chinese who were supported by some Arab seamen. The alleged causes were an escalating conflict initially generated on the ship *Skelton Castle*, which had sailed to London with 150 lascars and 20 Chinese seamen aboard, and jealousy over some local British women who were living with some but desired by others. Since many lascars and Arabs were Muslim, and most Chinese seamen were not, this was evidently not a religious conflict. In 1808, a quarrel between a drunken but armed British sailor and a single lascar brought 400 lascars out of Gole's barracks and into the streets in his support. A passing squad of British militia drove them by bayonet back into the depot, where they barricaded themselves in. In August 1813, Irish 'lumpers' (stevedores) fought street battles against Indian lascars. Thus, this large body of unemployed lascars led to frictions, especially with Britons who sought to exploit them and rival ethnicities among maritime workers.

Many others in the surrounding British community resented the large lascar presence in their midst. In December 1813, British vandals desecrated the graveyard where lascars buried their dead, disinterring four bodies.[57] Even while this violation occurred, the Rector, Warden, Overseers, and Trustees of the local Parish Church of St. George collected 192 signatures from their congregation against 'the inconvenience, and Nuisances which arise from the Lascars being accommodated in that Neighbourhood, and that the Property of the Petitioners has been much deteriorated and reduced in value'.[58] The directors responded that the outgoing ships of the season would soon sail, emptying the neighbourhood of lascars and therefore the 'Nuisances'.

This transient community of lascars also related in less violent ways with British society. During the first ten days of the month of Muharram, 1220 Hijri (1–10 April 1805), Shi'ite lascars supported by other Muslims and also Hindu lascars organised huge religious processions over several days through the streets of Shadwell. The response of the British public and press was quizzical but respectful.[59]

Over time, various British Christian evangelicals, other social reformers, and politicians interested themselves in this body of lascars. Christian missionaries sought to convert them. Among the various proliferating philanthropic societies that tried to assist and 'improve' them were: the Society for the Protection of Asiatic Sailors; the Society of Friends of Foreigners in Distress; the Society for the Suppression of Mendicity; the Distressed Sailor's Asylum; the Sailor's Home; the Society for Relief and Instruction of Poor Africans and Asiatics in London; and the Society for the Destitute. These and other groups repeatedly investigated and denounced conditions in Gole's barracks.

Parliament held the Company responsible for lascars but also rejected the Company's repeated requests for government support to control and maintain them. For example, in 1814, the directors vainly asked Parliament to establish 'a strong police to repress the irregularities of the natives [*sic*], to confine them within proper limits, and to prevent that intercourse between them and the lowest orders of society in this country, for which no endeavours of the Company have hitherto been effectual'.[60] Parliament did, however, work with the Company to reduce the number of lascars arriving by outlawing their employment except when it was 'impossible to procure a crew of British seamen'; yet the vital need for lascars continued.[61] While Parliament recognised that lascars should not legally be forcibly confined in the depot or expelled from Britain without due process of law, the vagrants among them could be deported.[62] Thus, the British Government, Company, seamen, and general population resented the presence of lascars in Britain but could not legally or economically eliminate them.

This ongoing lascar presence centred on Gole's barracks until 1834. When the Company lost its right to trade in India, it ended his contract to house and feed lascars. Then, this transient Indian community shifted eastward to London's Poplar and Limehouse districts (much closer to the East India Docks) as various private lodging-house keepers, including some Indians, provided for these lascars in what became known as London's Oriental Quarter (as we shall see in Chapter 4).

Shifting Receptions and Roles for South Asians in Britain

Over the decades discussed in this chapter, the effects of British colonial rule deeply affected the number, variety, and lives of Indians here. While most Indians came seeking employment or advancement, they virtually always came as dependents or appellants to Britons. In India, most Britons believed that their colonial rule required strong racial barriers against Indians. In Britain, the barriers that Indians faced were not so rigid, although some of these colonial attitudes were permeating British culture. Further, their identities as Indians were differentiated by class, gender, religion, and ethnicity. Individual settlers and visitors made choices about how Anglicised they wished to be, and faced different degrees of acceptance by different Britons. Some converted to Anglican Christianity, married, and merged into local society, with their lingering but fading Indian associations providing what was sometimes considered an attractive distinction from the other Britons around them.

As yet, most Indians here lived within British society rather than their own communities where they could live on their own terms. While lascars collectively formed a transient Asian communities in east London, their numbers and class status tended to cause distancing and friction with the British communities around them, both those Britons who serviced and exploited them and also the more respectable Britons who resented their presence. Over subsequent decades, all these factors would intensify.

Chapter 4

South-Asian Settlers and Transient Networks and Communities in Britain, 1830s–1857

Michael H. Fisher

The Developing Indian Presence in Britain

Over the decades leading up to 1857, the number and variety of Indians here expanded and they increasing socialised with each other, in different degrees according to their social class, religious community, gender, and relationships to Britons around them. Dozens of Indians settled here, some highlighting their Indian origins, others merging into society according to their respective classes. In the imperial capital, the households of Indian aristocrats and diplomats formed social centres where their numerous retainers, other visitors, settlers, and British hangers-on congregated for distinctive food, music, talk, and edification. In east London's docklands, lascars established an 'Oriental Quarter' – a substantial but transient community where Indian seamen and servants found companionship. Overall, as these cross-connections among Indians developed, they individually and collectively faced changing attitudes and conditions here, shaped largely by widening and deepening colonialism in India and also developments within Britain.

By 1857, all Indians experienced British colonial authority to varying degrees. In India, the British had annexed hundreds of kingdoms covering 1,577,000 square kilometres and containing some 165,000,000 people. Dozens of deposed and pensioned Indian dynasties still retained their royal status, but many grew restive at their confinement as virtual palace prisoners. Hundreds of thousands of Indian soldiers and officials sustained the colonial order (the Company's armies in 1857 alone contained 228,000 sepoy volunteers), although many grew dissatisfied with their degraded positions within it. India's other 800,000 square kilometres and 60,000,000 people remained under approximately 550 nominally sovereign Indian 'princes' who kept their thrones but struggled under British controls and feared annexation. They and their subjects lived under indirect colonial rule.

Especially from the 1830s onward, colonialism, with its relative impoverishment of India and enriching of Britain, made the latter appear attractive to many aspiring Indians. Various aristocratic and other elite Indian men viewed Britain as an accessible site for personal gratification and advancement, especially contrasted with the racial and other constraints on them in India. By 1857, at least thirty Indian royal or diplomatic missions had come to Britain, many lasting a year or so, others longer: envoys from Satara remained fifteen years (1838–1853). Discontented officials and soldiers, dispossessed landholders, and other aggrieved subjects failed to obtain justice from their new British masters in India, so some sought it here. Simultaneously, British efforts to make all things British – including technology, medicine, Christianity, and capitalism – appear universal roads to progress meant that Indian youths sought to study these directly in Britain. Indian seamen, servants, wives, and other employees and dependents of Britons also came seeking to better their lives. Some settled, marrying and merging into British society, many more stayed for a few months or for decades before returning. Increasingly, Indians wrote books about their lives here, either for Indian or British readers.

For virtually all Indians in Britain during these decades, however, their reception and roles differed from earlier times. Britain was itself undergoing social, cultural, economic, and political transformations. New opportunities for entrepreneurial activities emerged for Asians in Britain, now the dominant global power. Various British aristocrats continued a patronising recognition of their Indian peers. Many British women were receptive to Indians. Indeed, diplomat and scholar Lutfullah (1802–1874), like many other Indians, contrasted welcoming British society with the contemptuous attitudes of Britons in India: 'The fact is, that the more you proceed on towards England, the more you find the English people endowed with politeness and civility ...'[1] But, while British opinions about Indians here were never uniform, overall they changed adversely as colonialism and Britain developed. For many British elite and middle-class men, Indians, even royalty, had only vestiges of their earlier exotic attraction. Many British working-men, especially seamen, feared competition from Indians. Further, in 1834, Parliament suspended East India Company's Charter to trade in India for twenty years, thus legally removing its paternalistic responsibility for indigent Indians in Britain. Even after 1854 (when Parliament restored the Company's Charter for four years), the directors only marginally supervised or supported working-class and poor Indians in Britain as they had earlier.

The bloody fighting of 1857–1858 especially alienated Britons and Indians from each other. In India, the deaths of hundreds of Britons, including women and children, often carried out by Indian soldiers or servants who had worked under them or by Indian deposed princes, aroused British national horror and demands for retribution. British indiscriminate execution of thousands of Indian men, often without evidence or trial, and the looting of Indian property and assaults on Indian women, estranged many Indians against Britons generally. Following 1857 as well, Parliament formally took over the administration of India from the Company; the British Raj turned from policies of annexation, which intended to model Indians after Britons, to ones that relied on India's remaining princes as its 'natural leaders', presupposing that Indians were inherently inferior to Britons.[2]

In Britain as well, the events of 1857–1858 had deep impacts, reinforcing changing British concepts of 'race' as a biologically inherited and immutable identity which lumped all Indians into the same category as different from whites. Many Britons were coming to regard Indian men as physical threats, especially to white women. Thus, before and even more following the fighting in India, Indians here of all classes found far less sympathy. All these changing factors affected Indian identities and lives over the decades prior to 1857, binding Indians into greater solidarities – albeit ones cross-cut by economic class, religion, regional identities, and gender.

Aristocratic Settlers

As the imperial capital, London attracted dozens of Indian aristocratic men. In India, the East India Company customarily confined them to a luxurious but often constrained lifestyle as palace prisoners under British guardians. In London, they not only moved freely in the highest social circles, they often proved able to mobilise sufficient political support and recognition from British royalty and to enhance their pensions. Their wealth purchased the services of lower class Britons and sometimes the respect of middle class ones. Their lingering exotic associations attracted the attention of Britons, for better or worse. They also socialised with each other and bestowed patronage on other Indians. Rather than return to their relatively lower status back in India, several settled here, adding lustre to London and indulging in its pleasures and prestige themselves.

One such settler here was Mahomed Jamh ood-Deen (1792–1842), a younger son of the famous Tipu Sultan of Mysore. While British popular culture demonised Tipu Sultan more than any other Indian ruler (prior to 1857), his descendants found honoured acceptance in London society. British writers, dramatists, and painters portrayed Tipu as emblematic not just of oriental despotism but also, in his defeat and death in 1799, of British triumph. Indian travellers were guided by their British hosts to war trophies taken from Tipu and enshrined in Britain. After Tipu's death, the Governor-General pensioned but confined his dozen sons and many wives. As the family grew over time, these pensions stretched ever thinner to cover their aristocratic pretensions. Seeing the success of other Indian royalty in London, Jamh ood-Deen determined to resist his slide into obscurity by venturing here, where he could amuse and advance himself; his youngest brother would later emulate him.

Like the other deposed Indian royalty seeking such freedoms, Jamh ood-Deen had to persuade his British keepers in India to release him from internment. At age forty-one he claimed: 'for some months past I am frequently troubled with anxiety and restlessness of mind', therefore only four years in England's bracing climate would restore his 'impaired Constitution'.[3] When his British superintendent rejected this, Jamh ood-Deen appealed personally to Governor-General Bentinck. After two years' deliberation, Bentinck finally granted permission in 1833 and provided a letter of introduction to the British King. Jamh ood-Deen arranged to receive some £2,000 of his annual pension in Britain, while the remaining £450 would support his extensive household in India including: eight wives and mistresses, his senior mother-in-law, his own mother, his estranged adopted son, and seven bodyguards. Early in 1835, he sailed for Britain with only a European manservant to attend him.

Until his death seven years later, Jamh ood-Deen settled in British high society as 'the Prince of Mysore', even as he worked with substantial success to convince the directors that they owed him money. His family's status, and Bentinck's letter, gained a private audience with King William IV, to whom he proffered a book narrating his family's royal history. He also agreed to avoid politics. Jamh ood-Deen continued to meet with King William and then Queen Victoria, which firmly established his aristocratic credentials. He also secured the sympathetic support of powerful British politicians and the French and Belgian monarchs. The lingering notoriety of his father only added to his prestige.

Like other Indian royalty here, Jamh ood-Deen campaigned to enhance his pension. He employed Captain Grindlay (a former Company army officer whose agency later became Grindlay's Bank) and British lawyers to pursue his case before the directors and in British law courts. He argued that by treaty, when he had reached age fifteen, his pension should have been doubled to £4,800 annually, but less than half that had actually been paid by Company officials in India. Therefore he demanded the increase plus considerable arrears of £83,040 with compound interest. After hearing his arguments and receiving pressure from his influential friends for a year, the directors grudgingly accepted and paid his demands for the pension enhancement and arrears, but not for compound interest.

Funded by these sizeable payments and undiscouraged by the directors' refusal to do more, Jamh ood-Deen continued his demands. These, plus his refusal to return to India, frustrated the directors and Government, who could not legally deport him. Cabinet Minister and President of the Board of Control, John Hobhouse, wrote confidentially to the Governor-General in 1837:

> We have *our* grievances also ... we have the Mysore Prince who, having persuaded Lord W. Bentinck to allow him to come to England for his health, has turned the journey to account by raising his allowances, and now threatens me with an appeal to the H. of Commons, because I will not force the Court [of Directors] to pay interest on the arrears now granted to him. So I say, send us no more missions, and no more Mysore Princes, if you please.[4]

A few months later and frequently thereafter, Hobhouse privately directed the Governor-General to pressurise 'that wretched fellow' through his family:

> your Mysore Prince Jamh-ood-Deen is very troublesome and is going to bring his case before Parliament ... I do wish you would signify to him that unless he returns forthwith you will play the deuce with his wives and mothers of whom he is always talking

> to me – as if he had as many of the last as the first. You have no notion how very annoying he is, and I repeat my intreaties to you not to tolerate his absence any longer.[5]

So troublesome were Jamh ood-Deen and other Indian royalty and diplomats in their constant and often successful lobbying of Parliament and exposing of the Company's less savoury and legal actions in India, that Hobhouse warned the Governor-General against further annexations without strong justification:

> Each of the dethroned Princes will have Vakeels [Indian representatives] in England, and I shall have to fight the battles of the deposers in Parliament. I hope, therefore, you will be a little cautious in adopting such measures [annexations] and, if you do adopt them, at least send me over a defensible brief.[6]

While protests by deposed royalty and their envoys in London thus had political costs for Government, the pace of annexations and dethronements nonetheless continued apace until 1857.

Although his initial four year 'leave' had long expired, in 1841 Jamh ood-Deen savoured London life, arranging for more of his pension to be paid him here and less to his family in India. During this time, he lived in fashionable Albany Street, London, with a British maidservant, Rachel Loyd (*b.*1814). As a wealthy and well-known man about town, he socialised with British nobility. He also met frequently with Indian dignitaries, dining with the elite Muslims among them and patronising the others (as detailed in the Urdu personal diary of an Indian ambassador, Karim Khan).[7] One of Jamh ood-Deen's acquaintances and fellow Indian aristocrats, David Ochterlony Dyce Sombre (1808–1851), heir to Begum Sombre of Sardhana, was elected to Parliament from Sudbury, Suffolk, in 1841.[8] In November 1842, after seven years of this high society life, and still making occasionally successful further claims for augmentation of his pension, Jamh ood-Deen died while on a pleasure jaunt to Paris, where he was buried.

Before he died, Jamh ood-Deen had encouraged other Indian royalty to visit London, including his youngest brother, Gholam Mahomed (1795–1872), and relatives by marriage: Iqbal al-Daula (1808–1888) and Nepali Prime Minister Jung Bahadur Rana (1817–1877). During his visit (1837–1838), Iqbal al-Daula emulated Jamh ood-Deen in his high-society life and lobbied unsuccessfully for the Awadh throne, commissioning a book by cashiered Company army Captain William White: *The Prince of Oude* (London: William Strange, 1838). In 1850, Jung Bahadur received an even warmer welcome since he was the virtual ruler of Nepal.

Among the many other pensioned princes who followed Jamh ood-Deen prior to 1857 were the deposed Maharajas of Coorg, Veer Rajunder Wadiar (*r.*1820–1834, *d.*1859), and the Punjab, Duleep Singh (1838–1893, *r.*1843–1849) (see Chapter 5), as well as Mehdee Alee Khan Bahadur, son-in-law of the late Nawab of Rampur, and two descendants of the Nawab of the Carnatic, Hafiz Lodroo Islam Khan and Hyder Jung. Through two trips to Britain (1844 and 1853–1857), the son-in-law of the Nawab of Surat, Meer Jafur Ali Khan Bahadur (*d.*1863), turned a tenuous inheritance claim into secure, titled, handsomely pensioned status for himself and his daughters. Over the years, four aristocratic delegations from the large kingdom of Awadh arrived – the biggest and last of these with 113 men and women came in 1856, headed by the mother, brother, and heir of deposed Wajid Ali Shah (*r.*1847–1856), seeking to reverse the British annexation of Awadh. These pensioned royalty had to convince the British in India to grant them 'leave' from their confinement and travel to Britain; some, like Jamh ood-Deen, claimed that only the British climate would recover their health, others that they or a family member wished to become Christian or get an English education. Once in London, they enjoyed themselves, lobbied for more money or succession, published books to rally the British public and opposition politicians to their cause, sued the Company, and often successfully resisted British efforts to compel them to leave (at least until the events of 1857 made their situation particularly difficult).

Thus, over this period, Indian royalty and their entourages formed a continuous and controversial presence in London. Their wealth and royal status gained them personal access to the highest social and political circles in Europe, far higher than the British colonial establishment would allow in India. The men among them were empowered by gender over British women. Given the dozens of Indian dynasties deposed by the Company, however, the relatively modest number of Indian royalty in London speaks to the Company's effectiveness in confining its political relations with them to India, where its power was largely unchecked. Various middle and lower-class Indians who had settled in Britain found work with these royalty and embassies, as interpreters, guides, and servants; many others found congenial food and company among the members of these delegations who were of their own religious community and class.

Indian Intermediaries in London

As thousands of Indians tried to build careers as officials or scholars working under the British in India, many faced the frustrations of racial prejudice against them there. To advance their careers, and out of recognition for what the British had accomplished, many Anglicised themselves, at the cost of being alienated from their families and communities. While in India, they were never accepted as equals by Britons, in Britain, many proved able to combine their Anglicisation with their Indian identity which many Britons still appreciated and Indian aristocrats and diplomats here valued. These male intermediaries also found their gender and class elevated them over British women and lower-class men.

During this period, at least a dozen such Indian scholar-officials came to Britain to seek justice and advance their careers.[9] Among these was Mohan Lal Kashmiri (1812–1877) who came seeking honours for his diplomacy in Afghanistan. Another was Syed Abdoollah, who arrived in 1851 and settled here. Born at Pushkar, Rajasthan, around 1825, he had followed his father and other relatives into service to the British. He was an accomplished composer of Urdu and Persian poetry and prose. By 1851, however, he had only attained the modest office of 'Persian, Oordoo, Hindee, and English Translator to the Board of Administration for the Affairs of the Punjab'. He took two years leave at half pay and set out to advance himself in Britain.

Five months after arriving and exploring 'the English language, laws, and customs', Syed Abdoollah applied to the Company for appointment as 'Moonshee or Teacher of the Persian, Oordoo, and Hindee Languages' at its Haileybury or Addiscombe colleges. He enclosed glowing testimonials in support of his application, proposing:

> at least a trial as a Teacher to judge my capacity for a permanent Office in England; a Country to which I have become attached by my recent observation of its many noble Institutions and the kindness I have received from numerous persons of rank and worth. I am prepared to undergo an examination in the most difficult

> Persian and Oordoo works and I flatter myself that if I receive the appointment I seek the effect of my humble zeal and application will be apparent at the next ensuing College Examination in the improved pronunciation of such students as may be committed to my care.[10]

The directors declined his offer – as we saw in Chapter 3, both colleges had long refused to appoint Indians.

Meantime, however, Syed Abdoollah incurred 'heavy expenses of living in this Metropolis'. To generate income, he taught independently 'giving lessons in the Oriental Languages to gentlemen preparing to enter [Company] service'. He also taught Urdu for two years at Hanwell College and also at Grove, Blackheath.[11] Part of his expenses stemmed from his marriage, eighteen months after his arrival, to Margaret Wilson Henderson, the daughter of Royal Army Captain John Henderson. They wedded first in a civil ceremony and then, when her family objected, resolemnised it in St James Parish Church, Paddington.[12] In order to legally marry there, Syed Abdoollah swore under oath that he had become Anglican. They lived at 11 Bedford Street, Bedford Square, London.

In 1853, Syed Abdoollah renewed and reframed his argument for his appointment to Haileybury college:

> The importance of the acquisition of the languages of the East has been dwelt upon by successive [Company] Chairmen in their excellent and instructive addresses to the students of the Colleges and it has occurred to me that perhaps the assistance of a Native of the Country who has made philology his peculiar study would not be unacceptable to the students.[13]

The directors again declined his offer.

After this second rejection, Syed Abdoollah decided to return to India with his wife: 'As the love of one's country is great, and I have no permanent situation here'.[14] He applied to the directors for 'an appointment [in India] as Deputy Collector, Assistant Magistrate, or whatever other office your Hon'ble Court [of Directors] may think me fit to hold'. As usual, the directors redirected him to the Government of India. They did, however, provide free first class passage back to Jabalpur (where his father, Meer Syed Mohummud, was a Native

Magistrate) for him – but not his wife. He left England by steamer via the Cape, early in 1854. His return to India was brief. He visited his father presumably asking approval for all that he had done, including his marriage. He again reached England in August 1855, staying successively at Park Place, Paddington and later at 8 Grove-terrace, St John's Wood.

Syed Abdoollah resumed his career in London as a teacher and entrepreneur, based on his 'oriental' culture. He presented the directors with his translation of an erotic Urdu poem by the Awadh ruler Wajid Ali Shah, called 'Ocean of Love'.[15] He mixed socially with the large diplomatic delegation from Awadh, and sought a salaried appointment as its consultant, in vain.[16] He also proposed translating into Urdu Mountstuart Elphinstone's *History of India*; Elphinstone, however, declined paying him for this project and generally scorned Indian linguists.[17] Other Indian translators living in London were more successful; for example, Hafiz Ludroo Islam Khan (a descendant of the Nawab of the Carnatic) translated into Urdu and published in 1853 an abridgement of Oliver Goldsmith's 1764 *An History of England in a Series of Letters from a Nobleman to His Son*, which the directors graciously allowed him to dedicate to their Chairman.

Syed Abdoollah continued to seek work as a professor of Indian languages. In March 1858, he submitted to the directors a pamphlet arguing for the establishment of an 'Oriental College' in London (under his own direction). Indeed, as the Company terminated its colleges that year, other educational institutions, both private commercial and public, expanded their teaching of Indian languages to Britons going to India. One of the largest employers of Indian faculty became University College, London. Syed Abdoollah applied for and received appointment as Professor of Hindustani there (1859–1866).[18] His colleagues included R. Cowasjee, Lecturer in Gujarati (1866–1869), Ganendra Mohan Tagore, Professor of Bengali and Indian Law (1860–1865), Khitter Mohun Dutt, M.D., Lecturer in Bengali (1865–1866) and Hindustani (1867–1869), and D.K. Shahabudin, Professor of Hindustani, Gujarati, and Marathi (1871–1874). As we will see in Chapter 5, two other colleagues were G. Hyder, Lecturer in Bengali (1866–1871) and Hindustani (1869–1871) and a Parsi scholar and merchant from Bombay, Dadabhai Naoroji (1825–1917), Professor of Gujarati (1856–1866) – later 'Grand Old Man' of the Indian National Congress (founded 1885) and Member of Parliament (1892–1895).

Appellants: Visitors and Settlers

As the Company's colonial administration extended over the vast majority of Indians, many grew frustrated with its injustices. Nonetheless, many believed British dogma that the British Monarch and legal system, as fonts of justice, would right all wrongs brought directly before them. Indian appellants arrived seeking that justice throughout this period, including dozens of Indian soldiers and petty officers complaining against their British commanders, Indian officials seeking advancement or protesting their subordination by Britons, and an array of Indian landholders (or would-be landholders) seeking their property rights. Some found work to sustain their expensive appeals here. Enough gained a hearing and some recompense that this number continued to grow. Most, however, returned home unsatisfied and often impoverished. A few, although not granted what they had sought, nonetheless decided to settle here rather than return dissatisfied to India.

For example, in 1833, Mohammed Ibrahim Palowkar (1811–1855) arrived from Bombay with his father, Aboo Syed Palowkar (*b.*1786), and a suite of servants, claiming long-dispossessed landholdings. While their petition had no realistic chance of success, it reflected their desperate faith in British justice if only they could reach London. Ultimately, as their plight became more forlorn, their own unpaid servants themselves appealed against them to the directors, the father went home disappointed, but the son married a British woman and settled in London.

This family claimed origins in Arabia, indeed descent from the Prophet Muhammad, but had acquired its landholdings at Dabhol in 1685, at the peak of Mughal imperial expansion southward.[19] Although their lands lay in the heart of Maratha territories, the family held possession for fifty years. They also partly assimilated into the local culture, taking the Maratha-style family name: Palowkar. After losing these lands to Maratha rivals in 1736, they fled to Bombay, taking refuge with the Company, while struggling futilely for four generations to recover their property.

The Third Anglo-Maratha War (1817–1819) replaced Maratha by British rule in the region. Thereafter, much of the revenue from their lost lands went into the British treasury. However, British rule also created new possibilities for redress. For sixteen years, the Palowkars submitted appeals to the Bombay Government, hiring a British lawyer in Bombay to advance their claims. They sought not only restoration of the family's rights, but a century of rent arrears. The Bombay Government judged that the century-old dispossession was long past the statue of limitations but also conceded that the Company's directors in London could overrule this decision. The family understood this to mean that they should personally venture to London and there obtain redress.

Leaving behind the women and other family members, Aboo Syed brought his eldest son, Mohammed Ibrahim, and four servants to London. To pay for their passage, he mortgaged their three houses in Bombay. On reaching London in November 1833 (after an eight month journey via Egypt), they took respectable lodgings at 27 Haberdasher's Street, Shoreditch. They soon took legal advice from William Lyall, Esq. and then submitted their petition, requesting that the directors overrule the Bombay Government. Aboo Syed also borrowed money to sustain the family, using their expected compensation as collateral.

The directors quickly repulsed this appeal. Nevertheless, they understood how Aboo Syed 'seems to have understood the intimation made to him by the Bombay Government as an encouragement to proceed to this country'.[20] Nonetheless, the directors had no intention of undermining the authority of their Bombay Government by even officially considering Aboo Syed's case and used his increasing financial difficulties to induce him to leave London; to speed his departure, the directors were 'willing to incur a modest expense for defraying the charge of the passage of himself and family back to Bombay'. Aboo Syed, however, persisted. In June 1834, he appealed the directors' rejection, only to have it again rejected. The directors reiterated their proposed payment for his family's return 'provided he avails himself of their offer without loss of time'.[21]

Having learned in London about the Company's subordinate relationship to Parliament, Aboo Syed initiated a new campaign. He submitted his appeal, with all his supporting documents, to the President of the Board of Control, Charles Grant. Unlike Rammohun Roy's efforts, his appeal met only polite refusal – Grant's secretary referred him to the directors, urging him to accept their offer of return passage.

Over the months, the mission's financial situation deteriorated. In July, two of Aboo Syed's attendants, Munshi Haji Soolah al-Din (his secretary), and Shaik Sardar Haji (his cook), themselves petitioned the directors that Aboo Syed had stopped paying and even feeding them.

Consequently, they had moved out and taken humble lodgings at 10 Crutched Friars Street in the City. The Munshi asked the directors for employment in Britain, or else passage home. The directors refused to interfere in the matter of their wages, but did provide food, clothing, and lodging for these two men, as well as free passage back to Bombay.

As 1835 began, Aboo Syed appealed again with increasing desperation to both the directors and the Board of Control, not only over his original grievance, but also for an additional £600 reimbursement for his expenses coming to England. He pleaded that he was now faced with imprisonment for debt, so he would never be able to leave London. Further, should he return to Bombay not only empty handed but owing for the expenses of his coming here, he and his family would lose even their remaining heavily mortgaged property. Thus, he offered to exchange all his claims, which he asserted were worth £30,000, for a modest perpetual pension. He also moved into cheaper lodgings at 22 Jewry Street, Aldgate.

After eighteen months, Aboo Syed reluctantly agreed to return to Bombay with his plaint unsatisfied. The directors allotted him the 'modest expense' they had promised for his voyage, but routed him around the Cape. To maintain his status, however, Aboo Syed insisted on travelling to India via Egypt: 'by reasons of the many Inconveniences and Privations to which as Mahomedans they would be unavoidably exposed on board an English Ship [via south Africa]'. The directors granted him £300 (£50 less than he claimed necessary to sustain his status) and insisted 'that no part of the money be paid to Aboo Syed in this Country' lest he delay his departure any further or use the funds to renew his appeal. In July 1835, all these arrangements had been made, yet Aboo Syed's creditors in London insisted that the directors pay his debts (some sixteen months overdue) before he depart.

As Aboo Syed prepared to leave, his son, Mohammed Ibrahim, disappeared. Although his father unconvincingly denied knowledge of this, he had married a Protestant Irishwoman, Eleanor Deegan, at St Leonard's Church, Shoreditch, the previous February.[22] The directors, however, washed their hands of the matter, arranging that, should Mohammed Ibrahim ever reappear, Lyall would arrange his departure without any further expense to them. Aboo Syed and his remaining party reluctantly boarded ship in August 1835. Aboo Syed never recovered the claimed lands but his family apparently lived as merchants in Bombay.[23]

Mohammed Ibrahim, however, settled in London, running a tobacconist's shop until his death in 1855.[24] His three sons respectively became merchant's clerk, gas-fitter then electrician, and hatter. This family continues in Britain, with some branches taking the surname Wilson, but with few family traditions of their Indian origins.[25] Each member of the original delegation, like so many others, thus interacted differently with British society and authorities.

Indian Students Seek British Training in Technology, Science, and Christianity

Since the early seventeenth century, young Indian men have come here as students. With the British conquest over India, this number increased as Indians sought to gain mastery over the British scientific and technological accomplishments and cultural values that had allegedly made this conquest possible. During the period covered in this chapter, dozens of Indian students came to study engineering, medicine, Christianity, and British culture generally. Most then returned to India, applying and propagating their hard-earned knowledge and training there, others stayed on as settlers. Several wrote books about their experiences here, demonstrating their status as authors to the Britons with whom they studied and socialised and also informing their Indian audiences about what life in Britain was like for Indians.

Among the civil engineers who came were three cousins from the Parsi family that established and managed the Bombay shipyard. Jehangeer Nowrojee (1821–1866) and Hirjeebhoy Merwanjee (1817–1883) studied naval architecture here in 1838–1841 and co-authored *Journal of a Residence of Two Years and a Half in Great Britain* (London: William H. Allen, 1841). Ardaseer Cursetjee (1808–1877) studied maritime steam-engines here in 1839–1840 and wrote *Diary of an Overland Journey from Bombay to England and of a Year's Residence in Great Britain* (London: Henington and Galabin, 1840). Indeed, Cursetjee made three subsequent trips to Britain and died here. All applied the advanced technologies learned here in advancing the shipbuilding industry in Bombay and also their own careers working for the British.

British advances in medicine also impressed many Indians. In 1844, diplomat Lutfullah, for example, admired the surgery he observed in London, calling it 'the summit of the science of anatomy in both theory and practice'.[26] While Dean Mahomed was still practicing 'Indian' medicine but losing out to British practitioners, an increasing number of Indians were formally studying British medicine in India and in Britain. In 1845, four accomplished students from Calcutta Medical College (established 1835) agreed to accompany their British Professor of Anatomy, Henry Hurry Goodeve, to Britain for advanced training and qualification at University College, London.[27] In Britain, these Indian medical students – Dwarkanath Bose, Bholanath Das Bose, Gopal Chandra Seal, and Soojee Comar Chuckerbutty – competed successfully against British classmates and also practiced on British bodies, including women's bodies. Given growing British attitudes toward the moral and even physical inferiority of Indians, their British hosts were astonished that these Indians could surpass British classmates in a rigorous and scientific subject like medicine. College and Company authorities monitored both their academic progress and also their social life with the Britons around them. These four mostly spent their holidays with Goodeve touring Britain's countryside and industry. On one journey, they paid homage at Rammohun Roy's grave.

The youngest, Chuckerbutty, adapted himself most to British society. He also took a First Degree in the University College Batchelor of Medicine examination, with certificates in Anatomy, Physiology, Materia Medica, and Chemistry. He won the Gold Medal in Comparative Anatomy (judged best for the last ten years) plus the Silver Medal in Zoology. He specialised in Surgery, as Dresser and then Clinical Clerk. On successive six week annual holidays, a leading faculty member, Dr Grant, took Chuckebutty on study tours to Paris and then to central Europe. Chuckerbutty also decided to convert to Christianity. Although Goodeve claimed he had not pushed his students toward this, he was pleased. Chuckerbutty also added 'Goodeve' to his name. After his fellow students returned to Calcutta with their teacher, Goodeve-Chuckerbutty stayed on, since he was too young yet to receive the MD degree and wanted to pursue further specialised training. When he reached the legal age, he passed his examination and became a member of the Royal College of Surgeons. In November 1848, he requested a further two year extension of training in London. The directors agreeing his accomplishments had been 'praiseworthy', allowed him to study Pathological Anatomy for another fifteen months at his annual stipend of £160 plus fees. The directors did not, however, grant his request for £55 for the purchase of a 'Microscope, and the Medical Books ... with a view to the prosecution of Scientific enquiries'. In Fall 1849, he submitted his testimonials and certificates, and the directors recommended to the Bengal Government his appointment to a suitable post in the Calcutta Medical College with a salary 'commensurate with his high attainments'. In this way, he could 'have an opportunity of communicating to his countrymen the scientific knowledge and practical acquirements attained by him in this country'. After his return to Calcutta, he was appointed Assistant Surgeon in the Bengal Government medical service. Goodeve-Chuckerbutty himself regarded his own achievements as a proof of the success of 'one of the most arduous experiments every yet undertaken by our countrymen'.[28] In 1854, he returned to England to be examined and qualified by the Board of Examiners. He topped the list in the Indian Medical Service examination of January 1855. He published in the *British Medical Journal* and rose to be the first Indian Professor of Medicine and Materia Medica at Calcutta Medical College in 1867.

The superior performance of these students demonstrated to the British public, as well as the engineering and medical professions, that Indians were capable of 'acquiring the sciences and professional knowledge of the Western World, and that in such contests they are equal to their European fellow Subjects'.[29] They also reassured Indians that British claims of racial superiority were unfounded. Many other Indian students would follow over the course of the nineteenth century.

Despite the strong evangelical Christian orientation of many Britons, including colonial officials, relatively few Indians in India converted, although a high proportion of those in Britain did so. Some who did convert in India came here to be ordained. In 1843, a Parsi convert to Christianity, Dhunjeebhoy Nowrojee, travelled to Edinburgh, where he studied at the Free Church College, received ordination in 1846, and then returned to India to preach. He was followed by Wuzeer Beg, 'the son of a Mahomedan messman in Poona', who received ordination as a Presbyterian minister in Edinburgh, and then spent his career preaching in Australia. Ishuree Dass, an orphan who came from a north Indian agricultural caste, was raised and converted by British Christians in north India. After his visit to the West (1846–1848), he wrote: *Brief Account of a Voyage to England and America* (Allahabad: Presbyterian Mission Press, 1851).

Some Indians who had converted in India were disappointed in the limited acceptance they received here. In 1847, a Christian convert from Calcutta, A.C. Mazoomdar, who had settled in Bedminster (near Bristol), wrote plaintively to the directors for assistance. He explained that after studying in a Christian school in Bengal, he 'was led to renounce the heathen superstition of my fathers and embrace the Gospel of Christ'.[30] Disinherited by his wealthy family, he moved to Britain to be among supportive Christians. Instead, he found a 'strong apathy towards a stranger and a foreigner', which frustrated his search for employment. He used his (apparently English) wife's small capital in a business speculation that failed. Thus, he appealed to the directors for 'pecuniary assistance to alleviate our present misery'. He appealed in vain. As Shompa Lahiri and other scholars have shown for the later-nineteenth century, Indians who converted to Christianity often had quite different expectations about their roles than did British Christians.[31]

Indian Businessmen Come

As many Indian merchants entered the global capitalist system that enriched the British empire, they turned to London as its core. Various Indian businessmen had long been coming for redress of grievances, as we have seen. Increasingly during the early nineteenth century, Indians came here to advance their enterprises and obtain the social recognition they felt their wealth entitled but that British society in India was reluctant to grant.

For instance, one of Calcutta's leading merchants and civil leaders, Dwarkanath Tagore (1794–1846), decided to tour Britain and also improve his commercial and political influence here. He sailed with much publicity in January 1842 on his own steamship, the *India*, accompanied by his British personal physician, a nephew, and five attendants.[32] Like his close friend Rammohun Roy, Tagore arrived in Britain with an established reputation as a social reformer, as well as an entrepreneur. After his arrival, he received a distinguished welcome from Queen Victoria and many of Britain's prominent politicians and businessmen. In addition to talking to elites and enjoying London's tourist sites, he inspected British factories and mines, finding steam-powered printing presses particularly noteworthy. He made a walking tour of the countryside.

Based on his first trip, Tagore became more firmly convinced that knowledge of Britain would bring advantages for the next generation of Indians. In 1845, he returned here bringing young men for study and training: his youngest son, Nagendranath; his nephew, Nabin Chandra Mukherji; and the four Bengali medical students discussed above. Again in Britain, he resumed his munificent hospitality and elite socialising. He also honoured his late friend, Rammohun Roy, shifting his grave to Arno's Vale Cemetery near Bristol and erecting a monument. That proved prophetic, since Dwarkanath himself died in 1846, and was buried (without any religious ceremony) in Kensal Green, London. Thus, elite Indians interacted with people of their class in Britain and saw it as a site of advancement, as did many more working-class Indians.

London's 'Oriental Quarter'

Particularly after 1834, a transient Indian community, centred on lascars, evolved in London's East End. For many Britons, this area came to hold exotically both attractive and dangerous connotations as London's 'Oriental Quarter'. For many working-class Indians, however, it provided shelter, food, companionship, and opportunities to earn by serving the needs of other Indians.

Earlier, lascars in Britain had primarily dealt with the East India Company, as we have seen. In 1834, however, with the suspension of the Company's Charter, the directors ended their contracts with Gole's depot and other suppliers of medical care and clothing for lascars. Thereafter, many more British merchants entered trade with India, expanding shipping significantly, and bringing larger numbers of Indian seamen to Britain. While most Britons still believed that the Company had moral accountability for all Indian indigents in Britain, the directors did not live up to these expectations. In 1842, for example, Parliament lamented the 'large number of lascars wandering about London' and hoped that the Government and directors would somehow remedy 'the sufferings of these poor people'.[33] Under existing laws, arriving ship-captains had to report all Asian seamen aboard and were legally liable for their maintenance and return but, in practice, they often made no provision for them. Additionally, in 1844, the Government of India ended its system of taking bonds from departing captains for their Asian seamen, reducing the captains' financial commitment to caring for them in Britain (the system of bonds for Indian servants also had become less rigorous). When conditions worsened for many lascars in London, Parliament ordered the Royal Navy to assume responsibility for returning each

Asian (and also African) seaman who might be found in distress, charging the ship-owner who brought him.[34] This was not an effective arrangement, however, since the Admiralty had no real system for tracking or providing for these men, instead mainly responded to individual 'problem' cases.

In 1849, after heated debate, ship-owners who wanted cheap Indian labour overcame British seamen who feared that competition, persuading Parliament to repeal the Navigation Acts' limitation on Indian maritime employment.[35] Thereafter, the expense of employing lascars dropped by about half, since they could be worked on the passage home. Further, the concurrent emergence of steam-power on international voyages created the need for unskilled and poorly-paid workers to shovel coal into ships' furnaces. Many ships hired Indians for this torrid and dangerous task. Thus, as their cost and status declined, the number of Indian maritime workers reaching Britain rose significantly to 3–3,600 annually by the 1850s.[36]

Lascars and other Indian working-class people found a variety of occupations in London and throughout Britain. A few worked as artists' models, particularly when a British triumph in India was to be illustrated, or an exotic person to be depicted. When the 1853 Dublin Great Industrial Exhibition wanted to portray Indian folk-life, it recruited lascars from London to display working the *charka* (hand-spinning wheel). Indians came to predominate among the crossing-sweepers of urban Britain. Since horse-drawn transportation littered British streets with dung, respectable men and women (particularly in long skirts) tipped men with brooms to clear their path across the street. Possession of some crossings became recognised and even protected (presumably for a consideration) by the police. After British veterans of the Napoleonic Wars died off in the 1830s–1840s, Indians (and Africans) largely took possession of this niche. Indians were, of course, only a small proportion of the many indigents on London's streets.

In a widely publicised case in 1852, a blind lascar, Mahomet Abraham of Calcutta, was arrested for begging.[37] Mahomet had reached London in 1844 but, blinded during the voyage, was abandoned by his ship-captain. For eight years he had lived in London by begging, accompanied by his brown dog. What precipitated his arrest by officers of the Mendicity Society was the 23-year-old Englishwoman, Elizabeth Allen, found in his company. Elizabeth, the daughter of gentry, had earlier eloped with a married Englishman, been abandoned, and discovered by her parents in a workhouse infected with 'loathsome disorders'. After again escaping confinement by her parents, she worked for a milliner but, when that shop failed, lived by singing ballads in London's streets. As Mahomet described their meeting:

> I went out one night to buy some victuals for my dog. It was late, and I called out to the people I heard passing by, 'Where can I get any dog's meat?' At last, Eliza heard me, and she came and took me to a catsmeat shop, where I got what I wanted, and I asked her to come home and take a cup of tea with me, and I would try and make her comfortable. So she agreed to come home with me, and we had our tea, and then she said, as it was a quarter to 11 o'clock, she was shut out, and she did not know where to go.[38]

They lived together for nearly a year in a single room at 7 Little Halifax Street, claiming to have been wedded in nearby Whitechapel Church. She posted him outside the Sir Paul Pindar Tavern, Bishopsgate, with a begging petition pinned to his breast. He reportedly took home a substantial 7–15 shillings daily. Their 'perverted' relationship, however, drew the shocked notice of the Mendicity Society. *The Times* called him 'jet black ... a particularly revolting object'. Most troubling for London's Lord Mayor was why Eliza, who was of gentle birth and had inherited a small house in Devonshire, would accept living in sin with Mahomet; he chastised her for 'the disgrace with which you cover yourself and your family'. She responded by clasping Mahomet's hand and affirming that she had 'both respect and affection for him'.

These British authorities determined to separate them. Mahomet resisted returning to India and pleaded that begging in London was his only livelihood. Unable to deport him legally, the Lord Mayor sent him to the poorhouse. To 'redeem' Eliza, the authorities and her parents arranged her emigration, conveying marriage proposals from British 'tradesmen and others about to proceed to Australia and California ... [who promised] to treat her with the greatest kindness in [those] distant countries ... '.[39] Thus, these British authorities in the 1850s regarded her marriage with an unknown British white emigrant as far more appropriate than life with the Indian beggar she loved. Also problematic for British authorities were the growing numbers of street-children who were, from their physical features, visibly the abandoned children of Indian fathers and British mothers.

Many Indian seamen successfully entered British society, but others survived on the streets, were taken into workhouses or charity homes, or found places in the Oriental Quarter. There, a few entrepreneurial Indians joined Britons in running rooming houses which specialised in serving, and thereby profiting from, Indian visitors. Given the exclusively male population of arriving seamen and the common cultural expectation that women were necessary to provide particular services, a distinctive pattern developed: Indian male rooming-house operators with British wives/mistresses. As the Oriental Quarter developed, Indian servants from the increasingly numerous Indian diplomatic missions, as well as those working in British households, also participated in its cultural life.

Many male British elites, however, came to view the Oriental Quarter as creating new 'problems', especially what they saw as promiscuous mixing of Asian and British cultures and bodies there. Yet, despite the reformers' optimistic hopes of 'cleaning up' this area, it remained a centre for Indian lascars and servants as well as other Asian working men. In 1842, the Church Missionary Society surveyed and reported the 'State of the Lascars in London'. This led these evangelicals to propose a charity house, 'The Strangers' Home for Asiatics, Africans, and South Sea Islanders', collecting for it £15,000 (including Indian donations totalling £5,000) (see Chapter 5).[40] Since Parliament had in 1854 reimposed legal responsibility for indigent Indians on the Company, its directors contributed hundreds of pounds annually to this Home. The Home assumed many of the paternalistic functions of Gole's former depot, including identifying, maintaining, and managing lascars (and other indigent Indians), working with their serangs in prosecuting police and legal charges against defaulting ship-owners, and arranging for lascar employment or passage home. While the individual Indians living in the surrounding Oriental Quarter did not usually remain for very long, this area of London provided the first on-going community where they could interact on largely on their own terms.

Indian Networks in Britain

Over the decades to 1857, on the eve of 'high colonialism', significantly more Indians of various classes and backgrounds entered Britain, yet their receptions by Britons and their own attitudes toward Britain and other Indians here altered. The Anglo-centric world-system that extended colonialism and capitalism also enabled and enticed more Indians to travel to Britain. Increasingly, Britons regarded Indians collectively as inferior colonised peoples, although individual Indians in Britain established a range of roles, depending on their class, gender, ethnicity, and particular deportment and circumstances.

As Indian royalty learned about the sometimes conflicted political relationships among British authorities in London and in India, ever more Indian political delegations arrived and deployed a variety of strategies. Particularly charismatic and insightful envoys learned how to function here effectively. They employed experienced Indian experts in dealing with the British, consulted with each other and sympathetic Britons, and hired British lawyers and agents. The increasing involvement of Parliament in the affairs of India, at the cost of the authority of the directors, meant that new political arenas opened up for Indian missions. They petitioned, lobbied, and bribed rival British politicians, particularly those in opposition who were seeking ways to discredit the Government. They publicised their cases through articles, pamphlets, and books, and made sartorial and dietary choices that shaped their self-representations. Some Indian diplomats and royalty achieved much, particularly those who claimed legal rights using British law-courts or Parliament, or obtained the support of the British aristocracy. Others, especially leading up to and after 1857, faced antipathy among the British public; no longer attractive oriental rarities, they often seemed either picturesque or corrupting aliens. While many enjoyed the manifold pleasures of the British capital, living as men about town, they faced British constraints on them back in India.

Other classes of Indians in Britain also met with each other, and mixed with Britons as well. Anglicised officials went there to advance themselves. For those who sought to enter British society, marriages or liaisons with British women – often combined with conversion to Christianity – formed a prime means of assimilation. Their incomes often depended both on their entrepreneurial expertise in British culture and also their distinctive ability to convey Indian cultures and languages to Britons.

More numerous than ever before, Indian travellers and settlers in Britain formed their own social circles. Tens of thousands of Indian seamen arrived, working the ships that imported Indian raw materials and exported British finished goods. Many Indian servants found work in prosperous Britain not as available in relatively impoverished India.

Yet, following 1834, the East India Company's system of supervision and management of these arriving working-class Indians ended without effective replacement. Thus, they – and the British women and entrepreneurs who served their needs and lived off their wages – created an Oriental Quarter in east London which centred on them and other Asians, largely outside of British control. This transient community, and its cultural, racial, and sexual mixing, generated growing elite British disapproval. The Strangers' Home was a British effort to regain control over Indian working class people in London.

The events of 1857–1858, clearly altered the situation of Indians in Britain. Working-class Indians appeared to even more Britons as threatening aliens in their midst. Many Indians of all classes in Britain at the time were forced to protest their loyalty to the British and their hostility to Indians fighting against them in India; some delegations, including those from Awadh and Jodhpur, promised to devote all their resources to crushing the insurrection against the British. Yet, the Board of Control and directors increasingly pressured Indian royalty to leave, for example instructing Ali Morad of Sindh to go 'manifest your zeal and fidelity in the service of the British Government' there.[41] On their return to India, however, a few Indian envoys were arrested on suspicion of 'treason'.[42] These events also ended the East India Company, establishing the British Raj of crown rule over India.

For many Indians living in London, the degrading effects of colonialism reshaped their understandings of Britons and themselves. Mixing there with other Indians from many regions often overcame traditional cultural and political distinctions among them. Their common treatment by the British as 'other' made some conscious of their shared condition. Several explicitly expressed their hostility to the British; some fought the British in India during 1857.[43] Many leaders of India's later nationalist movements likewise had their political consciousness formed by their living and learning in Britain.

Chapter 5

Indian Victorians, 1857–1901

Shompa Lahiri

The Indian Uprising of 1857 was a watershed in Indo-British relations and the prelude to the transfer of India from Company rule to crown rule in 1858. These momentous events formed the backdrop to the opening of the Strangers' Home in London to cater for the spiritual and welfare needs of South-Asian seamen and the beginning of sustained missionary activity among working-class South-Asian men and women. Missionary conversion strategies and South-Asian resistances are present within missionary records and the private correspondence of, amongst others, feminist and social reformer, Pandita Ramabai.

The South-Asian Victorian social hierarchy in Britain ranged widely from aristocrats at one extreme to paupers at the other. As travel between India and Britain improved substantially after the construction of the Suez Canal in 1869 and prohibitions on Hindu sea voyage began to ease, the numbers and types of South-Asian visitors who crossed the 'Kala Pani' (black waters or oceans) which separated India and Britain increased, and now included a well-educated elite made up of students, social reformers, appellants, royalty and travellers. The published texts of these men and women provide revealing glimpses into the elite South Asians' encounter with Victorian Britain. The imperial metropolis of the day offered them unparalleled opportunities not just to study the mechanisms of British imperial power but to contest and reaffirm that power in a variety of public and private arenas: at imperial exhibitions, in connection with many different types of popular culture, in parliament (with two Indian Ministers of Parliament (MPs) being elected during this period), in the press and in the domestic sphere, for example at the home of pioneering Indian nationalist, W.C. Bonnerjee in the South London suburb of Croydon.

'Heathenism in the Inner Radius'[1]

In the Spring of 1857, the Indian Uprising was triggered by Indian soldiers or sepoys rioting in response to rumours that cartridges for newly issued rifles had been smeared with cow or pig fat, forbidden to both Hindu and Muslim elements of the army. The sepoy revolt put into motion other civilian revolts and for a while the British lost control of Northern India. By coincidence, 1857 was also the year in which W. Baker, Coroner of East Middlesex, reported that forty Indians had died of destitution and starvation in London.[2] Both these events formed the context to the establishment that year of the 'Strangers' Home for Asiatics, Africans and South Sea Islanders' (in the West India Dock Road, Limehouse, London) to cater for the spiritual and welfare needs of Indian seamen. *The Illustrated London News* reported that the object of the institution was 'to offer Indian sailors and other Orientals who come to Britain a comfortable and respectable lodging, with wholesome food, at a cost which shall render the institution self-supporting'.[3] Apart from providing food and accommodation, the institution also operated as a 'Repatriation centre',[4] ensuring that Indian seamen found work on board ships returning to India. South Asians, including servants, who became lost in the unfamiliar streets of the capital, were sent to the Strangers' Home by policemen until they could be restored to their employers – one servant who lost his way on a visit to friends in Brixton stayed in the Strangers' Home for three weeks until the address of his South Indian employers could be ascertained with the assistance of an interpreter.[5] Despite earlier missionary interest in Indian seamen in the first half of the nineteenth century, the Strangers' Home was the first national institution of its kind in Britain, accommodating approximately 200 people at a time. In the first two decades of its existence nearly 6,000 individuals passed through its doors. But why was a Strangers' Home *specifically for Indians* necessary, given that a similar 'Sailors home' already existed for seamen in general? Vice-president of the Church Missionary Society, Rev. Henry Venn, argued that 'the habits of strangers are so different from those of our countrymen that those excellent institutions which bear the name "Sailors Homes" are unsuitable for them'[6]. The desire to emphasise this difference between Indians and locals may have been influenced by the hardening of attitudes against India and Indians in the wake of the 1857 Uprising. Indeed, the title 'strangers' would remain in use even after the population of British India (as opposed to Princely India) came under crown rule the following year and even though individuals born in India but domiciled in Britain (such as Dean Mahomed and Dyce Sombre, mentioned in Chapter 4) had actually been British subjects since the 1840s.

The intention to provide for the South Asians' spiritual as well as welfare needs was a serious one. The London City Mission placed one of its many missionaries, Joseph Salter, at the disposal of the Strangers' Home, where he proselytised among a wide range of Indians, including ruined nobility, Indian apothecaries, interpreters and seamen. Salter's interest in South Asians stemmed from the time of the Nawab of Surat's residence in London, when the missionary had made himself familiar with the retinue of this and other royal parties, including the Queen of Awadh's, who had travelled to Britain to appeal against the annexation of her kingdom by the British and restore her son to the throne (see Chapter 4). By 1876, Salter claimed that 1,300 residents had been through the Home, the majority from India. After his replacement that year, he continued his work among Asian, African and Polynesian seamen until his retirement in 1898 and was therefore very familiar with them. Indeed, in his book, *The Asiatic in England* – the term 'Asiatic' encompassing Burmese, Malay and Thai as well as Indians – he provided a unique cartography of South Asians in Britain, systemically mapping the locations of those he found in workhouses, hospitals, jails and magistrates courts, not just in London but in the large towns of England and Scotland. Outside the capital he found an itinerant population of 'wandering asiatics' – also termed 'bedouins of England' – 'from Aberdeen to Hastings'. The terms adopted by Salter interestingly parallel those of contemporary social explorer, Henry Mayhew, who described indigenous Victorian vagrants as 'Nomads of England'. The nineteenth-century itinerant Indian also appears in Wilkie Collins' pioneering British detective novel, *The Moonstone* (1868), in which, as one critic has put it, 'the "East" erupts in the most intimate spaces of the "West" such as the Bedroom cabinet of a young lady in the most quintessential of English places, the country house.'[7] Some of these men had in fact married local women and had fathered children, to whom they sent money.

As part of a wider imperial ethos or civilising mission 'to convert sailors from savagery to civilisation'[8], several other missionary societies and individuals became interested in the salvation of the Indian lascar's soul, including Indian missionary Rev. Ebenezer Bholonath Bhose of the Lascar mission, St Luke's Victoria Docks, London. Adopting a variety of conversion strategies, such missionaries not only sought out Indians in distress but also made full use of Indian converts. Bhose, for instance, liked to cultivate the serangs who both recruited and supervised Indian seamen. For his part, Salter became conversant in a variety of Indian languages: learning Hindi in the London kitchen of the Nawab of Surat also gave him the opportunity to covertly teach his Indian language instructor the gospels. But constructing a vocabulary of conversion proved problematic: although missionaries were encouraged by Indians' apparent lack of resistance to religious tracts, the number of actual conversions was, in fact, negligible, and success proved elusive. Worse, as Mayhew reported in his description of 'Hindoo tract sellers', Indians appeared to be recycling the tracts and profiting at the missionaries' expense. 'I find that the tracts are given to them by religious people,' he wrote, 'and that they are bought by religious people, who are not infrequently the very same persons who provided the tracts'.[9] As one historian has astutely noted, in this way lascars turned 'spiritual into material sustenance'.[10]

Little is known of the 'Hindoo tract seller' depicted in Mayhew's *London Labour and the London Poor*: the non-availability of an interpreter prevented a statement being taken at the allotted time. However, it was estimated that there were approximately fifty religious tract sellers in mid–nineteenth century London, of which at least half were from the colonies and, more specifically, from the subcontinent of India. The 'Hindoo' in this context does not necessarily refer to the religious origins of the group, many of whom would have been Muslim, but to their geographical origins in colonial India or 'Hindoostan' as it was sometimes known.

According to the London City Mission, between 10,000 and 12,000 lascars had come to Britain by the late nineteenth century, the majority, but not all, from the Indian subcontinent. Most resisted conversion by both overt and covert means; some, particularly Muslims, the most numerous group, were extremely vocal in their opposition to Christianity. Salter was told: 'You Christians expect to live all your life-time in sin and when you are about to die and to account to God for your misdeeds, you expect to roll all your transgressions on to Christ, and stand before God as sinless.'[11] The greatest theological objection to Christianity was the doctrine of the Holy Trinity or the divinity of Jesus Christ, whom Muslims recognised only as a prophet. Lascars claimed that Christians had tampered with the New Testament, changing the message of God in the Koran to reflect Christian views. Some Indian seamen argued that translations of the gospel were 'utterly untrustworthy' and challenged missionaries to prove the superiority of Christianity. While some South Asians felt the need to defend their own faith, it was those (often Hindus and Buddhists) who neither defended nor explained their religion that particularly baffled and frustrated the missionaries. These subtle forms of opposition, which camouflaged the lascars' rejection of Christianity in a cloak of studied indifference, were particularly effective against missionary ambitions. The pluralistic view of religion adopted by many lascars naturally conflicted with the missionaries' narrow unitary stance. Asian seaman Monshee Syed was only one of those who claimed no contradiction in worshipping Christ in both the gospels and the Koran. However, the Lascar's pragmatic attitude to religion meant that while very few embraced Christianity wholeheartedly, neither were they willing to reject the possible benefits accruing from contact with missionaries. Total rejection of missionary overtures would have jeopardised access to the welfare facilities they provided, so Indian seamen tantalised them with the unspoken prospect of conversion, playing the role of the suggestible native just long enough to take advantage of the missionary in his capacity as secretary, social worker, translator, legal adviser and news provider. By manipulating the standard stereotype of the docile and exploitable lascar, they foiled missionary designs on their religious and colonial consciousness.[12]

In September 1863, the Indian Zoroastrian company Cama and Co. wrote to the London City Mission, offering to pay off the mortgage on the Strangers' Home, on condition that Christian instruction of Asiatics was immediately and permanently abolished. Although this attempt to pressurise missionaries to desist from proselytising was unsuccessful, it does show the financial leverage that a non-Christian Indian company, which was itself an important example of South-Asian business activity in Britain, was able to exert.[13] At the same time, South Asians pursued their own religions in various practical ways. The Zoroastrian Association was formed in 1861, and 1889 saw the beginnings of institutional Islam in Britain with the founding of the Shah Jahan Mosque in Woking, Surrey, by Dr G.W. Leitner, ex-Registrar of the University of the Punjab in Lahore, with the financial backing of the Muslim queen of the small Central Indian state of Bhopal, after whom the mosque was named.[14]

However, not all Indian Victorians resisted Christianity. During the nineteenth century, Britain became home to several Indian Christian converts from Calcutta including Dr Goodeve Chuckerbutty (whose career in Britain was highlighted in the previous chapter), Dr Rajendra Chandra, Rev. Philip Joguth Chandra Gangooly and Ganendra Mohun Tagore,[15] as well as two Calcuttan Bengali Poets: Michael Madhusadhan

Dutt, who went to London in 1862 to qualify as a Barrister, and Toru Dutt, who travelled to Britain with her parents and sister eight years later. The Dutt family lived in Cambridge and attended services at St Paul's Church. Both sisters studied at Cambridge University at a time when it was not possible for women to obtain degrees. According to a friend, the Dutts became 'a familiar sight in Cambridge'.[16] However, the relationship that Indian Christians and converts enjoyed with Christian missionary societies in England was not always harmonious. Two celebrated Christian South-Asian female social reformers, Cornelia Sorabji and Pandita Ramabai, who took up residence in south-eastern England at the end of the nineteenth century, both clashed with the missionary establishment.

Sorabji and Ramabai travelled to Britain in the 1880s from Western India, in search of educational opportunities not available to them at home. Sorabji enrolled at Oxford University in 1889 – the first woman to study law at a British university and the first Indian woman advocate. Ramabai, probably the first Indian woman to teach in Britain, spent three years (1883–1886) as student and teacher at Cheltenham Ladies College, where she converted to Christianity. Like other Indian women, including Rukhmabai, both had originally come to Britain to study medicine, but had changed career path. Despite these similarities, they were very different women, both in terms of their socio-economic background and political beliefs. Sorabji came from a relatively comfortable anglophile Parsee-Christian family. By contrast, Ramabai was born into an unconventional reformist Hindu family and had suffered extreme poverty as a result of famine, which resulted in the death of her family and later her husband by the time she arrived in Britain with her daughter and friend Anandibhai Bhaghat. Although both eventually returned to India, where they dedicated their careers to improving the lives of Indian women, ideologically they remained poles apart. Sorabji was a life-long conservative and supporter of British rule in India, opposing both Indian nationalism and the women's movement, while the radically inclined Ramabai spearheaded feminism, in both England and India.

Ambivalence and conflict characterised both Sorabji's and Ramabai's encounters with missionary societies in Britain. Sorabji's letters written during her time in Britain show that while she was keen to avoid becoming a tool of the Christian Missionary Society (CMS) – a feeling she revealed in a comment about a talk she gave at a CMS meeting in 1890 'I saw I had been placarded about'[17] – she was also concerned to maintain links with it for the sake of her parents, whose fortunes were tied to the CMS in Poona. Ramabai's correspondence with her spiritual mentors in England (Sister Geraldine, the Mother Superior of St Mary's Home, Wantage, and the principal of Cheltenham Ladies College, Dorothea Beale) exposes conflicts over theological questions such as the Holy Trinity and Immaculate Conception. Indeed, conversion did not lead to a resolution of Ramabai's spiritual dilemmas. She called herself a 'Christian outcaste' and, sometimes, a 'Hindu' – reference to her refusal to renounce vegetarianism and Indian customs. A sense of how highly she valued freedom of thought and action and her unwillingness to compromise her independence can be gleaned from a letter she wrote to Dorothea Beale dated 12 May 1885: 'It seems to me that you are advising me under the WE [the male leadership of the Anglican church] to accept the will of those who have authority, etc. This however I cannot accept. I have a conscience, and a mind and a judgment of my own. I must myself think and do everything which God has given me the power of doing.'[18] Ramabai was surprised and angry to discover the Anglican Church's objections to women teaching men, when no similar objections had been raised when she lectured to mixed and male-only audiences in India. Significantly, Ramabai supported herself through teaching in England. One of her main concerns was not to become financially dependant on missionaries; indeed, she paid her own way to England with the money earned from sales of her book, *The High-Caste Hindu Woman* (1887). Unwilling to submit to the authority of the Anglican church any longer, she finally left Britain and, after two years fund-raising in America, eventually returned to India.

Princes and Paupers

The historian Antoinette Burton's claim that 'colonial natives were to be found upstairs and downstairs in Victorian society'[19] is reflected in two familiar representative models of Indians in Victorian Britain, the prince and the pauper. But some South Asians crossed these class divides and could be found hovering on the staircase of late–nineteenth century British society.

The issue of princely travel to Britain started to attract interest in official circles at the turn of the century, although concerns about princes squandering their revenues in the great hotels of London had been expressed as early as 1874. Most South-Asian aristocrats visited Britain for purposes of health, leisure or education, factors which feature prominently in the Maharajah of Cooch Behar's justification for a trip to Britain, as they had done for Jamh ood Deen (see Chapter 4). 'I ask for Your Excellency's favourable consideration of this proposal on three grounds,' he wrote.

> First, that my income goes further in England than it does here; second, the opinions of two of the best London doctors that I am to avoid hot weather in a tropical climate, specially in India; and third, the education of my boys. If your Excellency desires it, I can send you letters from the doctors referred to.[20]

Despite the Maharajah's denial of princely profligacy, alleged by the British, his request was still declined. He had, in fact, visited Britain already, in 1887, travelling with his wife, Sunity Devi, daughter of social reformer, Keshub Chandra Sen, for Queen Victoria's Golden Jubilee celebrations. It is Sunity Devi who, in her autobiography, provides us with one of the earliest accounts by an Indian princess visiting Britain. Although she tells us she found aspects of British domestic life and adhering to royal protocol and etiquette demanding at times, nevertheless her audience with Queen Victoria accentuated her pre-existing loyalty to the empress, just two years after the seeds of Indian nationalism had been sown with the birth of the Indian National Congress in India.

> I looked at Her Majesty anxiously, and my first impression instantly dispelled my nervousness: a short stout lady dressed in mourning and kissed me twice ... I experienced a feeling, as did everyone with whom Her late Majesty came in contact, that she possessed great personal magnetism, and she certainly was the embodiment of dignity. Her conversation was simple and kindly and every word revealed her as a queen, woman and mother. I was delighted to find that I had not been disappointed in my ideal, and felt eager to go back to India that I might tell my countrywomen about our wonderful Empress.[21]

Many of the rulers of the princely states of India were presented to Queen Victoria when they visited Britain. Maharajah of Kapurthala, Jagatjit

Singh, also an empire loyalist, was presented to the Queen three times and was very impressed. In a few cases, where the atmosphere of a princely state was viewed by the Government of India as particularly unsuitable, or when the development of a prince had been impaired in some way, ruling chiefs were dispatched to England. The Chief of Junagadh, for example, was sent to Britain to protect him from palace intrigues, despite the threatened suicide of his mother, horrified at the prospect of him abroad. The Government of Bombay was implacable in its belief that the solution offered the best of both worlds: 'He should be trained in Britain while young and impressionable and then be brought back to India, on the verge of manhood to finish his training.' This is not to say that the Government of India was not concerned about the excessive anglicisation and sexual temptations that contact with British society could provoke. The case of the Raja of Pudukottai brought matters to a head. In 1897, the Government of Madras refused him permission to visit Britain for the Queen's jubilee. Describing him as 'an absentee chief unduly addicted to amusements', the government believed that the risk to him from European women would be simply too great. Improvement in the Pudukottai's state finances, however, softened their line, and, in 1898, they did allow the Raja to travel. But when, a year later, the Government of Madras once more acquiesced to the Raja's requests to travel, a storm blew up involving local and national governments. The Government of India objected to the decision on the same grounds as the original refusal; the government of Madras argued that if its decision were overruled, its imperial authority would be permanently damaged. Once again, the fortunate Raja was granted permission to visit Britain and Europe. But by now, the Viceroy of India, Lord Curzon had become infuriated by the whole episode, and, shortly afterwards, he issued a circular to local governments with the instruction that in future all applications from Indian chiefs to visit Europe should be sent to the Government of India well in advance, stating the object and reason for the trip, and emphasising that 'sanction should not … be given in advance, either conditionally or absolutely, by the local government'.[22]

Two other Indian aristocrats captured the Victorian imagination: Duleep Singh and Kumar Shri Ranjisinji. Duleep Singh lived in exile in Britain after his kingdom was annexed by the British in 1849. Separated from his mother, he became the ward of Dr John Login, relinquishing his own and his heir's rights to sovereignty of the Punjab in return for an allowance and the title Maharajah. This was standard practice: the British bought off Indian rulers by giving them pensions in return for not opposing annexation. Much later in the nineteenth century, Ranjisinhji, a Hindu heir to the princely state of Nawanagar, was also exiled to Britain as a teenager. Despite the time lag, their lives show clear similarities. Both gained celebrity status in Britain, Duleep Singh establishing himself as a favourite at court and in royal circles, and Ranjisinhji winning the affection of the British public by becoming the first non-European to play cricket at university, county, national and international level. Duleep Singh, known as 'Black Prince', bought a country estate, Elveden, and became a member of the landed gentry in England; as Lord of the Manor, he funded a village school and indulged his passion for hunting and shooting. Ranjisinhji too took up country pursuits as a country squire, first in Yorkshire at Gilling, later in Connemara, Ireland, where he purchased Ballynanich castle. The two men's spending habits also bear comparison. Both were extravagantly profligate, and both fell heavily into debt. Their relations to women, however, were strikingly different. Duleep Singh was both a family man and a notorious womaniser. He married twice, first to part-Ethiopian, part-German Bamba Muller, and, later, to chambermaid Ada Douglas Wetherill. Ranjisihnji, on the other hand, appeared outwardly to fulfil neither of these masculine roles – although his adoption of the Holmes family and the discovery of love letters between Mary Holmes and Ranjisinhji would suggest a much more complicated private life than suspected at the time.[23] There were also other differences between the two men. Unlike Duleep Singh, who struggled to regain his position as ruler of the Punjab, Ranjisinhji, who by all accounts was a much more canny individual, succeeded in becoming ruler of Nawanagar, despite the comparative weakness of his claim. Eventually, Singh dramatically transformed himself from Christian squire to born-again Sikh and critic of the British, claiming that they had stolen his kingdom and referring to Queen Victoria as 'Mrs Fagin'. The location of Ranjisinhji's loyalties remained much more ambiguous: at various times he exhibited affinity with both the British empire and Indian nationalism. Ultimately, when compared, Ranjisinhji appears to have been much more sophisticated at negotiating his various identities in Britain than Duleep Singh, who moved from one extreme to another, constrained by the limitations of his position as deposed ruler.

At the other end of the social spectrum, Victorian Britain was also home to South-Asian paupers. Salter's travels through Britain enabled him to visit some of the poorer sites of South-Asian Britain, such as the 'plague spots of Oriental Vice',[24] around Shadwell in East London (which he wrote about in language that reveals his contempt for South Asians). For Salter, the colonial Indian presence had transformed the imperial metropolis London into 'an Asiatic jungle of courts and alleys'.[25] Interestingly, the metaphors of contagion and invasion employed by Salter can be seen again less than a century later, in Enoch Powell's 'Rivers of Blood speech'. Like Powell, Salter frankly wanted South Asians out of Britain. 'I have a dislike to an oriental settling down in England,' he wrote, 'as with very few exceptions, I have never known them to be morally benefited by it'.[26]

The geographical boundaries of class were crossed when poorer Indians entered the service and homes of wealthier compatriots. Abdool Rheman's is a case in point. A Surati, he had started his career in Britain as a crossing sweeper in St Paul's churchyard and was then engaged by the Nepalese ambassador, before starting his own businesses running an opium/gambling den/lodging house, when the ambassador left. Ameen Adeen, who presumably came to Britain as a seaman, was for a while in the employ of the Queen of Awadh in London, though after his dismissal he became a hawker and eventually ended up in the Strangers' Home. Other examples of South-Asian poor noted by Salter included the Goanese steward Francis Kaudery, who had become a beggar but later rose to become manager of a lodging house. Another beggar, Shaik Boxhoo, described by Salter as the 'vilest oriental impostor in London',[27] pretended to be deaf and dumb, though he could speak both English and Hindi. Salter had a very low opinion of Indian beggars who, he believed, routinely practised deception in order to extract alms. It is possible, however, to view these actions as survival strategies.

Salter also came across destitute South-Asian women. One woman from Madras who Slater chose not to name was found on the streets of West London. He wrote: 'It was said she refused to work and therefore was dismissed by her employer. The fact was, she was a young mother who had left her three bairns in Madras, to whom she longed to return. She eventually returned to her family.'[28] His statement, apparently straightforward, is both ambiguous and intriguing. In it, the ayah (domestic servant), a figure so often invisible and voiceless within the public archives, is represented as wilfully work-shy only to be transformed into a symbol of unfulfilled maternity, deserving of pity. Ayahs often acted as nurses and attendants to British families on the long voyages to and from India, and, in 1858, the London City Mission estimated 140 of them lived in London, a figure which excludes ayahs residing with their employers for the duration of their stay in Britain. Sometimes they were found destitute on the streets of the capital. In 1897, an institution known as the 'Ayahs' Home' was formally established in Aldgate, London, to accommodate ayahs waiting for a return passage to India; it is possible that an informal structure existed to house them from as early as the mid-nineteenth century.[29] Certainly, destitute South-Asian women in Britain had come to the attention of the India Office, the government department with responsibility for India and Indians, by the late 1880s, when a list of destitute South Asians for the year ending 1886, compiled by the India office, cited two anonymous Asian women who had died in Camberwell infirmary. No details of their biographies are given, but they appear to have been long-term residents of Britain. Another case involved a 'Hindoo woman' named McBarnett, who came to Britain as an ayah in the service of an English family that later abandoned her. Unable to find employment to enable her to return to India, she was obliged to take refuge in a Manchester workhouse.[30]

Resident Indians sometimes alerted the British authorities to the plight of South-Asian paupers. The teacher Syed Abdoollah (see Chapter 4) retained an ongoing interest in the condition of other Indians in Britain: in 1856, he delivered a speech to the dignitaries gathered for the opening of the Strangers' Home,[31] and, in 1869, drew attention to the presence of Indian beggars on the streets of London in a letter to the India Office, which called for the re-introduction of the bond system to fund the repatriation of Indian domestics left stranded in Britain by their employers (calculated at 900), protecting them from destitution.[32]

Henry Mayhew's pioneering survey of the mid-nineteenth-century, *London Labour and the London Poor*, contextualised the presence of South Asians within a particular stratum of British society, and, in the testimony of two Indian paupers, afforded them a rare opportunity to speak for themselves. Indian cockney Joaleeka, born in Dum Dum, near Calcutta, had come to Britain as an interpreter to the servants of an Indian noble, after picking up English in the employment of a British officer in India. He formed a relationship with a British female servant who became pregnant, and, fearful of returning to India with his employer, despite the prince's promise to protect him when the scandal broke, he ran away and stayed with another British female acquaintance until the news of his employer's departure for India was announced in the

Illustrations

1. Anthony Van Dyck: William Fielding, First Earl of Denbigh. *c.*1633.

2. Peter Lely: Lady Charlotte Fitzroy and Indian. *c.*1674.

3. Sir Joshua Reynolds: George Clive, Family and Ayah. 1765–66.

4. Abdullah (a.k.a. John Morgan) and the Syagush (a.k.a. Caracal) in London. Anonymous etching reproduced in *The London Magazine*. November 1759.

5. George Stubbs: Cheeta and Stag with Two Indians. 1765.

6. William Thomas: Portraits of William Hickey, Esq., his favourite black servant, Munoo, and his dog. 1819.

7. Green Plaque commemorating London's first Indian restaurant, on the north side of George St. in the block between Gloucester Place and Baker St.

8. Mahomed's Baths, Brighton. Established 1821. Anonymous etching reproduced in S.D. Mahomed: *Shampooing, or Benefits Resulting from the Use of the Indian Medicated Vapour Bath* (1826).

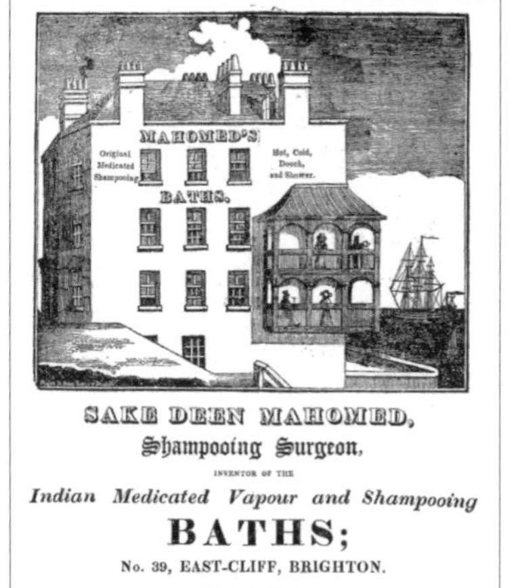

SAKE DEEN MAHOMED,
Shampooing Surgeon,
INVENTOR OF THE
Indian Medicated Vapour and Shampooing
BATHS;
No. 39, EAST-CLIFF, BRIGHTON.

THE soothing efficacy of the application of steam to the human body, has been long known in the eastern parts of the world. Medicated with fragrant herbs of peculiar virtue, the vapour is rendered more beneficial, whilst the addition of Shampooing the various parts of the body envoloped in steam, augments its sanative energies throughout the whole animal system. In Rheumatism, Parylitic, Gouty Affections, Asthma, Roughness and Diseases of the Skin, Stiff Joints, and Old Sprains, it is a safe and certain remedy; and in all cases of corporeal weakness, or where the circulation is languid, or the nervous energy debilitated, its effects have excited astonishment. Scarcely any disease, to which the human frame is liable, but may be relieved by the use of these Baths. They have been sanctioned by the first medical men in the united kingdom; and have been patronized by many of the nobility, both of England, France, and other places on the Continent, who have received relief from them in many hopeless cases, and whose written testimony of approval may be seen at the Baths.

The art of Shampooing first introduced into England, by S. D. Mahomed, in 1784.

☞ *Cupping performed by D. MAHOMED, Jun. late pupil of Mr. Mapleson Cupper to his Majesty.*

9. Advertisement placed in *Pigot's National Directory* by Sake Deen Mahomed. 1826.

10. S.D. Mahomed, Shampooing Surgeon, Brighton. *c.*1822. Etching by W. Maddocks. S.C. reproduced as the frontispiece of S.D. Mahomed, *Shampooing, or Benefits Resulting from the Use of the Indian Medicated Vapour Bath* (1826).

11. Sake Deen Mahomed in Court Robes, Brighton. *c.*1830. Anonymous etching reproduced in Erredge: *History of Brighthelmston*, vol. 4 (1862).

12. Sheth Ghoolam Hyder and Anonymous Students, East India College, Haileybury. *c.*1808. Detail of a drawing by Thomas Medland reproduced in Constance Mary Matthews: *Haileybury since Roman Times* (1959).

13. Rajah Rammohun Roy. Etching by Annin Smith reproduced as the frontispiece of Raja Rammohun Roy: *Precepts of Jesus* (1825).

14. Portrait of Mohan Lal Kashmiri. Etching by T. Peiken reproduced as frontispiece of Mohan Lal: *Life of the Amir Dost Mohammed Khan of Kabul* (1846).

15. Carl Hartmann: An Indian Crossing Sweeper, Berkeley Street. *c.*1847.

DOCTOR BOKANKY, THE STREET HERBALIST.

[*From a Daguerreotype by* BEARD.]

"Now then for the Kalibonca Root, that was brought from Madras in the East Indies. It'll cure the tooth-ache, head-ache, giddiness in the head, dimness of sight, rheumatics in the head, and is highly recommended for the ague; never known to fail; and I've sold it for this six and twenty year. From one penny to sixpence the packet. The best article in England."

16. Dr Bokanky, The Street Herbalist. From a daguerrotype by Beard reproduced in Henry Mayhew: *London Labour and London Poor* (1861).

HINDOO TRACT-SELLER.

[*From a Daguerreotype by* BEARD.]

17. Hindoo Tract-Seller. From a daguerrotype by Beard reproduced in Henry Mayhew: *London Labour and London Poor* (1861).

18. Strangers Home Annual Report for 1887.

19. Maharani of Cooch Behar. *c.*1893.

20. Indian suffragettes on the Women's Coronation Procession in London. 1911.

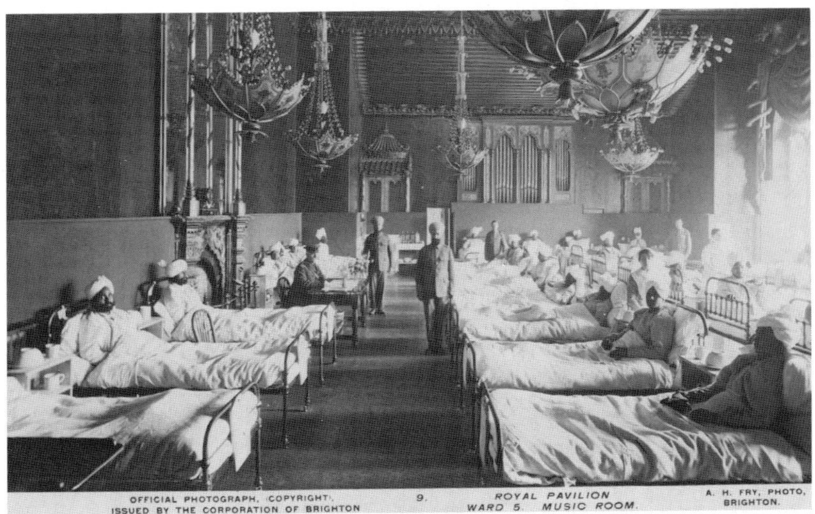

21. Indian soldiers in the Royal Pavilion, Brighton. *c.*1915.

22. Veeraswamy restaurant (established 1926), Regent Street, London. 1928.

PRINCES THEATRE
SHAFTESBURY AVENUE, W.C.2

Licensed by The Lord Chamberlain to BERT E. HAMMOND, O.B.E. Phone: TEMPLE BAR 6596
Direction: BERTRAM MONTAGUE

TUESDAY, DECEMBER 4th to SATURDAY, DECEMBER 15th

CONTINENTAL OPERA & BALLET ENTERTAINMENTS, Ltd present
(By arrangement with BERTRAM MONTAGUE)
DIRECT FROM INDIA
FIRST RE-APPEARANCE IN EUROPE OF

UDAY SHANKAR

RICHLY
COSTUMED
AND SUPERBLY
STAGED

SPECTACULAR
COLORFUL
EXOTIC

BEAUTY AND
EXCITEMENT

ALL THE
GLAMOUR
OF THE
ORIENT

The GREATEST of all HINDU DANCERS

WITH

A NEW COMPANY OF BRILLIANT DANCERS and MUSICIANS
OVER 100 ANCIENT INSTRUMENTS NEVER BEFORE SEEN IN EUROPE

FIRST PROGRAMME: DEC. 4th - 8th SECOND PROGRAMME: DEC. 10th - 17th
EVENINGS at 7.30 MATINEES: THURSDAYS & SATURDAYS at 2.30

TRIBE BROS., Ltd., London and St. Albans

23. Poster advertising Uday Shankar at the Princes Theatre, London. December 1917.

24. Princess Indira of Karpurthala.

25. Venu Chitale.

26. Refugees from Kenya arriving at London Airport. 1968.

27. Almost 15,000 people marched in memory of Blair Peach in Southall, London, on 28 April 1979.

28. A new building of Gurdwara Sri Guru Singh Sabha (originally established 1967), Havelock Court, Southall, London, opened 30 March 2003 at a cost of £17.5 million.

29. The Glassy Junction, South Road, Southall, offering Indian beers on tap and (reputedly) accepting payment in Rupees.

30. England captain Nasser Hussain in action at Headingley against the West Indies. August 2000.

31. A food stall during a Brick Lane Festival, Aldgate, London, 2005.

32. Protest against Rushdie's novel, *The Satanic Verses*, in Bradford, on 14 February 1989, the day a fatwa against Rushdie was proclaimed on Radio Tehran.

33. Annual Hindu Diwali festival of light has become a regular event at Trafalgar Square, London.

press. The woman, who would become his wife, taught him how to beg and persuaded him to become a Christian. Christianity being good for business, many South-Asian beggars claimed to be Christian converts to elicit the sympathy of potential donors. As Joaleeka admitted: 'I do not know what it means but I am a Christian and have been for years.'[33] By the time he was interviewed, he was over 50 years old and was married to an Irish woman with three children. As a result of anti-Indian sentiment following the Uprising in 1857, his earnings had declined. His nickname, Johnny Sepoy, was a reference to the sepoys involved in the Uprising, though his wife was sensitive to any suggestion that her husband might be unpatriotic and would assault the name-callers.

Despite his lack of oral fluency, Mayhew's unnamed Indian street performer, or 'Tom Tom player', vividly conveyed the indignities suffered by poor South Asians on London's streets: 'I put up many insult in dis contree ... De Boys call me black dis or de other.' The Tom Tom player had to swallow his pride to survive and support his wife and child even when times were hard after the Uprising. Diminished earnings forced him to resort to modelling for artists. Given their hardships in London, it is perhaps surprising that more impoverished South Asians did not take up or return to seafaring. But poor work conditions and the threat of violence at sea, confirmed by the Tom Tom player, acted as deterrents: 'Most of my countrymen in the street have come as Lascars, and not go back for bosen and bosen mate flog. So dey stay for beg or sweep or anything.'[34]

The Calcuttan Bengali hero, Colonel Suresh Biswas, who later rose to high office in the Brazilian army, lived as a pauper for a while when he first arrived in London in the late nineteenth century.[35] After a period of sleeping rough, Biswas found employment and lodgings with a newspaper seller and then became a street porter. His thriftiness enabled him to save enough income to survive periods of unemployment, but he was forced to leave the capital and tour the provinces as a peddler of Indian curios after becoming the object of amorous advances from a married woman. Here, his Indian origins gave him an advantage, as he was able to invent the provenance of common articles and pass them off as Indian antiques to his customers, who included farmers, villagers and local gentry. Within five months he made a dozen trips, earning £10 profit. Moreover, he found that peddling left him with free time to study mathematics, astronomy and astrology, later mastering ancient Greek and Egyptian in order to read original scientific texts. He continued his interest in athletics by becoming a member of an athletics club. A chance encounter with a travelling circus in Kent resulted in him joining the troupe as a gymnast and weightlifter, and, after two years' training as a lion tamer, he left England to tour Europe and America. Eventually he settled in Brazil, where he trained as a surgeon in Rio before joining the army. Letters to his uncle in India from the period of his stay in England have unfortunately been lost, but would doubtless have provided further insights into his remarkable life. Even with the evidence we have, his experiences in England reveal the fluid nature of South-Asian identities in Victorian England. Biswas' western education in India equipped him with linguistic and social resources necessary to climb out of poverty. Not all well-educated Indians were so fortunate, however. Many Indian students found themselves reduced to poverty in Britain. Both Womesh Chandra Bonnerjee and Michael Madhusadhan Dutt, who came to Britain to study in the 1860s, were forced to endure poverty and hardship until pecuniary assistance came from friends, family or, in the case of Dutt, from mortgaged property in India.[36]

Finally, some Indian paupers belonged to the 'petitioner class'. As discussed in the previous chapter, litigants who had unsuccessfully prosecuted land claims in Indian courts sometimes travelled to Britain to petition the Queen for legal redress. Of all the South Asians in Britain, they were regarded as the most troublesome by the authorities. One petitioner, Tulsi Ram, provoked particular consternation with his continual demands to 'meet the Queen' and his refusal to be silenced and repatriated back to India.[37] His pervading sense of injustice is palpable in his testimony:

> For ten months I have been going about trying to see the Queen, but a lot of people always collected near me and caused me to be locked up. I have been in about twenty courts and locked up. At one of the Courts one elderly gentleman offered me two hundred rupees to pay my passage back to India, but I told him I did not want money. I wanted justice and until I get that I will die sooner than return to my own country.[38]

Quite how this recalcitrant petitioner was transformed into 'Native 16: Sweetmeet maker from Agra' at the 1886 Colonial and Indian Exhibition in London is not entirely clear, but after a three weeks appearance at the show he was arrested for vagrancy and finally returned to India. Not before a parting shot, however, as he put on record his criticisms of imperial justice, which had brought about the drastic decline in his status from property-owner in India to landless peasant/criminal/religious outcast in Britain:

> The petition of my humble servant Tulsi Ram is that your worship's obedient servant is neither a rogue, a vagabond or a criminal of any sort nor is he a monomaniac of any description whatever. That ever since your worship's servant has set foot in this city he has been treated like a criminal ... for what crime he knows not. This cruel injustice has not only added his suffering but has defied him in a religious sense ... I prayeth that your worship's humble servant may no longer be treated as a criminal or madman but that he may be protected as a poor stranger in this strange land.[39]

His statement echoes the Tom Tom player's insistence that poor South Asians should not to be tarred with the brush of criminality: 'Dey are never pickpockets dat I ever hear of.'[40] And it was the same story for Oomar Khan, who also came to Britain to see the Queen, to appeal against a legal decision concerning a land suit in 1891. Like Ram, he resisted the attempts to deport him and was regarded as 'dangerous' by the British authorities.

However, while both Oomar Khan and Tulsi Ram struggled in vain to gain an audience with the Queen, another Indian, Abdul Karim, succeeded. Karim arrived in Britain from Agra and rose within the Royal Household from menial servant to the Queen's teacher of Hindi, for which he was known as the 'Munshi'. He later acquired the title 'Indian secretary'. As Sushila Anand has written, 'little by little he progressed from blotting letters to discussing their content'. Indeed, Queen Victoria's description of him as a 'friend more than servant'[41] indicates that he had perhaps crossed the line between subordinate and associate. Was Abdul Karim then a genuine bridging figure, a commoner who moved in royal circles? Or did his servitude symbolise India's dependent position within the imperial relationship? The hostility and suspicion that he provoked suggests that, for Queen Victoria's advisors and household at least, the Munshi had become too powerful and needed cutting down to size. Every opportunity was taken to discredit him in the Queen's eyes, and his position was eventually reduced.

The destruction of Abdul Karim's papers after his death deprives us of his voice and thoughts. However, a surviving document written by him reveals a thoughtful, politically informed and critical, but not necessarily treacherous subject. The opinions expressed in this note suggest that Abdul Karim did not hide his concerns about British mismanagement of India, which he discussed openly with Lord Hamilton. Whether such views were influenced by Rafiuddin Ahmed, co-founder of the Muslim League, failed MP, barrister, journalist and secret agent who, according to British Intelligence, was Karim's mentor, is unclear. What is clear is that Karim criticised British rule on several fronts. Writing about the excessive power of the British Resident in India's princely states, he observed that 'they act as if they themselves were the head of the states'.[42] According to Karim, 'Famine never occurred in India as frequently, nor so severe before, as they do now.' Inadequate government pensions and the import of foreign goods were identified as sources of poverty, and the revival of traditional handicrafts within educational institutions was offered as a solution to unemployment and the decline of India's indigenous industries.

Travellers' Tales

In the year of the opening of the Suez Canal (1869), as travel to Britain from India promised to become easier, the British Indian Association, an association loyal to British rule in India, established a department for encouraging both Muslims and Hindus to travel to Britain, not for trade or legal reasons, but for educational and scientific purposes.[43] There was tremendous breadth of support in India for such travel, highlighted in the first edition of the Allahabad Review, in 1890:

> A voyage to Europe certainly enlarges the mind and as far as the advantages of culture, and experience of the world are concerned, a lengthy stay in the modern cradle of civilisation is to be recommended for everyone who can afford the time and has the means for it. The fact remains that some of the most coveted offices under the Government can only be obtained by passing certain examinations held in England and England alone.[44]

Similar enthusiasm also developed in Bengal, particularly among high-caste Hindus, despite opposition from orthodox family and friends, a key feature of autobiographies, diaries and travelogues of the period.

But, just when travel to Britain was becoming more desirable, feasible and – for the elite seeking careers as barristers and civil servants – essential, working class South Asians faced more legislative restrictions in the form of the 1869 Revised Emigration Act which baldly stated: 'England is not a place to which emigration from British India is lawful.' 'Emigration' in this context referred to 'departure from India for the purpose of labouring for hire'[45] – though curiously this did not seem to apply to servants or maritime workers.

Travellers, who often wrote travelogues and memoirs (some of which first appeared as letters in Indian newspapers), are hugely important to our understanding of the encounter between South-Asian men and women and Victorian Britain. Increasing numbers of them, especially from British India's western-educated urban elite, came to Britain in the late nineteenth century to study, travel for pleasure, engage in social reform or advance their careers. Given the highly influential roles played by those who then returned to India – Mohandas K. Gandhi, Jawaharlal Nehru and Mohamed Ali Jinnah all studied in Britain and qualified as barristers – the importance of travel to England takes on an added significance.

Two of the most informative travellers were women. Pothum Janakummah Ragaviah, who described herself simply as 'a Hindu lady from Madras', travelled to Britain with her husband in 1871. Her book, *Pictures of England* (1876), was based on letters she wrote in Telugu to the *Madras* newspaper. Not only did she describe the many places she visited in Britain and give her – largely favourable – impressions of British society, she also provided personal insights into her daily routines, including walks in Hyde Park, visits to public baths and regular trips to the theatre. She was accompanied not just by her husband but also by Indian servants. What did Ragaviah's ayah make of Britain, and how did her experiences and reactions differ from those of her mistress? Unfortunately, lack of testimony makes supposition difficult. Krishnabhabini Das (1864–1919) also travelled to England with her husband in 1882 and stayed for a further eight years in London. Her book, *Englande Banga Mahila* [A Bengali woman in England], was written in Bengali and published in Calcutta in 1885.

The Indian visitors' first impression of Britain came when they disembarked at London, the largest city on earth for much of the Victorian period. Their opinion of the imperial metropolitan capital depended on their own urban backgrounds. Most came from the

Presidency cities of Madras, Bombay and, in particular, Calcutta, the capital of British India until 1912 and home of the Bengali Hindu middle class or *Bhadralok*. At first sight, many of these writers were over-awed by the sheer scale of London, its dazzling lights, ceaseless motion of traffic and clean streets crowded by all manner of people. Das wrote:

> On arriving in London from India one feels sort of dazed ... for everything looks so different – dress, way of speaking, houses, traffic – all seem to be entirely new. At first sight someone might call it a 'city of shops', or a 'city of theatres' or a 'city of riches'. But after staying here for some time I have failed to decide as to how to name it[46]

Ragaviah also struggled to find words to describe the metropolis. But Bengali writer Amrit Lal Roy was much more determined to define the city for his Indian readers: 'London means the centre of the world-wide empire ... a repository of wealth and a reservoir of energy ... a whirlpool of activity and a deep sea of thought, a point where the ends of the world may be said to meet.'[47] Other aspects of Victorian London life to impress visitors included the Underground and London policeman, who helped to navigate them through the city's streets. Curiously, many travellers were attracted to the British Museum, the symbol of imperial knowledge and conquest. The adopted son of the Maharaja of Burdwan, Bijoy Chand Mahatab, described how the artefacts he saw took his breath away. In contrast, the young Rabindranath Tagore, later a Nobel prize–winning poet, writer, artist, educationalist and humanitarian, found London's dark, foggy winters depressing compared to Calcutta's temperate winter weather. Both Bipin Chandra Pal, who came to Britain on a scholarship but soon took up lecturing on religious and political issues, and Bijoy Chand Mahatab remained unmoved by London's grandeur. Outside the city, however, Indian travellers often found much to admire, discovering in rural England the pastoral idyll they had first encountered back home in the romantic poetry of Wordsworth, Keats and Shelley.

Several of the travellers commented upon the political freedoms enjoyed by the British, which were denied to Indians as colonial subjects. Trailokyanath Mukharji, assistant curator of Calcutta Museum at the time of his visit to Britain in 1886, who took part in the Colonial and Indian exhibition, described the free discussions of the Home Rule Bill for Ireland which he witnessed in theatres, trains, omnibuses, workshops and restaurants 'as a treat for an Indian'.[48] Romesh Chandra Dutt noted the public interest and enthusiasm generated by the 1868 General Election:

> Go and speak to the commonest greengrocer, the commonest boot maker in London, and he will tell you the amount of national debt, he will tell you who introduced such and such bill, and what likelihood it has of passing, he will argue with you as to the good or evil effect of a bill lately introduced in Parliament. Your cabman will tell you that this bill will pass and t'other bill not, and the boatman will inform you that the conservatives are no good ... Such is England, a country where people govern themselves – what wonder if such a people have secured for themselves an amount of political liberty which is nowhere else to be found on the face of the globe, America alone excepted.[49]

Nevertheless Dutt, a civil servant, economist and historian, who taught briefly at the University of London and was president of the Indian National Congress, was also aware that political freedom was tempered by the power of class interests and, at a domestic level, family voting patterns. Eighteen years later when fellow Bengali Lal Mohun Ghosh (unsuccessfully) contested the Deptford election in 1886, Dutt was able to observe an Indian participating in, not just commenting on, British parliamentary democracy.

For women commentators, concerns about liberty were not just confined to issues of citizenship and politics, but resonated at a personal level. Krishnabhani Das wrote of how she had come to view England 'as the land of freedom and India as one of servility'.[50] For Das, a Bengali middle-class high-caste Hindu housewife, or *Bhadramahila*, who had travelled to England with her husband against the wishes of her ultra-conservative in-laws, the contrast between the restrictions and social incarceration of her life in India and the relative latitude of her life in Britain was much sharper than that experienced by her male contemporaries who travelled to Britain. But, for Das, freedom came at an extremely high price: separation from her daughter, Tilottma, who remained with her grandparents in Calcutta when they refused to allow her to travel with her parents. On return to India, Das was unable to see her daughter who had been married off against her wishes. The poetess Toru Dutt, who as a Christian led a much more socially and geographically unencumbered life in Calcutta, also lamented the loss of the mobility she had enjoyed in Britain. After returning to India, she wrote to her friend, 'We all want so much to return to England. We miss the free life we led there, here we can hardly go to the limits of our garden.'[51] As Inderpal Grewal has shown, 'what is evident here is the equating of "free life" with England and its walks' – an aspect of the English Romantic tradition.[52]

While Indian visitors was struck by the energy and vitality of British people, the warmth of the middle-class home, the technological and scientific achievements and democratic freedoms, neither were they blind to what they perceived as British faults. Seeing below the surface of British society, they discovered – in one traveller's words – that all that glittered was not gold. In typical Victorian phraseology, every virtue had a corresponding vice. Many Indian writers observed how material prosperity in Britain masked abject poverty, and some used this to challenge the British ideology of imperial progress and 'civilising mission' in India. Rabindranath Tagore was shocked at the deprivation of the working classes: 'I feel a shiver when I see the faces of some of them ... and I cannot tell you how dirty they are!'[53] The dehumanising aspects of British poverty were also apparent to Bombay social reformer and journalist, Behramji Malabari:

> Men and women living in a chronic state of emaciation, till they can hardly be recognised as human, picking up, as food, what even animals will turn way from; sleeping fifty, sixty, eighty of them together, of all ages and both sexes, in a hole that could not hold ten with decency; swearing, fighting, trampling on one another; filling the room with foul confusion and fouler air. This is not a picture of occasional misery; in some places it represents the every-day life of victims of misfortune.[54]

Witnessing gypsies scrambling for food thrown at them from the carriages of the wealthy at Epsom Downs, Bijoy Chand Mahatab noted that in Britain the feeding of the poor was a spectator sport for the rich, and he was, like Malabari, thankful that such grotesque spectacles did not exist in India. Romesh Chandra Dutt painted an equally harrowing picture of the tragic consequences of alcoholism in a London labourer who, unable to support his large family, habitually resorted to one of the capital's many public houses, which resulted in his violent and premature death and the destitution of his children. Several visitors commented on Britain's 'drink problem'. Lala Baijnath wrote: 'drink mocks the legislator, the philanthropist and the patriot'.[55] Trailokyanath Mukharji, who described poverty in Britain as 'a crime ... of the deepest dye',[56] recommended (somewhat naively) importing Indian pulses and vegetables to meet the need for cheap and nutritious food for Britain's poor, in the hope that it would reduce the cost of living in Britain and enrich India. In fact, it would have further encumbered India's already overburdened peasantry.

Most writers blamed the glaring inequalities of British society, summarised by Ragaviah as 'astounding wealth and wretched poverty', on the class system. Romesh Chandra Dutt was disappointed to see that even in 'enlightened England' class prejudice survived. On a lecture tour of Britain, Bipin Chandra Pal, ex-student turned Brahmo Samaj missionary/lecturer, observed these distinctions at first hand. During a visit to a Utilitarian chapel meeting in Birmingham, his host consoled Pal, saying that he 'had quality in the morning [a reference to the fact the chapel was located in an affluent area] and ... I would have quality in the evening'. Pal remarked:

> These experiences brought home to me the very wide differences between India and England. The humanity of the British people is skin-deep, they have no castes, it is true, but the class feeling among them is really even worse from the humanitarian point of view, than our caste feeling.[57]

Krishnabhabini Das was equally repelled by British class pride: 'In this country, a dunce who happens to be rich thinks himself a very great man and hates a poor but learned man.' Like Pal, she believed that class divisions were more damaging and divisive than caste distinctions: 'In our country we only hear of rich men and poor men, but in England we often hear of gentlemen and vulgar men ... without money it is impossible to be recognised as a gentlemen.'[58] Several Indian observers agreed that materialism lay at the heart of many of Britain's problems. Krishnabhabini Das and Lala Baijnath compared the acquisition of money in Britain to a religion. Das was particularly sensitive to the foreign policy implications of British avarice:

> In making money they care not for virtue or vice. Even if they make money by wrongful means in a foreign country, they feel

> no compunction or self-reproach ... How much money have they spent and how much blood have shed in order to force opium upon the unfortunate Chinese! ... Such is the despotic hold of the demon of wealth upon the English people.[59]

Das, like many of her male compatriots, expressed the belief that the advancement of material interests inevitably sacrificed moral and spiritual values. This superiority of Indian spiritualism over western materialism was also annunciated by Gandhi in the twentieth century.

If, in the view of some South Asians, British prosperity found its negative expression in British greed, in a similar way British self-reliance seemed to some (such as Romesh Chandra Dutt) unattractively offset by British self-love – a lack of demonstrable interest in neighbours or even family members. Several visitors claimed that such promotion of self-reliance was incompatible with charity (though Dutt argued that the mutual dependence of Indians and their expectation of assistance hindered the development of a national character). Bengali travellers, in particular, contrasted the lack of charity in England, where compassion had been eroded by competition and materialism, with the Bengali propensity to be driven by the dictates of the heart. Mukharji took the moral high-ground when he wrote, 'We in this country know better how to treat our poor than the people of Europe.'[60] The British spirit of independence had failed to counter a contradictory element in British life, he thought, namely the tyranny of fashion. This observation was part of a wider complaint about the artificiality of British society, in which external behaviour and appearance was valued above internal merits. Adopting a characteristically robust tone, Das noted: 'Very often they have one thing in their minds and another thing in their mouths. Their gentlemanly behaviour is often external and not sincere.'[61] Similar criticisms were made about British hygiene. In a letter home in 1878, the teenage Rabindranath Tagore wrote:

> Appearance takes precedence over cleanliness. One would have thought that a spittoon for use when people have coughs and colds would be highly necessary here, but such an unsavoury article in the room would not be acceptable – so a handkerchief has to suffice. Our codes of cleanliness would prefer a spittoon in the room, and we would shrink at the idea of keeping filthy substances in our shirt-pockets. But appearances are supreme here. No one sees

> a handkerchief, so it causes no offence. If you keep your hair neatly combed and your hands and face well scrubbed, people are quite satisfied: there is no great need to have a bath ... The female servants here wear an apron tied round their waists and there is nothing that they do not rub with it. The gleaming china dinner-plates that you see in front of you have been polished by that all-purifying apron. But there is no harm in that, because you don't see anything unpleasant. The people here are not unclean, but they are very unhygienic. If we could marry our ideas of cleanliness and theirs, that would be a most beautiful and complete combination.[62]

Not surprisingly, clear gender differences emerge over the issue of a woman's position in British society. As one of the few women to write about her residence in Britain, Krishnabhabini Das was vociferous in her condemnation of the failings of Hindu Bengali domesticity and gender relations, painting the British equivalent in glowing terms. Three main areas reflected the gender equality enjoyed by English women: marriage, domestic life and sibling relations. Das was impressed by the freedom of choice granted to children by their parents on the subject of marriage. She claimed that parents usually consented to their children's choices of partners, very rarely opposing their children's wishes. Not only did she approve of the English system of courtship and marriage but, crucially, she also approved the right of British women to put an end to a bad marriage by instituting divorce proceedings. Das' observations led her to conclude that English parents treated their children with greater care and affection than Indian parents. She also praised the custom of the nuclear rather than the extended family, on the grounds that while it reduced intimacy between parents and married offspring, it also lessened domestic tensions. The equal treatment given by British parents to both boys and girls produced more harmonious sibling relations than the rivalrous ones which Das believed were common in India. Her position on the women's question was influenced both by her own experience as a wife, daughter-in law and mother and by her feminist advocacy of female emancipation in India developed along the lines of the suffragette movement in Britain. Ragaviah also praised the freedoms enjoyed by British women, in contrast to the relatively circumscribed existence of middle and upper class women in India, posing the question: 'When will my Indian sisters enjoy such a noble position in their households, as do ... sisters of the west?'[63]

Both Behramji Malabari and Romesh Chandra Dutt were committed to female suffrage at a time when such views had few male supporters in either India or England. As a social reformer, Malabari argued for the expansion of women's rights, equal pay for men and women and an equitable sexual morality. He stood in marked contrast to the conservative A.K. Ray, whose view – much more typical of Indian male visitors to Victorian Britain – was that the 'beautiful utopia' of gender equality was 'not within the domain of practical politics'.[64] It was Dutt who provided the most sophisticated analysis of the plight of both British and Indian women. He claimed that, while British women occupied a superficially more favourable position within society than Indian women did, the need to marry diminished their freedom. As employment was closed to them, British women – according to Dutt – either were obliged to marry or were 'shelved', forcing them into dependency on their parents. Other Indians also wrote about the 'hide and seek' tactics employed by British women to catch a husband. In Dutt's view, the freedom to select a life partner did not necessarily guarantee connubial happiness, as a young man in England knew as little about the real character of his betrothed as an Indian groom. The inadequacies of British courtship and wedlock did not, however, lead Dutt to promote the Indian system of marriage, in which Indian women were subjected to the traumas of child marriage and confined within the zennana. Instead, he advocated economic independence and the opening up of the professions to women.

Overall, in comparing Britain with India, the writers of travelogues frequently found Britain wanting. Though they could be deferential, they were also capable of criticism, particularly when discussing the drawbacks of the nuclear family or individualism, lack of spirituality, excessive preoccupation with material acquisition, poverty, the class system, alcoholism, sanitary habits, love, romance and fashion. By highlighting the gaps between appearances and reality in Britain, they both demystified and domesticated the country for their elite Indian readership back home.

Public Sphere and Domestic Space

In the nineteenth century, South Asians frequently appeared in imperial exhibitions as craftsmen, performers and musicians, in London and elsewhere, as far north as Glasgow. In 1885, the London department store, Liberty, attempted to recreate an Indian village at the Albert Palace, Battersea Park, with performing craftsmen and entertainers, including women dancers, male acrobats and jugglers. But, as Saloni Mathur has shown, it turned into a financial and public relations disaster when the poor treatment of the Indian artisans and performers was exposed in the Indian and British press.[65] The following year, 1886, the Indian and Colonial exhibition opened at Earl's Court, London, running for six months. Trailokyanath Mukherjee, mentioned earlier, who travelled to Britain to oversee one section of the exhibition, wrote about his experiences in *A Visit to Europe*, recording what it felt like to be put on public show in the imperial metropolis. 'Would they discuss us so freely,' he wondered, 'if they knew that we understood their language? It was very amusing to hear what they said about us.' His sharp irony, which continued in his satirical writing after his return to India, made his observations very lively:

> Once I was sitting in one of the swellish restaurants at the Exhibition, glancing over a newspaper which I had no time to read in the morning. At the neighbouring table sat a respectable-looking family group, evidently from the country, from which furtive glances were occasionally thrown in my direction. I thought I might do worse than have a little fun, if any could be made out of the notice that was taken of me. I seemed to be suddenly aware that I was being looked at, which immediately scared away half a dozen eyes from my table. It took fully five minutes' deep undivided attention to my paper again to reassure and tempt out those eyes from the plates where they took refuge, and the glances from them, which at first flashed and flickered like lightning, became steadier the more my mind seemed to get absorbed in the subject I was reading. The closer inspection to which I submitted ended in my favour. Perhaps, no symptom being visible in my external appearance of cannibalistic tendencies of my heart, or owning probably to the notion that I must have by that time got over my partiality for human flesh, or knowing at least that the place was safe enough against any treacherous spring which I might take into my head to make upon them, or owning to what other cause, the party gradually grew bolder, began to talk in whispers and actually tried to attract my attention towards them.[66]

Mukharji's response to being put on show for public consumption was to 'return the metropolitan gaze' and subject Britons to his own satirical inspection.[67]

It was the British press that catapulted South Asians into the public sphere either as the subject or as producers of articles. *The Times* newspaper devoted considerable space in the court and social pages to the visits and extended sojourns of Indian aristocrats and the public speeches of Indians in Britain. Similarly, other Victorian newspapers, such as *The Illustrated London News* and *The Graphic*, frequently contained photographs or sketches of visiting or resident South Asians. Pieces written by South Asians for outlets such as *Pearson's Magazine, The Nineteenth-Century* and *Fortnightly Review*, included an exposé of female poverty in London by the Anglo-Indian Olive Christian Malvery, a discussion of Indian women and property law by Cornelia Sorabji, a defence of Islam by Syed Ameer Ali (an early leader of Britain's Muslims), and a critique of the Hindu child marriage system and the promotion of female emancipation in India by Rukhmabai.[68] The British press also picked up on the satirical figure of the 'The Babu', who first appeared in the magazine *Punch* and was then republished in book form under the title *Baboo Bungsho Jabberjee, BA London in* 1897. A fictional creation, the Babu was a figure of ridicule – an Indian (specifically Hindu Bengali) student in Britain, exhibiting a stereotypical misplaced intellectual and linguistic vanity, cowardice and comically superficial knowledge of British customs and society.[69]

Several South Asians who came to Britain in the nineteenth century captured the public imagination and, trumpeted in the newspapers, gained celebrity status. Keshub Chandra Sen, leader of the reformist Hindu sect the Brahmo Samaj was one. He travelled to Britain in 1870, in the wake of fellow Calcuttan Brahmo social reformer Ram Mohan Roy (see Chapter 4), who had died during a visit to Britain and had been buried in Bristol. Like Roy, Sen found himself in great demand as a public speaker and dinner guest in Britain and was even presented to the Queen. Also like Roy, Sen attracted intense public scrutiny. One newspaper even published a poem satirising his popularity.

Have you heard – if so where and when –
Of BABOO KESHUB CHUNDER SEN?
The name surpasses human ken –
BABOO KESHUB CHUNDER SEN!

To write it almost spoils my pen:
Look – BABOO KESHUB CHUNDER SEN!
From fair Cashmere's white-peopled glen
Comes BABOO KESHUB CHUNDER SEN?
Or like 'my ugly brother Ben'
Swarthy BABOO KESHUB CHUNDER SEN?
Big as Ox, or Small as Wren,
Is BABOO KESHUB CHUNDER SEN?
Let's beard this 'lion' in his den –
This BABOO KESHUB CHUNDER SEN
So come to tea and muffins, then,
With BABOO KESHUB CHUNDER SEN[70]

His visit filled newspaper columns and he became a topic of conversation among the chattering classes fascinated by his vegetarian-eating habits and his physical appearance, which attracted many female admirers. It has been claimed that Sen's talks were attended by as many as 40,000 people.[71]

But it was not just South-Asian men who became recognisable figures, a few women did too, including Ramabai, Rukhmabai and Sorabji (who, claiming to hate publicity, nevertheless recognised that it was essential to control her public image). Rukhmabai came to Britain in 1888 to study medicine under the sponsorship of suffragettes Eva McLaren and Dr Edith Pechy Phipson. She was a Hindu child bride who had refused to live with her husband, provoking a famous court case and heated public debate in Britain, where her stance was supported by the press and the suffragette movement. Graduating from the London School of Medicine in 1894, she became medical officer at a hospital for women and children in Surat.[72] Rukhmabai's friend and contemporary at the London School of Medicine for women in London, Dr Louisa Martindale, remembered her fondly 'as a very charming Indian',[73] and visited her in India many years later.

South Asians became highly visible within British political life when two Indian MPs were elected to the House of Commons in the late nineteenth century. Although Indians had contested seats before (Lal Mohan Ghosh, for instance, or Womesh Chandra Bonnerjee), and a South Asian of mixed descent, David Octerlony Dyce Sombre (see Chapter 4), had actually been elected to Parliament in 1841, the real breakthrough came in 1892, when Dadabhai Naoroji was elected liberal

MP for Finsbury Central in London, an event that stands as a milestone in the history of South Asians in Britain. Shortly afterwards, in the year that Naoroji lost his parliamentary seat, another Indian, Mancherjee Bhownagree, became conservative MP for Bethnal Green. Although Naoroji and Bhownagree were both Parsees (an ethnic and religious minority) from Bombay and went on to lead the London Zoroastrian Association, in every other respect they differed substantially. Naoroji was born into a comparatively poor family, whereas Bhownagree was the son of an affluent merchant. By the time Naoroji was elected to parliament he had already established himself as a pioneer in many fields: he had been the first Indian to be appointed to a professorship at Elphinstone College, Bombay, and, when he went to London in 1855, he became a partner in the first Indian company established in Britain: Cama & Co. Bhownagree, on the other hand, was a journalist, then the agent of Bhavanagar, before arriving in London in 1882 to study law.[74] The two men's careers and politics also diverged. Naoroji, a critic of empire and a politically moderate Indian nationalist who led the Indian National Congress a record three times, had a short parliamentary career, lasting only three years. By contrast, Bhownagree, a supporter of British imperialism, represented his East London constituents for over a decade, gaining a reputation as a good local MP. But it was Naoroji who enjoyed the most fame, as a result of the unprecedented national and international publicity surrounding his election campaign, during which Conservative Prime Minister, Lord Salisbury, made the provocative statement: 'however great the progress of mankind has been and however far we have advanced in overcoming prejudices, I doubt if we have yet to go to that point of view where a British constituency would elect a black man'. The public debate that followed made Naoroji into a household name, and, it has been argued, contributed towards his election victory.[75] In such comments as Salisbury's, and the reactions to them, we see both sides of the British imperial debate about 'race'.

The family history of early Indian nationalists offers particularly fascinating insights into both the private and public lives of South Asians in Britain. The Bonnerjee family is a case in point. Womesh Chandra Bonnerjee came to Britain in the mid-1860s on a scholarship to study law, becoming, in 1867, only the fourth Indian to be called to the bar. As his daughter wrote, 'My father had made many friends in England and was deeply impressed by English freedom.'[76] One of Bonnerjee's closest friends was Sir Tarak Nath Palit, who, like Bonnerjee, had his children educated in England. Bonnerjee, who co-founded the London Indian society with Dadabhai Naoroji in 1865, became a member of the small coterie of men who together presented the public face of moderate Indian nationalist politics in Britain. Unlike Dadabhai Naoroji, however, Bonnerjee failed to fulfil his political ambitions, unsuccessfully contesting two seats for the Liberal party (though in 1885 he was elected as the first president of the Indian National Congress).

Bonnerjee's remarkable home in Croydon was well known within the South-Asian community. The privileged domestic life he enjoyed and shared with his wife and children at 'Kidderpore', was the source of childhood memories for his daughter, Janaki Agnes Penelope Majumdar, who lived in it as a child:

> Sundays were special days at Kidderpore. They were started with breakfast in bed, as when the elder sisters began their medical work in London they had a very early start and a late return all the week and liked to get up late on Sundays to make up and we younger ones thought it a marvellous idea, so my mother would send up as many as six trays sometimes! Attendance at the Iron Room [meeting house of the Christian sect, the Plymouth Brethren, to which Mrs Bonnerjee belonged] was compulsory for the younger ones and on our return we usually found two or three young Indian students and other friends awaiting us who had arrived for lunch – Mr K.N. and Mr O. Chaudhuri were frequent visitors, also Basanta Mullick and his brothers, Sir B.C. Mitter, Sir B.L. Mitter, Mr C.C. Ghose and a great many others. After lunch some of us always had to go with my mother to the cemetery and then there was a 'spread tea' in the dining room and after that 'Hymn' in the drawing room ... Immediately after this ceremony my mother used to go down to the kitchen to cook a real Indian dinner and as soon as I was old enough I always used to help her. The servants were all given the evening off and we used to dish and carry up the things ourselves – my Aunts always sent spices to us ready ground in tins and we and our visitors all greatly enjoyed this meal. Sometimes my father would come and help and I remember him and Mr R.C. Dutt once spending the whole evening cooking wonderful duck curry which no one could eat because it was too highly spiced (jhal!). At first the servants were rather 'superior' about Indian food and my mother always left plenty of cold meat and pudding out for their

> supper. But she gradually noticed that however many curries might be left over on Sunday nights, there was never anything on Monday morning, and at last a deputation came to her from the servants asking her to cook just a little more of everything if she didn't mind, as they all enjoyed it so much![77]

This recollection provides several insights into both upstairs and downstairs experiences in the affluent Bonnerjee household, not least about an Indian family's relationship with their servants and the domestics' 'conversion' to the delights of Indian cuisine, which in some ways mirrors Hemangini Bonnerjee's own conversion from orthodox Hinduism to orthodox Christianity in Britain. While, outwardly, the three-storied home appeared to be a model of Victorian middle-class domesticity, re-fashioned to resemble the family mansion in Calcutta (also named 'Kidderpore') with its fashionable furnishing, solid wooden furniture and army of servants – all presided over by the Matriarch, Hemangini Bonnerjee – the image of the 'jhal' duck curry being consumed by frock-coated men and crinolined women[78] shows that the family's anglicisation was never complete, but selectively adopted.

A school friend of Susie Bonnerjee who witnessed the Sunday gatherings reflected: 'What an oasis Kidderpore must have been to the dozens of young Indian students in London who came there on Sundays and were transported in spirit to their own country!'[79] In fact, as Antoinette Burton has argued, 'No. 8 Bedford Park functioned as more than a gathering place for expatriate Indians.'[80] Hemangini Bonnerjee had succeeded in transforming a part of London's metropolitan suburban landscape, as much as she contributed to the development of Indian nationalist politics in Britain.

Family life in Britain was not always so convivial for the Bonnerjee children, however. Nolini (Nellie) Bonnerjee recalled being left with the Wood family when her mother returned to India for her confinement: 'It was always impressed upon us that we being Indians were inferior and our parents paid too little for us in return for what we got, that our hands could not be clean being dark-skinned.'[81] Nolini had to endure severe punishments at the hands of the Woods, which ranged from being locked in a dark cupboard to assaults. Both the physical and mental scares of this abuse would remain with Nolini until her death. In a poignant statement, she noted that her mother had returned from Calcutta 'too late to undo the harm' inflicted by the Woods. Her testimony is a reminder of the physical and emotional cost that Britain sometimes exacted from some of its Indian residents.

The Victorian era saw many changes in South-Asian experiences in Britain. By the time of the Queen's death in 1901, a much greater variety of South Asians had taken up residence in Britain – including seamen, ayahs, domestics, social reformers, princes, paupers, petitioners, professionals, servants, travellers and politicians – though they were not always comfortably at home. Although relatively few in number, they were highly visible, and could be found in slums, workhouses, factories, boarding houses, the London docks, hospitals, law courts, prisons, Inns of Court, medical schools and universities. They were seen begging in the streets, strolling in parks, travelling in omnibuses and carriages, riding on the London Underground, parading in political and royal processions, performing in exhibitions, serving and meeting the queen, visiting the seaside, tourist sites and theatres and addressing Parliament. The lives of these 'brown' Victorians, both 'heathen' and Christian, straddled both poverty and affluence, and were played out in both public and private spheres. By commenting on these varied experiences themselves, they found much to both appreciate and regret.

Chapter 6

From Empire to Decolonisation, 1901–1947

Shompa Lahiri

In the first decades of the twentieth century, South Asians became increasingly visible in the social, cultural, political and institutional life of Britain. This is not to say that attempts to quantify this nascent 'community in the making'[1] have proved easy. For one thing, the census is an unreliable guide to the exact size of the South-Asian population in Britain, as name and place of birth do not necessarily indicate ethnicity. South Asians who married Britons and who travelled frequently between India and Britain do not always show up in the records. In fact, only one attempt was made to accurately measure the scattered South-Asian population of Great Britain, by the Indian National Congress, which calculated that in 1932 there were 7,128 Indians living in Britain. But this statistic is difficult to validate and is likely to be too cautious. What is more certain is that, as the research of Rozina Visram and Michael Fisher has shown, some South-Asian families already had very long roots in British soil. Generations of the same family would often return to Britain. The Dutts are one example. Leading British communist Rajani Palme Dutt was distantly related to both Romesh Chandra Dutt and Toru Dutt, who had spent long periods in Britain previously; Rajani's father, Upendra Krishna Dutt, had settled permanently in Cambridge, where he had established a medical practice.

To anyone familiar with the history of South Asians in Britain during the early twentieth century, various themes are obvious. One is the state scrutiny to which they were subjected, both in groups and as individuals, in the form of 1907 Lee Warner Committee on Indian students, the 1910 Committee on distressed Colonial and Indian subjects and the high-profile George Edalji criminal case. Governmental intervention continued during the First World War, when Indian soldiers, sent to the South Coast to receive medical treatment, were deliberately sectioned off from the British public. Such events highlighted the issue of identity for South Asians in Britain. In the interwar period, Indian seamen fought to maintain their rights as imperial subjects when their citizenship was challenged by the state via the Coloured Alien Seamen's Order. At the same time, other

Indians sought to relinquish imperial subjecthood in favour of independent Indian nationhood, through organisations such as the India League – their activities were closely watched by British Intelligence. The development of South-Asian organisations in Britain is indeed another feature of the period: Indian women's political and feminist activism, for example, was nurtured by the formation of various networks, friendships and associations. Reflected in the increase in the number of organisations is the widening variety of careers of South Asians in Britain during the early twentieth century, indicated by the number of different occupations noted in the passports granted to Indians travelling to Britain in the 1930s. A particularly significant profession for South Asians in Britain is medicine, and the activities of one Indian doctor, Dr Buck Ruxton, is an example of another feature of the period – the cause célèbre, a stark contrast to the hidden lives of other South Asians, who remained anonymous and forgotten. Towards the end of the period, the conflicting loyalties of some South Asians in Britain were exposed during the Second World War. While many were keen to join the war effort, others rejected participation in an 'imperialist war'. Still others worked in the Indian section of the BBC, led by the writer George Orwell, broadcasting radio programmes from London to win Indian support for the Allied cause. Through all this, the campaign for decolonisation in the Indian subcontinent grew, to culminate finally in Indian and Pakistani independence in 1947.

Under the Spotlight

State interest in the activities of Britain's resident Indian population was stimulated by the fear that politically subversive students, desperate indigents and insurgent soldiers would return to India to destabilise British rule. The official spotlight was first placed on Indian students in 1907, when a government committee chaired by Sir William Lee Warner was set up to investigate the issue of Indian students in Britain. A reference in *The Times* to the 'Indian student problem' indicates that students had provoked attention before 1907, but this was the first time that the issue was deemed serious enough to warrant a government inquiry. As a result, thirty-five Indians in London, Cambridge, Oxford and Edinburgh and sixty-five British witnesses gave oral and written testimony to the committee. Some of the students felt that there was no justification for the inquiry; others viewed the committee as a cover for government surveillance. In fact, when the Lee Warner Committee finally completed its report, all sides agreed that the nature of the findings warranted its suppression. There was consensus that passages in the report, open to misrepresentation, could offend Indians. This, however, merely delayed its appearance. Despite continued opposition from the Government of India, it was published as an appendix to the 1922 Lytton committee report, which re-examined the position of Indian students in Britain.[2]

One of the main components of the 'Indian student problem' identified by the Lee Warner Committee was the further radicalisation of Indian students in Britain. This was partly, the report suggested, a reflection of the political climate in India in the wake of the 1905 Partition of Bengal. Equally, it was the result of the politicising effects of the students' residence in Britain, where the education they received highlighted the obvious contradiction between theories of democracy, equality and civil rights, and the realities of imperialism in India, not to mention their exposure to negative representations of India and Indians in the British press. The Lee Warner report revealed British fears that disaffected students would embrace radical nationalist politics, and the presence in the metropolis of Indian revolutionaries with effective recruitment techniques seemed serious enough to Scotland Yard to justify their surveillance of the students. Consequently, students were routinely shadowed and their mail intercepted. Particular watch was kept on India House, a building in Highgate, London, which was the headquarters of a group of revolutionary Indian students led by Shyamji Krishnawarma. He had started a scholarship scheme for Indian students, and in the journal *Indian Sociologist*, which he edited, he frankly stated that his aim was to frustrate the British government's attempts to wean young Indian students in England from the nationalist cause. The figure of the discontented Indian revolutionary plotting the violent demise of the Raj in the capital city of the empire was sufficiently resonant to appear in British fiction of the period, including Mason's *The Broken Road* and Edmund Chandler's novel, *Siri Ram, Revolutionist: A Transcript from Life, 1907–1910*.

Another aspect of the Lee Warner Committee's report was its concern about the susceptibility of Indian students to so-called 'immoral influences', specifically their co-habitation with, and marriage to, white women. In a climate of heightened anxiety after the assassination of a British official, Sir William Curzon Wyllie, by Indian student Madan Lal Dhingra, the guardianship of students was no longer left to unofficial associations. The Indian Student Department and the Bureau of Information provided an official framework of control and a means of curtailing seditious influences. In addition, a secret quota system was imposed by higher education institutions to limit the number of students from India.[3]

The issue of destitution and homelessness among South Asians domiciled in Britain, which had concerned the British government in the nineteenth century, continued to concern them in the twentieth century and resulted in a government committee – the Committee on Distressed Colonial and Indian subjects – which published its findings in 1910. The comparatively small number of cases – only 250 Indians for the period 1888–1910 – posed no difficulties, but the diversity of cases was considered a problem. Destitute Indians comprised seamen, litigants, domestic servants, students and Indians who came to Britain 'for spectacular purposes', that is, to appear in exhibitions. These entertainers enjoyed protection under legislation introduced in 1902, and Indian seamen (who formed over half the cases of destitution) were satisfactorily protected by Merchant Shipping legislation: deserting Indian seamen were repatriated by Superintendents of the Mercantile Marine under the direction of the Board of Trade. But Anglo-Indian sailors were not protected by any shipping legislation because they were engaged under European rather than Indian articles, a reflection of the British government's limited racialised understanding of mixed descent and the boundaries of Indianness. The Committee recommended that masters of vessels carrying Anglo-Indians should be required to give an undertaking to repatriate them.

Repatriation agreements also became compulsory for British employers of Indian domestic servants in Britain. Disappointed litigants such as Tulsi Ram, discussed in Chapter 5, who sought legal redress in Britain and became destitute, should, the report stated, be given further warnings not to prosecute cases in Britain. University students in India were also to be discouraged from coming to Britain by publicising the difficulties faced by students already here. For those students in Britain who became impoverished, a private fund for temporary relief (in urgent cases) would, together with public funds from Indian revenues, fund repatriation costs.[4]

War Effort

During the First World War, 1.27 million Indian soldiers fought on the Western Front in France. Of 14,514 Indian soldiers invalided, some were brought to England, 'as it was found inconvenient to move them by rail to the South of France'.[5] The Indian connection with the seaside town of Brighton, epitomised by the famous baths of local Indian celebrity Sake Dean Mahomed (discussed in Chapter 4), continued when the Brighton Pavilion, workhouse and local school were hastily converted into hospitals for the wounded Indian troops. Two similar facilities were established at Brockenhurst and a convalescent home at New Milton. In order to maintain sepoy loyalty – to inoculate them against anti-British sentiment – great pains were taken to cater to the soldiers' religious, dietary, social and linguistic needs. As David Ommisi has noted, 'the British had no desire to provoke another mutiny like that of 1857 by tampering with what the soldiers held sacred'.[6] Caste committees, religiously sensitive cooking arrangements, ritual slaughterhouses and places of worship were set up within the hospitals, and a burial ground for Muslims was established near Woking Mosque. Hindu and Sikh soldiers were cremated on the Sussex downs, above Patcham, a site marked by the Chattri Indian War Memorial built in 1921.[7]

Indian home-front support for the war was considerable. The hospitals were staffed by serving and retired members of the Indian medical service; 198 students acted as interpreters, dressers, dispensers, clerks and superintendents of the Indian hospital kitchens. When the First World War broke out, Mohandas Gandhi, in Britain, canvassed support for the war effort at a meeting of South-Asian students and professionals in Britain, and 281 Indian students formed the Indian volunteer corps, representing all provinces and religions. While the male volunteers undertook a six-week training course in first aid and military drill, Indian women in Britain, led by Sarojini Naidu, the poet and budding nationalist leader, made clothes and dressings for the troops. Gandhi himself was happy to comply with Naidu's demands to sew clothes together from a pattern: 'I welcomed her demand,' he wrote, 'and with the assistance of friends got as many clothes made as I could manage during my training for first aid'.[8] The war effort was not without racial difficulties, however. Gandhi had been chairman of the volunteer corps for a short time when a dispute erupted concerning the right of Indian volunteers to elect their section officer, rather than have the commanding officer impose his choice, to whom Indians frequently objected. Eventually, after lengthy correspondence, a compromise was reached, and the corp sent on to Netley hospital (without Gandhi, who was suffering from pleurisy). Difficult compromises were struck elsewhere too. In 1915 the Union of East and West presented four Indian plays adapted from Rabindranath Tagore and the Hindu epic Mahabharata at Chiswick Town Hall in aid of wounded Indian troops, directed by an Indian, but performed by a white cast.[9] At the time, other groups of Indian artists were performing in London, including Hazrat Inayat Khan's Royal Musicians of Hindustan.[10]

Indian support for the war did not go unnoticed. Colonel Sir Walter Lawrence, Commissioner for sick and wounded Indian soldiers in England and France (1914–1916), noted the self-sacrifice entailed by such 'work which in India would have been scorned' for western-educated, high-caste/class men. At the end of the war, Lawrence concluded that the students had behaved well in spite of their anti-government views. 'There is no doubt,' he wrote, 'that the war has brought out their better qualities and I have heard of many instances of real self-sacrifice and fine loyal spirit'.[11]

During the course of the war, additional personnel were brought from India including barbers, tailors, cooks, washermen, sweepers, clerks, storekeepers, orderlies and surgeons. It was not, however, always necessary to look as far as India when more menial positions could be filled by the South-Asian residents of the Strangers' Home in London's East End. A shortage of labour led both Indian seamen and non-seamen in Britain to be recruited in munitions factories, sugar refineries, and shipbuilding and engineering firms. Sometimes there were disputes over pay. On one occasion, discontent was inflamed when Indian soldiers learnt that a sweeper, working at one of the Indian hospitals, could expect to earn triple the salary of an Indian soldier.

The most contentious issue regarding hospital personnel concerned the deployment of white female nurses to treat Indians. The paranoia concerning miscegenation (inter-racial sexual union) was deep-rooted in the British imperial and domestic psyche. The colonial South-Asian male – student, prince, seamen or soldier – had always excited considerable trepidation. Like other non-Europeans in Britain, they were viewed more often than not as sexual predators threatening the honour of white women. The British Empire was based on social distance, the separation of the ruler and ruled, and it was thought that any bridging of that gap would compromise British imperial prestige and authority. Tied to imperial anxieties about racial degeneracy, which had surfaced in the Edwardian period, were concerns voiced by British officials about uncontrolled female sexuality, which revealed the wider gender dimension of the issue. A year before the war broke out, a government circular was sent to Registry offices in Britain warning white women against marriage to Hindus or Muslims. In this climate of anxiety, those who wanted to keep British nurses out of Indian hospitals appear to have won the argument. Only the Lady Hardinge hospital employed British nurses, and they were placed in a supervisory capacity, leaving the hands-on nursing to British male orderlies, minimising physical contact with Indians and diminishing the possibility of what was euphemistically described as a 'scandal'. As one Indian noted bitterly: 'you take our men and money and yet deny us good nursing'.[12]

Indian anger grew when British concerns about fraternisation with local women resulted in draconian restrictions on Indian freedom of movement and association. Extreme measures were taken to prevent Indian soldiers and staff from leaving the hospitals unchaperoned: not only were no women permitted within the Kichener Hospital precincts, but a stringent system of passes was introduced. Those permitted to venture outside the confines of the Kitchener Hospital in Brighton had to travel in groups for promenades along the seafront and organised trips to London, escorted by a British officer to prevent communications and gifts being passed between the Indian soldiers and the British public. Barbed wire, fences and sentries further emphasised the impression of an impregnable fortress. Of the seven Indians who tried to escape these confines, six were flogged and one was imprisoned for six weeks. Complaints about restrictions led to the establishment of a committee of enquiry, but predictably it concluded that the hospitals were homes-from-home for Indian soldiers, a part of India transferred to British soil, fulfilling all an Indian soldier's wants and making frequent excursions unnecessary. The feelings of the Indian soldiers were plain, however. They likened the hospitals to prisons, comparing England to the colonial Indian penal colony on the Andaman Islands. One concluded: 'We have found our convict station here in England'.[13] The anger of an Indian surgeon at his forced incarceration boiled over into violence when he shot British officer, Col. Bruce Seton.

After the War: Politics of Citizenship and Gender

In the aftermath of the 'Great War', South Asians in Britain laid claim to the fruits of imperial citizenship and British subjecthood earned in military service. They were severely disappointed. Indeed, the British government took the opportunity to adopt more restrictive measures to limit their employment and travel rights. Betrayed by both the wartime compact and the imperial rhetoric of a multi-racial empire, South Asians in Britain became more determined than ever to claim their imperial rights.[14]

Gradually, the British government took measures to strip South Asians and other non-European colonial residents of their rights as British subjects. The most important of these was the 1925 Coloured Alien Seamen Order, despatched by the Home Secretary to regional police authorities, which requested the registration as 'aliens' of any 'coloured' seamen who could not produce documentary evidence of British subjecthood. The onus was on the seamen to prove their status as British subjects – but, as documentary evidence of nationality was very rarely issued, many of them found themselves in trouble. Despite their status as British subjects, seamen from British India and the princely states were frequently classified as aliens, criminalised and threatened with deportation. In some cases, documents were even tampered with or confiscated by local police. Protests by Indian seamen – who employed the services of solicitors, complained to the India Office and the press, and went on mass rallies – were strong and well organised. They even managed to have the matter raised in parliament. Crucially, as it turned out, the case of the Glasgow Indian peddlers, who had been registered as aliens, attracted widespread negative publicity in the Indian press, and in an attempt to placate hostile opinion in India, the order was ameliorated, though not completely abandoned, and a certificate of nationality and identity was introduced instead, described by one historian as a 'second-hand passport'.[15]

Another example of South-Asian attempts to stake a claim to imperial Britishness and the benefits of British subjecthood can be seen in their resistance to the 1935 British Shipping Assistance Act. The legislation reintroduced a colour bar against South-Asian and other non-European seamen, resulting in the formation of the Coloured Colonial Seamen's Association, a body incorporating Indians, Arabs, West Indians, Africans,

Chinese, Malays and Cypriots. A radical Indian nationalist group, the Indian Independence League (also known as the Indian Swaraj League), called for the end to discrimination at a political conference, sponsored by the communist party of Great Britain in 1936. One Indian delegate at the conference exposed the British Labour party's double standards and class bias by drawing attention to the fact that the first South-Asian hereditary peer, Lord Satyendra Prassano Sinha, was permitted admittance into the House of Lords without birth certificate, 'but the Labour party would take no steps to assist ordinary Indian seamen and peddlers who were also unable to produce evidence of birth'.[16]

It was not just Indian seamen whose right to live and work in Britain came under threat. Other working-class Indians, particularly peddlers, found themselves attracting unwelcome attention from the British government. From the 1920s, Indian peddlers (mainly from the Punjab) selling cotton, silk, voile and woollen goods from door to door became an increasingly common sight in Britain. The origins of these early peddlers actually lie in the First World War, when demobbed Punjabi soldiers chose to remain in Britain and took up peddling in the Scottish Highlands. According to Roger Ballard, they were joined there by a hereditary caste of peddlers known as Bhadra Sikhs, who developed a clientele in England's seaports and larger cities.[17] The India Office believed that Indian peddlers were signing on as lascars and then, on arrival in Britain, deserting in order to become peddlers, thereby bypassing British attempts to restrict the entry of working-class economic migrants from South Asia. Under the Merchant Shipping Act of 1894, the only offence a lascar committed when he deserted a ship in Britain was that of breaking his contract with the Shipping Company that employed him. After deserting, the lascar would usually find accommodation at one of the Indian lodging houses in the areas around the docks, such as Limehouse, where the wholesale dealers of silk goods could be found. Then he applied for a certificate to work as a peddler. The 'nully' or record of service was his only identification. The India Office made a distinction between the two types of would-be settler: 'the Sylhet man hopes to obtain sea employment on European wages and resorts to hawking and peddling as an interim measure only, while the Punjabi does not seek sea service.'[18] The regional origins of these peddlers are significant, as Sylhetis from Bangladesh and Pakistanis and

Indians from the Punjab form two of the three main components of Britain's contemporary South-Asian population. The third numerically significant group is the East African Asians, many of whose origins lie in the Indian state of Gujarat.

Along with the employment restrictions, new travel restrictions were introduced too. In 1929, the shipping licence companies reported only eighty desertions, but the India Office believed many more had slipped through the net, and, as a result, the police were asked to scrutinise applications for peddling licences and sea-service records to check for deserters.[19] A year later, passport controls were introduced for rural working-class Indians seeking to engage in petty trade in Britain. Although no similar sanction was placed on elite groups of South Asians, stop-lists existed for politically motivated travellers. Nevertheless, despite British attempts to restrict the settlement of working-class Indians in Britain, growing numbers of families made Britain their temporary or permanent home. Interracial family histories from this period reveal the multicultural origins of Britain's pre-war population.

At the same time as seamen and peddlers were fighting for imperial citizenship, another group of South Asians were fighting against it in favour of a different type of belonging – national citizenship within an Independent India. Their activities and organisations were closely watched by British Intelligence services, in particular the India League, which brought together diverse groups of seamen, students and professionals under the charismatic leadership of Vengalil Krishan Krishna Menon, who rallied many to the cause of Indian self-rule in the 1930s and 1940s. Through its various local branches, it attracted both South Asians and Britons. Between 1930 and 1949, it had a membership of approximately 180, over half of whom were Indian, including women such as Savitri Chowdhary, wife of a doctor. Despite its clear ideological association with the Indian Nationalist Congress, it was in fact an independent organisation, founded in 1912. But it only became a serious political force in Britain after Krishna Menon became Secretary. Menon mustered the support of various sorts of working-class Indians in Britain, for example the Muslim Sylheti seamen who settled in London during the 1930s, such as Sheikh Abdul Majid Qureshi, attended and co-chaired League meetings. The League's twin aims were to acquire support in parliament and from the British public. Their tactics included lobbying MPs and key figures in the Labour movement such as Harold Laski, Bertrand Russell and Fenner Brockway, and raising political consciousness with information campaigns and public meetings.

The India League was only one of several radical political organisations, which includes the Indian Freedom Association, the British Branch of the Indian National Congress and the London Branch of the Indian National Congress. All were subject to the surveillance of the Indian Political Intelligence (IPI) and struggled with the problem of finding suitable accommodation for their meetings. In an effort to control their costs, the Indian Freedom Association held its meetings at Hyde Park, the India League met in Indian restaurants and the London Branch of the Indian National Congress shared its headquarters with the League against Imperialism. Frequent changes of address and anonymous donations helped frustrate the Intelligence operatives. However, the problems of underfunding, fluctuating membership, political in-fighting and clashes of personality frequently resulted in the Indian political factions breaking up and reforming, showing how unstable, if dynamic, South-Asian radical politics was in Britain at this time.

British-based Indian nationalist politics exhibited strong internationalist sympathies with wider anti-colonial and communist movements. The Indian Freedom Association, for example, included Egyptians, Somalians, West Indians and Malaysians among its members. Two of Britain's leading communists were Indian: Shapurji Saklatvala, the communist MP for Battersea (1922–1929), and Rajani Palme Dutt, one of the leaders of the Communist Party of Great Britain from the interwar period to the 1960s.[20] A group of left-wing Indian students known as the London Majlis formed links with the Communist Party of Great Britain; one of them, Jyoti Basu (who edited the group's journal and went on to become chief minister of West Bengal in India) later recalled how the group's members used to meet at a London bookshop, Bibliophile, owned by Dr Sasadhar Sinha.[21] Many such groups took initiatives to bridge class, gender, regional and religious divisions, and to strengthen community bonds around a radical nationalist agenda. The Majlis, for instance, initiated a literacy campaign in East London aimed at Indian sailors. Indian women members of the Lascar Welfare League, mainly wives of Indian residents and students, fund-raised on behalf of Indian seamen.

In rather different ways, Lord Satyendra Prassano Sinha, Britain's first South-Asian Peer, mentioned above, developed Indian involvement in British parliamentary politics after he was awarded a peerage and took his seat in the House of Lords in 1919. Born in 1863 in Calcutta, he had studied for the bar in London, then established a successful career in India as a barrister, becoming the first Indian Advocate General of Bengal. Together with other moderates, he left the Indian National Congress in the year of his elevation to the British House of Lords, having already been awarded a knighthood in 1915. Although an establishment figure, he was nevertheless a pioneering Indian presence in the administration of British India, achieving high office as parliamentary under-secretary of state for India and becoming the first Indian to become governor of an Indian province.

The surveillance reports on Indian political activities in the interwar years show that political debates were not the exclusive preserve of men. Indian women, such as Mrs Haidri Bhattacharji, often chaired meetings, were elected to committees, gave speeches and sang patriotic songs. Indeed, the names of certain women appear regularly in the records. At the Labour Party conference on self-government for India in 1930, it was noted that the radical (or, from an IPI perspective, 'extreme') views of Miss Nur Jehan Mohammed Yusuf, who was in favour of full Indian independence, clashed with the moderate stance of Begum Meenakshi Faruki, who spoke in support of dominion status for India within the British Empire. Who were Miss Nur Jehan Mohammed Yusuf, Begum Meenakshi Faruki and Mrs Haidri Bhattacharji? Unfortunately, the records give few clues.[22] But women like them claimed voting/citizenship rights and fought for gender equality in their participation in women's suffrage and feminist politics in Britain. In contrast to the maharanis who were so often photographed for the British press as traditional symbols of Indian womanhood, in 1911 three Indian women – Mrs Roy, Mrs Bhola Nath and Mrs Charulata Mukerjee – were pictured marching in a suffrage procession in London, representing a radical vision of diasporic Indian feminism. The most prominent Indian suffragette, however, was Sophia Duleep Singh, the youngest daughter of Maharajah Duleep Singh. An ardent, active member of both the National Union of Women's suffrage Societies and the Women's Social Political Union, she fund-raised and sold copies of the suffragette newspaper outside her home, Faraday House, in Hampton Court. But it was her refusal, as a member of the Women's Tax Resistance League, to pay tax which brought the most publicity for the cause of British female enfranchisement when she ended up in court. She remained committed to the women's movement all her life.[23]

It was a meeting with Sophia Duleep Singh in Kashmir that encouraged Mithan Tata and her mother Herabai, members of the legendary Parsee business dynasty of Tata Ltd, to pursue their interest in women's rights. After the First World War, they travelled together to London as delegates of the Southborough committee charged with petitioning parliament to amend the Government of India Bill and grant Indian women the vote on the same terms as men. As Geraldine Forbes has noted, both mother and daughter worked tirelessly for the enfranchisement of Indian women in Britain, making contact with the leaders of the British women's suffrage movement, researching and preparing reports, speaking at public meetings and lobbying MPs.[24] Their work was financed by Tata Ltd and Mithan's father. Despite support for the amendment among British feminists, who crowded out the visitor's gallery in the Houses of Commons to hear a forceful speech by the Assistant Secretary of State of India, in the end it failed to be passed. But the two women's extended stay in London was not wasted. Mithan Tata enrolled in a two-year post-graduate course at the London School of Economics, while her mother studied social work at the same institution. On completion of her masters, Mithan Tata joined Lincoln's Inn in April 1920 and became the first Indian woman to pass bar examinations and practise law in India. [25]

Another notable event was the foundation, by Mrs Charulata Mukerjee, mentioned earlier, and the Dowager Maharani of Cooch Behar, of the *Sisterhood of the East*, an association open to Indian and other Asian women as an informal forum in which to debate issues of mutual interest with like-minded British women. Mrs Mukerjee described the association to her daughter as 'most definitely a progressive movement', though she added, 'but we do not intend to have any men at our parties, so that women who observe purdah may belong. Most of the "sisters" enrolled do not observe purdah.'[26] Another member of the *Sisterhood of the East*, Avabai Wadia, gave a vivid impression of the meetings as consisting of: 'Bright saris, colourful lace, and chiffon dresses and dainty hats.' She went on: 'Most of the Indian women were painfully shy, but they were put at their ease by more knowledgeable ones, often the wives of officials who were used to entertaining. Some of these meetings … were held at the Lyceum Club in Park Lane.'[27] The great cachet of the Mayfair address reflected the social standing and affluence of the club's Asian and British patrons.

Wadia was one of the most remarkable South-Asian women in Britain at this time. Born in 1913, in Colombo, Sri Lanka, to Parsee parents, she was the daughter of a shipping company executive, and her life provides not just a glimpse of how South-Asian feminist networks operated, but an insight into how an elite Parsee woman experienced and made a temporary home in interwar Britain.

In 1928, she and her mother sailed for Britain, where her elder brother was already a student. As she wrote in her autobiography: 'Going to England was a great act of faith for my parents, my mother especially, with her poor command of English and with a naïve 14-year-old in tow.'[28] But Wadia's mother was determined that her only daughter should receive the education that she herself had been denied. Fore-warned that Britain was a gastronomic wilderness, especially for vegetarians, the Wadias took with them large bags of rice, dhal (lentils), ghee (clarified butter) and spices, to make their stay more palatable.

Wadia's background and training was very similar to Mithan Lam's. Both were from elite business Parsee backgrounds; both had liberal and supportive parents, who sponsored and encouraged their education. Wadia's descriptions in her autobiography of her time at Brondesbury and Kilburn High School, where she was the only South-Asian pupil, are particularly revealing. Rather than attempting to hide Avabai's difference from her classmates, Mrs Wadia decided her daughter should accentuate it by wearing a sari, which she thought would not only keep her warm but also earn her respect. Wadia made up for her lack of skill in physical education by performing well in academic studies, acquiring top grades in English, History and French, and eventually gaining admission into the Inns of Court in London to train as a barrister. Although the Inns of Court were a popular destination for Indian male students (it is no coincidence that many of the key players in South-Asian colonial and post-colonial politics studied for the Bar in London, including Jawaharlal Nehru, Mohandas Gandhi, Mohammed Ali Jinnah, Subash Chandra Bose and Dr Bhimarao Ramji Ambedkar), the law was still – despite the pioneering Cornelia Sorabji – an unconventional choice of career in the 1930s for a South-Asian woman. Most South-Asian women studied medicine, teacher training, or took undergraduate courses (Mrs Wadia kept herself busy by enrolling at Regents Street Polytechnic on a handicrafts course). Despite being one of only a handful of women and non-Europeans enrolled at the Inns of Court, and having to submit to frequent informal racial segregation, Wadia described this period as one of the happiest times of her life. Having completed a law degree at University of London in 1934, she became the first Sri Lankan to be called to the bar in 1935, and although many of the chambers she applied to were reluctant to take on an Asian woman, she eventually found one willing to accept her.

From the time of her arrival in London, Avabai Wadia and her mother had been involved with British women's organisations, including the Women's Freedom League and the British Commonwealth League, campaigning for gender equality, attending conferences and speaking at gatherings. Looking back, Wadia wrote: 'This was a fight we understood well and when we found that as Indian women we were welcomed into such bodies, it meant a lot to us in terms of intellectual stimulation and friendship.'[29] Even before she left school, Wadia had been invited to join the London Committee of the Women's Indian Association, which championed a feminist agenda in India, and she was astonishingly active on their behalf, travelling extensively on bus and train to distant suburbs and into London's impoverished East End to advocate adult female franchise, equal rights to education, entry to the professions, and property and inheritance rights for South-Asian women. Later, she was actively involved with many groups, including representing the Six Point Group, which campaigned for equal rights for men and women, at the League of Nations, as well as the Labour party and the Indian nationalist movement. Britain was the place where she served her political apprenticeship, before returning to South Asia, where she would become an internationally recognised pioneer in the family planning movement.

Interestingly, Wadia's description of British-based Indians in this period as a 'tiny minority', comprising professional/business people, with or without families, and students, reflected her own middle-class background and experience. She failed to take into account the working-class groups, which constituted a numerically sizable component of the South-Asian population in Britain. In contrast, her use of the term 'Indian' is deliberately inclusive. As she explained, 'When I write "Indian" I include people from Ceylon and Burma as well, not in any chauvinistic manner but because they were far fewer and were usually taken as part of the sub-continental scene.'[30]

The truth, however, was that the relationship between South-Asian and British feminists in interwar Britain was not always so cordial. Mrs Dhanvanthi Rama Rau lived in Britain, with her two daughters and husband, during the 1930s. Her husband, Benegal Rama Rau, was financial adviser to the Simon Commission, which had been established to investigate constitutional reform and the prospect of self-rule for India. In her autobiography, Mrs Rama Rau claimed that, to her surprise, her offer of assistance at an all-Indian women's conference in London was flatly rejected. Angry at the snub, she publicly criticised the right of British women to speak for Indian women, a protest which heralded her explosive entry onto London's political stage. Over the next few years, she received numerous invitations to work on committees and give lectures to British women's organisations. Coming to believe that the internationalist outlook of the women's movement was crucial, she started a new association, the Women's Indian Association in London, to keep India alive in the mind of Indian and British women in Britain.[31]

Cultural and Social Life in Britain

There is no getting away from the fact that racism was a fact of life for many South Asians in Britain. Rama Rau wrote about the difficulties she and her husband faced finding a flat to rent in London.

> The colour prejudice in London was very strong, and it took us several weeks of answering advertisements, visiting landlords and landladies, only to be told over and over again that, yes, there were flats available, but no coloured couples could be accommodated. I was both furious and humiliated, for we certainly had not come to England for our own pleasure.[32]

After thirty-five refusals, the couple finally found a flat in South Kensington. Wadia, who also encountered racism, believed that South Asians were united by the overt and covert discrimination they faced, though this did not always prevent contact and even friendships with the host community. She and her mother were members of several social clubs in London, including the British Indian Association that held social gatherings, which were much appreciated by Wadia. 'For us Indians,' she wrote,

> these were very welcome since we were able to meet our few scattered fellow Indians ... Visiting dignitaries from India, British or Indian, were feted at dinners or luncheons at some good hotel

> and this provided a real social occasion ... the Cecil Hotel in the Strand was a favourite place.[33]

However, not all social encounters held such pleasant memories. Despite initial contact with the Theosophical Society, and attendance at their garden parties, Wadia and her mother found little in common with the people they met there; they soon abandoned the club although they maintained personal contacts. Their attendance at Zoroastrian House in Kensington (founded by the Parsee Association of Europe in 1909), which held fortnightly meetings and organised festivities, was more successful. After passing her bar examinations, Wadia was elected treasurer, and her contacts with the association helped her secure appointment as confidential secretary to the manager of the State Bank of India in London.

Wadia and her mother were keen radio listeners and enjoyed London's cultural life, regularly visiting the cinema, concerts and theatre. At the Arts Theatre Club, they saw Uday Shankar's celebrated dance ballet. Shankar, who had been trained in both India and London (at the Royal College of Arts), had revolutionised classical Indian dance, bringing it to a western audience for the first time. After the First World War, he partnered Anna Pavlov, for whom he created two ballets on Hindu themes. At the end of a decade of European and American tours, he returned to India to establish a troupe of dancers and then headed back to England, where his 'Hindu Ballet' appeared in London theatres throughout the 1930s.[34]

Between the wars, the South-Asian presence in the British performing arts was strong. Indian theatre companies, such as the 'Indian players', produced Indian plays and novels. Shankar's father, a notable impresario, produced several plays and ballets and organised concerts in London. In 1922, a mainly Indian cast appeared in two special matinee performances of Niranjan Pal's *The Goddess*.[35] As mentioned earlier, Hazrat Inayat Khan and his brothers formed the Royal Musicians of Hindustan, playing at charity concerts, music halls and operas houses. In this period, Devika Rani, India's first film star, studied at the Royal Academy of Dramatic Arts (RADA). And, in one of the most gossiped-about events of the decade, the Indian princess, Maharajkumari Indira Devi of Kapurthala, took to the stage.

Determined to be an actress in London, she had saved her allowance in secret and abruptly escaped aristocratic obligations and impending matrimony by enrolling at RADA – ignoring the advice of Hollywood director, Alexandra Korda, who told her to abandon acting, and spurning the influential show business contacts of her mother, the Maharani Brinda Devi of Kapurthala. In 1938, her stage debut as a 'Turkish slave girl' in the play *The Heart Was Not Burned* at the Gate Theatre Studio, London, made her, according to *The Oriental Post*, 'the most talked of subject' in London's 'Indian colony'. Unfortunately, she was ultimately disappointed in her acting ambitions. After the war, she confided in her mother, who visited her in her Chelsea flat: 'I wanted to be an actress. But I am not an actress. The theatre is so difficult. I have not had the success I wanted.'[36] Princess Indira, as she would later be known, did remain in the theatre, however: she was one of London's 'Angels', a theatrical term for individuals who formed small syndicates and invested in the staging of plays in the 1930s.[37]

A glimpse of how elite South Asians socialised in the interwar period can be gleaned from the first issue of the journal *The Indian* which reported on a lavish garden party held by the British Indian Union, attended by 200 mainly Indian guests – 'the first time that sweets and savouries have been provided at a garden party of this size in London'.[38] At the other end of the social scale, Sylheti-owned restaurants and lodging houses in London's East End catered for the religious, social, cultural and material needs of Asian seamen from East Bengal (Bangladesh), who had docked and sometimes settled in London, the precursors of Britain's modern-day Sylheti community, who still dominate the 'Indian' restaurant sector, satisfying Britain's continuing appetite for South-Asian cuisine, albeit in a hybrid form. Several central London Indian restaurants were established by enterprising North Indians and Calcuttan entrepreneurs – such as Shafi, Kohinoor, Durbar, Dilkush, Shalimar and the still-fashionable Veeraswamy – between the wars. They were not just eateries, but venues for South-Asian political meetings, community social gatherings and parties. The YMCA Indian Student Hostel, established in London in 1920, also had a dual function, serving as a social and cultural centre for Indian students and holding receptions for eminent Indian politicians, including Gandhi and Nehru. In an act of generosity to the fledging Sikh community, Maharajah Bhupinder Singh donated his London residence at 79 Sinclair Road, Shepherds Bush, for use as a *Gurudwara*, the Sikh place of worship – the first in the United Kingdom. Sikh peddlers arriving in Britain in 1920s used it as a religious and cultural refuge from an often hostile society.

Causes Célèbres and Hidden Lives

South Asians did not usually enter the historical record unless they became famous, or by publicly campaigning on political and employment issues or, especially at the beginning of the twentieth century, if they were viewed by the state as a problem. Most remain today barely visible on the historical map of imperial Britain, appearing fleetingly, if at all, in obscure public archives and family histories. The Sri Lankan J.W. Pieterz is typical. As mentioned in surveillance reports, he earned his living mainly as a walking advertisement, though in 1926 he paraded London's streets dressed as a Native American for a film company. He had lived in Britain for eleven years and was married to an Englishwoman with one son. After serving in the Army during the First World War, he became a pot-washer, a demotion for a man who had come to Britain with a college education.[39] No more is known about him.

George Edalji, on the other hand, became the subject of one of the most intriguing and highly publicised cause célèbre of Edwardian Britain (and more recently the subject of Julian Barnes' novel, *Arthur and George*, which recreates the case) with his arrest, conviction and imprisonment on a charge of animal maiming. Edalji was the son of Reverend Shapurji Edalji, an Indian Zoroastrian convert to Christianity, and his English wife Charlotte Stoneham. In 1873, Reverend Edalji had become the Vicar of Great Wyrley, a small village in Staffordshire, where, for nearly two decades, he and his family were subjected to a sustained campaign of malicious anonymous letters, practical jokes and pranks, culminating in 1903 with the accusations which led to George Edalji's arrest and imprisonment. An outcry followed, led by a press campaign in which ten thousand people signed a petition demanding that the case be retried. Edalji's cause was championed by none other than Arthur Conan Doyle, creator of legendary fictional detective, Sherlock Holmes, and an amateur sleuth himself, who sent his findings to the *Daily Telegraph* newspaper and the Home Office, forcing them to establish a committee to re-investigate the case.

Doyle was interested in several peculiarities of the case, first and foremost being Edalji's father's ethnicity. Despite the fact that two Indians of Parsee origin (like Edalji's father) had been elected to parliament in the late nineteenth century, it seemed to Doyle inevitable that an Indian clergyman would excite animosity among the villagers of the 'rude, unrefined parish' of Great Wyrley. George Edalji's character was firmly established as irreproachable: his old headmaster and his colleagues at the firm of solicitors where he worked all gave him glowing references, testifying to his 'mild tractable disposition'. In any case, his severe myopia prevented him from seeing beyond 6 yards, particularly at night, making it all but impossible for him to have committed the crime. He even had an alibi, his father swearing an oath that Edalji had not left the locked bedroom he shared with him.

Obviously, the case was permeated by strong racial undercurrents. The benefits of education, a successful career, middle-class status and religious compatibility had not protected George Edalji and his family from personal and financial ruin. 'Race,' it seemed, was still a barrier to complete acceptance in Edwardian society, a point highlighted by both Edalji's supporters and detractors. With so much written about him, it is a shame that very little of Edalji's own voice and opinions are available in the surviving historical records: it would be good to know more of what he himself thought of his experience. After three years, he was freed, though he remained under police supervision as a discharged convict. Eventually he received a pardon – but no compensation for three years false imprisonment and loss of name and reputation. The case, however, would leave a profound legal legacy. Together with the Adolf Beck case, it led directly to the establishment of the criminal court of appeal in England.[40]

Another cause célèbre – and gruesome murder case – involved the Indian-born Dr Buck Ruxton, who, like Edalji, achieved notoriety to the extent of becoming the subject of a popular rhyme. Ruxton, born in Bombay of Parsee origins in 1899, was given the name Bukhtar Rustomji Ratanji Hakim, or Buck Hakim for short. Later, he anglicised his name by deed poll to Buck Ruxton. He had graduated in medicine from the University of Bombay and served in the Indian Medical Corp before travelling, first to London, where he worked as a locum while pursuing his studies, then to Edinburgh, where he failed examinations for the Royal College of Surgeons. In time, he settled with his wife and three children in Lancaster, building up a thriving medical practice with over 2,000 patients. But his marital relations deteriorated after he became convinced that his wife was adulterous, and the police were called in to investigate violent arguments in the family home. In 1935, the dismembered bodies of Mrs Ruxton and her nursemaid were found. Pioneering new forensic techniques were used in order to identify the bodies and convict Ruxton of the double murder. Although the exact circumstances of the killings remained unclear, it was assumed to have been a crime of passion. The infamous doctor was convicted of murder and hanged, despite a petition for clemency signed by 10,000 people.

Although George Edalji and Buck Ruxton were not unique, relatively few South Asians in Britain experienced the British criminal justice system first-hand; of those that were charged with serious offences, few were convicted or hanged. An interesting feature of the Edalji and Ruxton cases is that, while they led to a negative portrayal of the South-Asian community in the tabloid press, the Indian defendants themselves drew support from the British public. Many people signed petitions for them, including, in Ruxton's case, his loyal patients. When, in 1920, Dr Devi Sasun was convicted of murder and procuring illegal abortions, he was able to rely on the support of his East End patients, who testified in court on his behalf. Similarly, the terrible crimes of Indian Physical Education teacher, U.R. Biswas, who went on the rampage with a gun (killing two members of his Scottish wife's family, his baby and a Glasgow taxi driver), did not prevent his pupils from speaking highly of him to the press.

Occupations, Associations, Journals

Surviving duplicate passports for Indians travelling to the West provide a valuable, if incomplete, record of the type of the men and women who journeyed from South Asia in the 1930s to early 1940s. Roughly 80 percent of the passports belonged to men, reflecting the masculine nature of travel of the time. Analysis of the 1,849 passport holders of 1932 reveals that the main groups of South Asians travelling to Britain comprised students, doctors, merchants, civil servants and aristocrats (seamen did not require passports to enter Britain). In total, over a hundred different occupations were recorded, demonstrating the diversity of Britain's colonial South-Asian population, which also represented every layer of Indian society, including the traditional ruling elite (landowners, nobility and priests), the urban professional middle class (teachers, engineers, accountants – and even an archaeologist) and, at the bottom of the hierarchy, labourers, performers and domestic servants.

As noted before, medicine was a popular profession among South Asians in Britain. Indeed, several practitioners were celebrated in their fields. Dr Chowry Muthu, though unnoticed by the British press, was praised in the Calcutta journal *Modern Review* for his successes in treating tuberculosis. In his article 'An Indian Tuberculosis Specialist in England', British-based Indian journalist, Nihal Singh, described Muthu as 'an eminent specialist in tuberculosis, who for twenty years has been maintaining one of the largest and most up to date sanatoria at Wells, Somerset'.[41] Born in Madras in 1865, of Christian parents, Muthu had graduated from King's College, London, and first practised in a London suburb. Having made a study of the Indian system of medicine, he came to the conclusion that tuberculosis could only be eradicated by dealing with environmental factors which encouraged the disease, such as poor housing. At his sanatorium, he tried to create an oasis of calmness, peace, wholesome food, light exercise and fresh air in order to build up his patients' immune systems. Somewhat ahead of his time, he placed particular emphasis on a holistic Indian-inspired treatment, which treated the mind as well as the body, viewing his role as both psychotherapist and physician.

It is more difficult to identify Indian women doctors in imperial Britain, though South-Asian women certainly came to study medicine before returning to India. Nolini Heloise (Nellie) Bonnerjee (see Chapter 5) qualified as a doctor from the London School of Medicine for Women and the Royal Free Hospital in 1899, though, settling in Liverpool with her husband George Blair, her medical career failed to flourish. Instead, in the words of her younger sister Janaki Agnes Penelope Majumdar, she 'did such medical works as came her way and also a great deal of social work for the Baby Clinics'. Nellie's other sister, Susila (Susie) Anita Bonnerjee, also faced difficulties in her attempts to find employment as a doctor in Britain. Janaki Majumdar believed it was her sister's 'nationality', which prevented her from obtaining a hospital post or entering into partnerships with other medical women in Britain, 'as they preferred British partners'. Nevertheless, Susila was able to secure a temporary post of home surgeon in a Bristol Hospital for six months during the First World War.[42] In general, South-Asian women journeying to Britain fall into several groups, including wives, domestic servants (ayahs), female royalty, students, teachers and a handful of other professionals including a social worker and a lawyer.[43] The most unconventional occupations undertaken by South Asians in Britain at this time included flying instructors, auctioneers, animal caretakers, sculptors and authors. At least ten Indians came to work in the British film industry.

This occupational diversity is reflected in the increase in different professional associations, including the Indian Chamber of Commerce in Great Britain, which was established in 1928 to promote the interests of Indian traders and merchants in Britain; by 1930, its membership had risen to 296. Indian doctors in Britain formed the Indian Medical Association in 1929, and both the Indian Workers' Association (IWA) and the Indian Seamen Union were established in this period.

At the same time, several South-Asian English-language journals, targeted at western-educated South Asians, came into existence, though they were often poorly funded and consequently short-lived. *Hind* described itself as the 'Indian organ of the United Kingdom', and there were also *Indian and Colonial Journal*, *United India* and *The Indian: At Home and Abroad*, which devoted sections to British Indians. While broadly political in flavour, these periodicals also covered cultural, social and religious events in the lives of Britain's Indian residents and sojourners. So, in November 1938, *The Oriental Post* reported on both a dinner for 250 guests and 'a sherry party'[44] to celebrate Divali, the Hindu festival of lights at Shafi's restaurant, as well as covering the preparations for Eid – the feast which marks the end of the Muslim festival of Ramadan – at Woking Mosque. Likewise, *The Indian* reported the establishment of a Hindu temple in London in 1929 (which may have been a reference to the Arya Bhavan in Belsize Park). New associations came into existence too. In its 22 August 1922 issue, *Hind* listed a wide array of religious, social, cultural and political Indian associations under the heading 'Indian Colony in the British Isles':

> The Indian YMCA, the Woking Mosque, the Putney Mosque, the London Dharmsala, the London Indian Association, the Indian Conference, the Bharat Conference, the Central Islamic Society, the Indian Majlis at various University centres, the Workers Welfare League. Indian Muslim Association, Indian Social Club, Parsee Association, Indian Information Bureau, Bengal Literary Association in London and some Urdu Literary Societies in Cambridge and Oxford.

As the journal was keen to emphasise, the list was far from exhaustive, and new associations continued to appear: in 1935, the well-established Central Hindu Society was joined by a rival organisation, Hindu Association of Europe. The South-Asian community was beginning to create bodies to protect and advance the interests of its various diverse components. An older London-based South-Asian religious association the Parsee Association of Europe (formed in 1909) served as a guide to the new organisations.[45]

Obituaries appearing in the journals provide valuable biographical detail about individuals. For example, in 1951, *The Indian: At Home and Overseas* contained an obituary of Rajani Nath Majumdar, who had established himself in early–twentieth century Britain as a successful businessman. The obituary represents a classic migrant tale of rags to riches. Majumdar, originally from Chittagong, now in Bangladesh, arrived in Britain in 1910, having travelled the world to seek his fortune. Little was known about his early life and family background, but by 1912 he had managed to save enough money to take over a small teashop. From these humble beginnings he prospered, eventually buying the Hotel Regina in London, which was to become his home, and extending his business empire to the Caledonian Hotel in Bloomsbury and the Metropole Hotel at Bexhill on Sea. Despite continuing ill health, he regularly inspected his London and South Coast hotels and took working holidays in Paris for inspiration. Majumdar was also involved with Indian politics in Britain and a close friend of Indian communist MP, Shapurji Saklatvala. In the last years of his life he struggled to win compensation for damage done to the Metropole Hotel during the Second World War.[46]

The Second World War

The outbreak of war in 1939 abruptly initiated a new phase in the experience of British-based South Asians. Many of them – their numbers swelled by South Asians stranded in Britain when shipping routes to India were bombed – were keen to join the war effort. The Indian Ambulance Unit was established in London to complement the valuable civil defence work done by Indian air raid wardens, and a charity, the Indian Troops Comfort Fund, was set up, supported by several Indian women residents, to provide food, clothing and treats for Indian prisoners of war captured by the Axis powers. Excursions and entertainments were organised for Indian soldiers, seamen and industrial trainees stationed in Britain.[47]

Colonial India contributed the largest volunteer army in support of the Allied cause in the Second World War, approximately 2.5 million men and women. For their part, many South-Asian British residents volunteered to join the Merchant Marine and the armed forces. One was Vilayat Inayat Khan, son of Indian Sufi Mystic, Hazrat Inayat Khan, and his American wife, Nora Baker. He applied to be a pilot in the RAF, was grounded due to faulty eyesight, and transferred to the Royal Navy, where he became a minesweeping officer and participated in the Normandy landings. The dentist Shanti Behari Seth (uncle of author Vikram Seth), enlisted shortly after the war broke out, joining the Army Dental Corps. After training in Cardiff, he was sent to North Africa and the Middle East, gradually moving up the ranks to Captain. At the battle of Cassino in Italy, his arm was blown off, and he was discharged with a disability pension (though remarkably he overcame his handicap to prosper in his profession, setting up his own dental practice in London in 1948).[48]

South-Asian women were also involved in the war effort. Perhaps the most remarkable was Vilayat Inayat Khan's older sister, Noor Inayat Khan. Trained in Britain as a Special Operations (SOE) secret agent, she became the first wireless operator to enter occupied France and was possibly the only Indian secret agent in Europe during the war. Her arrival in the summer of 1943 coincided with the Gestapo's arrest of the resistance group, which she had been sent to join. Successfully evading capture, she continued transmitting to London, providing for four months the only means of contact with Paris, until she was betrayed, arrested and incarcerated by the Gestapo. After several unsuccessful escape bids, she was transferred to Pforzheim prison in Germany, where she was manacled, tortured and kept on starvation rations in solitary confinement. Finally, nearly a year after her capture, she was sent to Dauchau concentration camp, where she was brutally killed. Khan's exceptional courage earned her one of only three George Crosses awarded to SOE women agents during the Second World War. In total, twenty-eight Victoria crosses were awarded to Indians, most of whom had served in the Indian Army, in the Far East.

South-Asian involvement in the war effort was not restricted to the battlefield, but extended to the home front. As the defence programme developed, Indians throughout the United Kingdom found employment as casual labourers. Some secured work constructing military camps and aerodromes; others became unskilled labourers in factories in the Midlands. Indian seamen, living precariously in the East End of London and in other big port cities after their ships had been torpedoed and sunk, found employment in some industrial capacity, gravitating in large numbers towards Newcastle, Glasgow, Manchester, Sheffield, Birmingham and Coventry. Cities such as Leeds, short of labour during the war, relied on seamen from Mirpur to fill the gap in the city's foundries: it was the beginnings of one of northern Britain's largest modern Pakistani communities. In Birmingham, the South-Asian population reached around 7,000. Once there, some of the men continued the well-established tradition of marrying British women.[49]

The war produced many new experiences in the domestic sphere too. Dhanvanthi Rama Rau, mentioned earlier, arranged to keep her family's London home intact, so that her daughters could continue their education. She was helped by the arrival of a young Jewish refugee, Lilian Ulanowsky, the daughter of concert musicians, who had been recommended to Mrs Rama Rau by the Refugee Committee. Lilian, whose brother was in Daccau and her mother in Austria, waiting for his release, rapidly became a member of the family, taking on the role of surrogate older sister to the Rama Rau girls, especially after Mrs Rama Rau left London to accompany her husband on his new posting in South Africa.[50] This innovative and pragmatic reconstructing of the diasporic home met the challenges of displacement and exile, and went some way to supplying the reciprocal emotional, domestic and academic needs of all involved.

Also responding to the crisis of war, the Princess Sophia Duleep Singh opened her home in the village of Penn, Buckinghamshire, to evacuees. John Sarbutt, who found refuge there with his family, has left a description of himself, his two elder sisters, his mother, Princess Sophia and her three dogs all sheltering from the nightly air raids in a purpose-built shelter within the grounds of Rathenrae House.[51]

The issue of the conscription of Indians domiciled in Britain, often contentious, came to a head with the trial of Suresh Dowlat Jayaram Vaidya, a journalist and political activist in Britain, who was arrested in 1944 for ignoring the call-up. Claiming that he was not 'a British subject by choice, or by consent',[52] he endeavoured to secure exemption as a conscientious objector. After a tribunal rejected his plea, he refused to undergo a medical examination and was arrested. When, finally, he submitted to a medical examination, he was found to have defective eyesight and be suffering from tuberculosis, and was officially declared unfit for military service. Nevertheless, his case provoked other Indian in Britain to protest against their conscription. For their part, the British authorities viewed Vaidya as clever troublemaker and, when he applied for a passport, they quickly expedited his return to India with his English wife and two children.

South Asians resident in Britain for more than two years were officially liable for national service. According to the India Office, all Indian conscripts were enlisted into the 80th Pioneer Indian Company, which consisted of 235 men, two-thirds of them volunteers. The majority of recruits were Muslims, with a handful of Sikhs (out of an estimated 1,000 Sikhs in the country), though the India Office made distinctions between South Asians not on grounds of religion, but according to education ('The greatest number of educated Indians in the company was 18,' a report stated). The term 'educated' referred to 'businessmen, doctors, barristers'. 'Uneducated' referred to 'seamen, deserters, waiters, labourers and hawkers.' The India Office was keen to emphasise that the majority of Indians in Britain had not been called up, and were free to study or earn a living: 'For every Indian serving in the Pioneer Company there are at least six earning a livelihood in Great Britain who have not been conscripted.'[53] One such group was formed of the Mirpuri seamen-turned peddlers, who had spotted a gap in the market and were profiting by selling nylon stockings to British women at a time when they were in short supply.

Not all South Asians in Britain accepted participation in what some considered an imperialist war, particularly after the launch of the Quit India movement in 1942, when Indian National Congress leader, Jawaharlal Nehru, called on Britain to leave India – an act which resulted in the arrest and imprisonment of the Congress leadership. This led to some conflicted loyalties. Writer Mulk Raj Anand was torn between allegiance to the Indian National Congress and his desire to fight Fascism. Some Indian workers in Britain resisted the burdens of imperial citizenship by adopting low key tactics to weaken the war effort. Surveillance reports suggest that the IWA functioned to protect Indians against conscription, which, according to the association, most Indians regarded as a great hardship, objecting on political and economic grounds and delaying registration until compelled to do so by the authorities. Some argued that the war was not their business and that their stay in Britain was only temporary. Official concern about the political fidelity of some Indians in the event of a German invasion of Britain and the threat posed to domestic and imperial security led the security services to draw up contingency plans for the possible internment of six Indians.

These fears had been fanned when Udham Singh, a Punjabi Sikh, assassinated Sir Michael O' Dwyer, former Governor of the Punjab, and wounded three other British officials, in London in March 1940, as revenge for the 1919 Amritsar massacre, which O'Dwyer had publicly supported. The massacre, which had occurred when British troops fired at a crowd of 10,000 unarmed men, women and children, leaving many dead or injured, and the subsequent declaration of martial law in the Punjab, had irreparably damaged Indo-British relations (and had formed the prelude to Gandhi's civil disobedience movement to end British rule in India). Singh, who had travelled the world, including Europe and America, was influenced by revolutionary anti-imperialism. He worked for a while as a peddler and film extra in Britain, and wandered the Midlands gaining a reputation among his countrymen, particularly at the Shepherd's Bush *Gurudwara*, as a 'fiery speaker' with a deep-seated hatred of British imperialism (but, crucially, not of British people). He was sentenced and hanged in Pentonville Prison, so following in the footsteps of fellow Punjabi, Madan Lal Dhingra, who had also assassinated a high-ranking British imperial bureaucrat in London in 1909. To many Indians in Britain, particularly Punjabi Sikhs, who collected funds for his defence and petitioned for clemency against the death sentence, Singh was a hero. Many Punjabi Britons remember Singh today as a Patriot Martyr in the struggle against British rule in India, and a conference is held annually in his memory by the IWA.[54]

One of the most interesting and revealing aspects of the South-Asian war effort relates to the Indian section of the BBC's Eastern Service. Led by Z. A. Bokhari, who later become head of Pakistan Radio, and staffed by Indian residents, the service broadcasted radio programmes apparently giving an account of the war 'through eastern eyes' (as one of the programme series was called), though scripts were in fact often written by George Orwell. From August 1941 to November 1943, Orwell was the Talks Assistant, and later Talks Producer, in the Indian section, and his job was to write programmes to help win Indian support for the Allied cause. Once they were written, they were translated by Indian members of staff, and then checked by Orwell before broadcast. In order to conform to government directives on censorship, the BBC employed a switch censor to monitor all broadcasts, who had instructions to interrupt any attempt to deviate from his scripts. It was noted that the BBC had difficulty recruiting Indians to do the job of 'switch-check'.[55]

Although Orwell's role in the Indian section has attracted some scholarly interest, comparatively little is known about the Indians employed by the BBC, which included several women, including Princess Indira of Kapurthala, mentioned earlier (who also drove an ambulance in London during the Blitz), Mrs Damyanthi Sahni, who had come to Britain with her husband in 1940,[56] and Venu Chitale, who had been studying teacher training (or Montessori) at University College London.[57] Chitale's first job at the BBC was to assist Orwell with both English and Hindi language programmes. Later, she became a full-time member of staff devoted solely to programmes in her mother tongue, Marathi. Her presence helped to maintain the equilibrium between Hindu and Muslim staff employed by the BBC. She also wrote pieces for the BBC's magazine, the *Listener*, and her recipe for 'Bean Sausages and Mash' – a vegetarian version of the British staple 'Sausage and Mash' adapted to meat-deficient wartime rations – provides a rare and fascinating example of an Indian woman writing confidently for a domestic British reading public, her tone (which may have reflected her radio voice) light, frothy and engaging. The recipe also shows how a vegetarian Indian could reinvent a Western Indian diet to suit the dietary restrictions of wartime Britain.[58]

Not all Indians in the Eastern service were resident in Britain before recruitment: some were brought over from India for the duration of the war. But by September 1942, there were fourteen full-time and fourteen contract Indian members of the BBC staff. All had been carefully vetted. Indeed, specific enquiries were made about M.R. Kothari, who was known to be in touch with the India League, when he was put forward as a translator and announcer for the BBC weekly Marathi Programme.[59] The eventual team included both well-known names, such as writer Mulk Raj Anand, and more obscure individuals, including the grammar school teacher and meteorologist Sharatchandra Gopal Sathaye.

Throughout the war, the Indian section put out a wide variety of programmes. Some were personal, the staff describing their experiences in wartime London, including the Blitz, to their Indian audience. English-language radio programmes also included 'The Names Will Live' (a series of biographical sketches on political personalities of the time), 'Today and Yesterday' (discussions of social changes in Britain as a result of war), 'Women of the West' (arranged as a letter to a friend in India from Venu Chitale), 'The Debate Continues' (a breakdown of parliamentary news broadcast by House of Commons correspondent Princess Indira) and Mulk Raj Anand's 'A Day in My Life', in which he interviewed ordinary people taking part in the war effort. The Eastern Service of the BBC also broadcasted Indian-language programmes in Hindi, Gujarati, Marathi and Bengali: news commentaries, features, talks and music, as well as a message service for Indian soldiers to their families in India. One of the most popular Hindi programmes was a children's series featuring Salamo, an Indian mouse, who came to England in the suitcase of a Bevin Boy (the name given to Indian industrial trainees who came over to be trained, under a scheme initiated by Minister of Labour, Ernest Bevin). Salamo's adventures enabled him to see a great deal of British life.[60] Unfortunately, Hindi language programmes suffered from a shortage of female presenters. Princess Indira was one of the most popular, her voice enhanced by her drama-school training in Britain, but when the Eastern service suggested recruiting suitable female candidates from India to make up the numbers in the Hindustani Repertory Company, which consisted of one member, the idea was discouraged.[61] Perhaps the single most interesting broadcast during the war was the 1943 documentary drama 'India Speaks: Map of India' by Mulk Raj Anand, produced by the radical British Unitary theatre company and performed by an all-Indian cast. Taking the dramatic form of a 'living' newspaper, it vividly depicted the political situation in India, in particular the devastating 1943 *man-made* Bengal Famine – highlighting how Indians strove in creative and imaginative ways to keep Indian politics on the British metropolitan agenda.[62]

Towards Nationalism

In many ways, the nationalist struggle to mobilise support for Indian self-rule united the disparate groups of South Asians in Britain, usually divided by class, religion, region, gender and language. After the Second World War, however, the British South-Asian community split along sectarian lines, replicating the politics of the subcontinent. Among Muslim seamen, support for the Muslim League began to grow. Sylheti sailors such as Nawab Ali and his friends had regularly attended India League meetings organised by Krishna Menon at Hyde Park Corner in the 1930s, and were staunch supporters of the Indian National Congress. But as support grew in India for a separate Muslim state – Pakistan – Indian Muslims in Britain started to question their allegiance to a united India. A party given by Muslim seamen to mark the London visit of the leader of the Muslim League, Mohammed Ali Jinnah, ended with the public pledge of their support for Pakistan.

Sectarian developments aside, the general move was strongly towards independence, and South Asians in Britain were caught up in it. A group pivotal in promoting decolonisation, particularly among Punjabis, was the Indian Workers' Association, mentioned earlier. According to one source, it was formed in the 1930s by a group of businessmen, students and professionals in the London area. Others, however, claimed it was formed in Coventry in 1938 by Punjabi peddlers. Either way, it seems to have been instrumental in introducing Punjabi labourers, who, prior to their arrival in Britain, had little knowledge of Indian politics or nationalism, to the idea of independence. Anant Ram, one of the founders of the IWA, told an interviewer how he had joined the association at the beginning of the Second World War:

> Since we were all from small villages in the Punjab and had no idea what freedom and slavery was, we came as labourers and had very poor knowledge of the world ... IWA meetings were about telling those who attended about such matters ... Our aim was to voice a concern for Indian freedom.

He nostalgically recalled the day India achieved independence: 'No one called us "Blackie", even if the children said something to this effect the parents would forbid them, so it was a great day for all of us.' Though marred by the violence which accompanied the partition of the Indian subcontinent into two successor states, India and Pakistan, Independence Day had great practical, symbolic and mythic value for South-Asian residents in Britain.[63]

Chapter 7

Migrating to the 'Mother Country', 1947–1980

Shinder S. Thandi

In the three decades after the Second World War, migration from South Asia to Britain surpassed anything that had occurred in the previous 300 years. The make-up of migrants arriving in the UK was different too, with a higher proportion of manual workers and fewer members of elites. Furthermore, after the partition of India, settlers were now coming from newly created nation states (of India, Pakistan and East Pakistan – Bangladesh after 1971). This new development is especially important in understanding the eventual pattern of South-Asian settlement in Britain, the evolution of identity politics and the persistence of a 'homing desire' among some British-based South Asians.

The 1950s and 1960s were decades of uncertainty and despair for many of the new migrants still unsure of their long term plans. But, seeing the prospects of a better life in Britain and needing to take a decision ahead of impending restrictions on further immigration, many of them decided to make Britain their home and asked their wives and children to join them. Thereafter, settlement expanded rapidly, through family reunion and natural increase, and this was given a further boost by fresh immigration from East Africa in the early 1970s. Starting small at the beginning of the 1950s, but growing fast, sizable and visible South-Asian communities developed in the major metropolitan areas of Britain – predominantly in England.

In the 1970s a British-born second generation of South Asians emerged. Their values were derived both from their home culture and those of the dominant British community, and it was hard to tell how they would develop – though academics and policymakers of the day, pre-occupied with the idea that the new generation was 'between two cultures', predicted inter-generational conflict and assimilation of the younger South Asians into 'British' society. In fact, at the same time as putting down roots in Britain, newly-confident South Asians began to campaign for their economic, social, political, cultural and religious rights. Many of these struggles – especially for Muslims and Sikhs – would take years to win because, causing high-profile controversy and

Map 3: Origins of Settlers in Britain from the Indian Sub-Continent, post-1947.

Map 4: South-Asian Presence in Britain, post-1947.

involving legal changes at the highest level, they challenged the very notion of Britishness. Over time, however, South-Asian communities won important victories and, simultaneously, there was a growing understanding and tolerance of cultural diversity. Thus, by the 1980s, the foundations of a vibrant, urban, multicultural, multireligious and multiracial Britain were fully laid.

Looking at these decades as a whole, three broad features stand out. First, the distinctive settlement pattern – the concentration of different South-Asian migrants in specific localities of Britain. Second, the dramatic life-changes of these new migrants (often originally from small villages in South Asia) in their new big-city environment. And third, the struggles they undertook to secure their cultural and religious rights.

Decolonisation and Migration: Unwelcome Guests from the Colonies

Although the causes of South-Asian migration to the UK are varied, complex and – indeed – contested, the dominant narratives of post-war migration emphasise the interplay between the push and pull factors.[1] The primary push factors included South-Asian demographic pressures, economic dislocation caused by events such as the construction of the Mangla Dam in Pakistan, low levels of income, lack of employment opportunities and political tensions, as for example in Sri Lanka. The main pull factor was the increased demand for labour in war-devastated Britain. Insufficient supplies of home workers meant that many manufacturing industries, especially those requiring unskilled labour, and public services, such as the newly created National Health Service and the public transport system, needed 'ready-made' labour. To fill such vacancies quickly, government departments actively promoted immigration.[2] It is hardly surprising, therefore, that most of earlier settlers from South Asia ended up in three economic areas of the UK in urgent need of extra manpower: the textile mills in northern cities in Lancashire and Yorkshire, the metal-bashing foundries and hosiery industries in the West and East Midlands and the light manufacturing industry and transportation systems in the Greater London area, particularly Southall and Hounslow, which are close to Heathrow airport.

The Midlands provides a good snapshot of the situation at this time. Here, Coventry was a favourite destination for migrants. A rapidly expanding local economy, boosted by reconstruction work and an emergent car industry, created employment opportunities for unskilled labour, and many South Asians took jobs in the local foundries of Sterling Metals, in Dunlop, Dunns and at toolmaker, Alfred Herberts. Later, in the same area, South-Asian women worked for General Electric Company, manufacturing and assembling light telecommunications equipment. In Birmingham and other key Midlands locations such as Smethwick, Dudley, Darlastan and Walsall, a (disproportionately) large number of migrants were employed in the metal-bashing foundries which served the manufacturing industry of the region.

Many of these settlers came from rural areas of South Asia – Punjabis, predominantly Sikhs (with a smaller number of Hindus), from the central districts of East Punjab (known as *doaba*), Muslims from Campbellpur in West Punjab, Kashmiri Muslims from Mirpur district, Muslims from Sylhet, a north-eastern district of Bangladesh and Sri Lankans, mainly Tamils fleeing ethnic conflict in the Jaffna province. Historically, most of these districts shared an imperial connection with Britain: for generations Sylheti seamen had worked on East India Company ships and Punjabi soldiers had served in the British Indian army. But, unlike many earlier migrants (except perhaps lascars), most of these post-war pioneer migrants were relatively young men in their early twenties, illiterate or semi-literate, with predominantly farming or rural backgrounds. Although it would be true to say that they were relatively poor, by no means were they 'pushed' out of their homelands due to poverty. They were, in fact, economic migrants *par excellence*, with aspirations to better themselves. They were joined by other sorts of migrants, such as retired soldiers of the British Empire who, since the First World War, had been given special dispensation – 'vouchers' – to enter Britain. Professionals, such as doctors, and political refugees from the Punjab, Kashmir and Bengal also migrated to Britain at this time, but they were in a minority.

Previous chapters have shown that the Indian presence was traditionally concentrated in London and other major port cities such as Bristol, Cardiff, Manchester, Liverpool and Glasgow, though the numbers of people were relatively small, and some of these 'British Indians' moved frequently between Britain and India. After the Second World War, the situation was quantitatively, as well as qualitatively, very different. Not only was there a sharp rise in numbers, South Asians also began to penetrate the interior counties of England (though concentrating only in a few of them). Census data show that the total South-Asian population rose from 43,000 (of whom 31,000 were Indians, 10,000 Pakistanis, 2,000 East Pakistanis/Bangladeshis) in 1951 to just over a million by 1981 (676,000 Indians, 296,000 Pakistanis and 65,000 Bangladeshis). This remarkable rise, due to both the increase in British-born Asians and fresh immigration, was to have a permanent effect on the socio-economic and religious landscape of the inner-city areas receiving them.[3] But how do we explain the concentration of specific communities in particular geographical localities? What led Pakistanis to settle predominantly, not just at first but later too, in the textile mill towns of northern England, or Sikhs to settle in West London and the 'black country' of the Midlands or Bangladeshis to live mainly in East London? Naturally, access to employment opportunities was paramount. But, for a more nuanced understanding we need to explore the dynamics of chain migration.

Often, chain migration had its roots in villages, where the first steps to migrate to Britain were taken. A villager received information (about the British government's 'labour vouchers',[4] for instance) from a travel agent in a local town, or in a letter from a friend or relative from the same village already living abroad. Family and local ties were crucial. Many aspiring migrants were sponsored by their friends and relatives, and, once they had arrived in Britain and secured a job, they would quickly send letters to friends or to other members of the kinship network, extolling the virtues and benefits of living in *Vilayat* (a common word used for a rich western country, but Britain in particular). As a result, dense patterns of emigration developed in those villages with information networks (while excluding villages in which information networks were not in place). So, in the case of the pioneer Sikh settlers, whose kinship relations were mainly spread over the two neighbouring central districts of doaba – Jalandhar and Hoshiarpur – it is not surprising that most of the earlier migrants came predominantly from villages located in these two districts, the former being particularly important.[5] Even within Jalandhar district, migrants came predominantly from a few particular *tehsils* – Nurmahal, Phagwara and Nawanshahr – reinforcing the point that it was kinship networks which determined who was included, and who was excluded, in the chain migration.

This had important implications at the receiving end too. It was not uncommon for migrants to arrive at seaports or airports with hardly any money or belongings except a handful of addresses or old letters.

Since the date of arrival was often uncertain, their kinsmen were seldom there to meet them at their port of entry, and many had to make a long and uncertain journey alone to the address of the nearest acquaintance. In many cases, the first address was only a temporary abode: it could be weeks or months before a close relative could be contacted and informed about the new arrival.[6] Their final destination, however, tended to be in an area where their closest relatives or village kinsmen were already settled – which reinforced the conspicuous settlement patterns of different South-Asian communities. It is interesting to observe that these early patterns still remain the dominant patterns of South-Asian settlement in Britain today.

It is also important to note that it was not always the intention of migrants to settle permanently in Britain. Far from it, the initial aim, more often than not, was to earn as much money as possible and return with it to South Asia. Getting a job was the first priority. Since most of the early migrants were relatively young, healthy men and largely unskilled, the vast majority of them ended up in what may be termed as '3D' jobs – dangerous, dirty and demanding (and offering low pay). These were the jobs routinely offered to South Asians – to the dismay of the minority of educated migrants, those with BA or MA degrees for instance, whose qualifications were not recognised and who were often forced to take work as bus conductors or teaching assistants. Many qualified teachers contested their case with local authorities, with some winning recognition later, but even then they found themselves employed only as teachers of remedial English or of community languages. Other South Asians worked anti-social hours, often night shifts, readily taking advantage of whatever overtime was offered to supplement their meagre wages, built up their savings and sent regular remittances back home. In the 1950s, many of these early migrants lived in all-male households, usually Victorian two-up, two-down terraced houses in run-down inner city areas, where low cost, rented accommodation was to be found. Shift work and over-time allowed multiple occupancy of rooms and beds and communal living kept expenditure to a minimum. Since a major objective of the migrants was to accumulate as much money as possible before returning home, home-ownership was not considered a viable option. It is only later on, with the 'myth of return' receding and settlers no longer perceiving their stay in Britain as temporary, that we witness a period of family re-unification, causing those individuals who had the means, especially those from the Indian community, to buy their own houses. No doubt the impending immigration laws of 1962 designed to curtail primary migration also helped in this decision-making.

The 1960s was a crucial period in the development of South-Asian communities. Family re-union prompted South Asians to engage in new spheres of British life as users of public services such as schools or the health service, and later, through increased female participation in the labour market. Each of these new engagements brought a fresh set of problems both for migrant families and local authorities. It was a period of social adjustment and cultural adaptation, in which wives, mothers and children had to acquaint themselves with local school procedures, learn how to access health care through their General Practitioners, and deal with the administrators of social services and welfare benefits – all formidable tasks. With their propensity to acquire new language skills more quickly, it was often the migrant children who acted as intermediaries or translators for their parents in such situations.

As colonial subjects, most migrants admired the British system of education, and were keen for their children to benefit from it. A good education was seen as an important vehicle for upward social mobility, and many South-Asian parents began to make strategic choices, 'pushing' their children to gain the right school qualifications for entry into 'ideal' and 'highly respected' careers. Within two decades or so, the first crop of 'home-grown' doctors, dentists, pharmacists, lawyers, accountants, engineers and teachers began to emerge from the child migrants and second generation, British-born children. Despite these successes, however, the actual number of high-achieving children, relative to the total number of South-Asian school children, remained – and still remains – low. More precisely, though children from India and Sri Lanka have excelled, Muslim children both from Pakistan and Bangladesh have tended to lag behind in educational achievement at all levels.[7] This failure has had repercussions on their employment opportunities and labour market experiences.

The next major phase of settlement starts with the arrival of migrants, mostly of South-Asian origin, from East Africa – 'East African Asians' – who were to have a significant impact on both the socio-economic composition and future evolution of the British South-Asian community, providing an important new impetus to an emergent South-Asian business sector.

The history of South Asians in East Africa is somewhat complicated, but an understanding of it is important in appreciating the manner of their arrival and their reception in Britain in the early 1970s. During the heyday of the British Empire a hundred years earlier, the British administrators of East Africa had recruited thousands of Indians from southern, western and eastern states through what was known as the 'indenture system' to work on the tea, rubber and sugar plantations,[8] and later, drawing on skilled artisans and administrators from the Punjab and Gujarat to build the East African railways. After this policy was terminated in the 1920s, many contracted workers stayed in East Africa where they were joined by their relatives on a voluntary basis. Over time, therefore, a significant South-Asian community, divided into distinct religious and kinship groups, had developed in Kenya, Uganda and Tanzania. There, with their specific craft and administrative skills, they began to dominate local petty trading and came to occupy an intermediate socio-economic status above the indigenous Africans but below the white colonial masters – the middle layer of the 'colonial sandwich'. It was a precarious position: the resentful Africans blamed them for their economic problems and the British colonial masters excluded them from government. When the British finally left in the early 1960s, politically independent African leaders found it expedient to generate anti-Indian feeling, and in 1972, pursuing a policy of Africanisation, Idi Amin, the new President of Uganda, decided to expel all South Asians, even those who had taken Ugandan nationality at the time of independence. Involuntary mass migration followed. Some South Asians went back to the Indian subcontinent; others preferred to go to UK, the perceived 'mother country', especially those who had taken British citizenship at independence and were entitled to make the move.[9]

Despite their rights, these 'twice migrants' experienced growing hostility from some sections of the British population. They had arrived at a time of increased anti-immigration feeling. As early as 1962, the first Immigration Act had sought to limit numbers of immigrants. Six years later, in a matter of days, Parliament rushed through the 1968 Immigration Act, which effectively institutionalised racial discrimination, removing the automatic right of entry to British passport holders whose parent or grandparent were not born in the UK. A further Act followed in 1971, redefining British citizenship by clearly demarcating between patrial overseas British passport holders (whose parents or grandparents were born in Britain) and non-patrial passport holders (whose parents or grandparents were not). Since the parents or grandparents of most East African Asians were born on the Indian sub-continent, this had an immediate effect on them. Though they held British passports, they were rendered stateless (not possessing dual African or Indian nationality). Furthermore, they were divided from their families living in India, East Africa, the USA or previously settled in the UK. Under international pressure, the British government allowed some East African Asians to settle in Britain, but under a strict quota system which did not allow them entry for a number of years. The damage had mainly been done.[10]

The outbreak of the Ugandan-Asian crisis and the new influx of immigrants to Britain caused panic and anger amongst British politicians and anti-immigration lobbyists. It was not surprising that East African Asians should sense a high degree of hostility on their first entry to Britain (and recently released Cabinet papers reveal that their fears were not entirely unfounded[11]). Their sense of unease was reinforced by new resettlement procedures introduced by the government which restricted their destinations to 'green zones' (a euphemism for areas where there were no or very few South Asians), away from 'red zones' (areas considered already 'swamped'[12] by too many immigrants). This policy fitted neatly with changing theories of race relations. Under the new Labour government, the old belief in gradual assimilation (over time, new immigrants naturally adopting the British way of life in all its forms) was giving way to a policy of integration (that it was necessary to create an integrated society in which there is an acceptance of cultural diversity and equal opportunity for all within an atmosphere of mutual trust): the first signs of multiculturalist thinking which would dominate the 1980s. In the majority of cases, however, it proved to be a total failure at implementation stage. One major problem was that very few local councils were prepared to accept new migrants for fear of an electoral backlash. Second, the migrants themselves showed a strong preference for moving into neighbourhoods where they already had friends and relatives. Hence, in the early 1970s, a large number of East African Gujaratis moved to Leicester and Wembley, and Punjabis to the west London boroughs of Ealing and Hounslow or to the Midlands, perpetuating the earlier pattern of spatial distribution.[13]

British Responses: From Hostility to Reluctant Accommodation

From the beginning of the 1950s, the arrival of thousands of new migrants had evoked a largely negative response both from local communities and politicians. At the local level, certain stereotypes developed about the new neighbours: they 'smelled of curry', were 'dirty', wore 'funny' clothes, lived like 'sardines', 'talked funny' (in accents later mocked by the comedian Peter Sellers) and had 'strange' religious traditions and customs.[14] Popular TV shows such as *Love thy Neighbour*, *On the Buses*, *It Ain't Half Hot Mum* and *Please Sir* reinforced the racist stereotype of the 'comical' South Asian. In reality, South Asians experienced discrimination in housing and employment; their access to social services and educational provision was restricted; and they suffered verbal and physical racial abuse. Property damage, street muggings and stabbings were common occurrences, with the tabloid press often blaming the victims. In many cases, far-right groups such as the National Front actively sought to provoke a violent reaction by deliberately operating in areas of South-Asian settlement. At the infamous National Front meeting in Southall on 23 April 1979, they succeeded. They had been granted permission to hold an election meeting in the town hall, despite opposition from local community groups. On the day of the meeting, local residents organised a peaceful protest but, as a result of media coverage, a large number of anti-racist groups also joined in, creating – according to the police – a potential law and order problem. Overreacting to the situation, and spearheaded by the Special Patrol Group (SPG) of Metropolitan Police, officers used violence mainly on the unarmed and peaceful protestors, and one of them, Blair Peach, a school teacher from East London, was fatally struck on the head with a truncheon. His assailant was widely believed to be a member of the SPG, although no police officer was subsequently charged.[15] This was a crucial turning point in the politicisation and mobilisation of second-generation London Asians against racist organisations, and many joined the Asian Youth Movement or other anti-racist groups such as the Anti-Nazi League.

In response to the growing problem, organisations such as the Institute of Race Relations began to monitor racial violence and harassment in a more systematic way.[16] In fact, racial hostility was not altogether surprising, given that this was the first time provincial British communities had been exposed to South-Asian migrants who were often perceived as 'natives' or 'strangers' from the colonies with little to do with the British communities. Since these new immigrants were moving into already disadvantaged and depressed working-class areas with their overcrowding and housing shortages, limited job opportunities and poor access to public services, it was not surprising that these problems should quickly become associated with their arrival. New immigrants were convenient scapegoats for local politicians, community and trade union leaders. Local political discourses became increasingly racialised.[17] In some localities, white workers staged strikes to protest against the employment of Indian workers, for example in Nuneaton, near Coventry.[18] As South-Asian settlements grew, many members of the dominant white community moved out of the inner-city neighbourhoods which created space for more South Asians to move in, consolidating their position in these areas. It was only gradually – and more through perseverance and determination rather than welcome – that South Asians began to gain acceptance as normal, hard-working, law-abiding citizens – the first necessary step in the process of building friendships with the communities, sharing communal activities and celebrations such as Christmas, *Eid, Diwali* or *Vaisakhi* and, eventually, inter-racial marriages.

Throughout this period, the British government adopted a dual approach towards immigration, on the one hand pandering to calls from right-wing politicians and the general public for more stringent immigration controls, and on the other upholding liberal values of equality and fairness by outlawing racial discrimination and promoting good race relations. As we have seen, the 1962 Commonwealth Immigration Act was the first important piece of legislation passed. It was very much a response to growing political unease about the levels of immigration and its potential effects on race relations, and it effectively curtailed most primary migration, limiting it to dependents and potential spouses (though Category C vouchers continued to be issued for highly skilled workers such as doctors, scientists, engineers and nurses). The first Act to promote good race relations was passed in 1965, the second in 1968 and third, and most important, in 1976. The Race Relations Act 1976 (later amended and strengthened by the Race Relations (Amendment) Act 2000 and the Race Relations Act 1976 (Amendment) Regulations 2003, incorporating European Union directives) made it unlawful to discriminate against anyone on grounds of race, colour, nationality (including citizenship) or ethnicity. More important, it also created the Commission for Racial Equality (CRE) and a network of over one hundred local Racial Equality Councils, largely funded by the CRE. Thus, the 'race industry' grew rapidly after 1976, continually expanding to cover wider areas of peoples' lives.

Transplanting Roots (1): Development of Asian Business

The emergence of sizable localised communities offered niche entrepreneurial opportunities to more enterprising South Asians, especially those seeking self-employment and a more independent lifestyle. As a result, South-Asian-owned grocery stores began to appear in major locations of settlement, stocking ethnic foods and spices, particularly tropical vegetables which were hard to acquire from mainstream shops. Following this development in retail, other entrepreneurs invested in food production and distribution, sometimes importing in bulk and packaging under their own brand labels, such as East End, Bestway, Natco, Tilda and S&A Foods. Some business owners expanded further or diversified into other sectors. In this way, starting from humble beginnings, a number of South-Asian businessmen went on to become multimillionaires, achieving high civic and state honours and featuring prominently in the annual British and Asian Rich lists.[19] There are numerous rags-to-riches stories involving the migrants of the 1950s to 1970s. Avtar Kang, a rural migrant from Jalandhar, opened a corner shop in Coventry in 1962 and went on to develop a large wholesale food business in the Midlands under the name Sandhar and Kang. He later diversified his portfolio to include commercial property in Birmingham. Tirlok Singh Wouhra founded his family business East End Foods in 1972 and rapidly developed it to become a major wholesale distributor in the Birmingham area, supplying imported pulses, rice, lentils, peas, spices, chutney and pickles under its own brand. Laxmishankar Pathak's story is even better known. He arrived from Kenya in the late 1950s with his wife and six children, almost penniless and unable to find a decent paying job. In 1956, taking matters into his own hands, he set up a company, Patak, to sell authentic South-Asian food – cooking sauces, pastes, poppadoms, chutneys and pickles etc. – from a small basement in his rented house in Kentish Town, London. Soon he opened a shop in Euston and, later, a factory in Brackley, Northants. In the course of time, the business expanded further, managed by his son Kirit and his wife Meena Pathak, operating from a larger food-processing factory in Leigh, near Wigan. Today, Patak's is one of the best-known brands in the UK ethnic food sector and an exporter to over 40 countries worldwide. Perhaps, however, the most remarkable story of all is that of Sir Mohammed Anwar Pervez, a farmer's son who arrived from Pakistan in the 1950s and worked as a bus conductor in Bradford before moving to London to open up a corner grocery shop. In 1976 he was in a position to find his own cash-and-carry company, Bestway Holdings, and by the end of the century it had grown to be one of the UK's biggest cash-and-carry businesses, making Pervez Britain's richest Asian Muslim in the process. The business now employs 4,250 people in the UK in cash-and-carry and retail businesses and has also diversified into property, cement and import–export trade.

Not all South Asians went into food, wholesale and retail. Many took on newspaper shops, ethnic clothing or textile shops, butcher's and later post offices, travel agencies and off-licences. The South-Asian 'open-all hours' corner-shop, offering many or all these services, and located at end of a street of decaying Victorian or Edwardian terrace houses, has become a common sight throughout the UK. Some budding entrepreneurs also ventured into the fast-food business, especially fish-and-chip shops, which they modified over time, offering ethnic snacks for those preferring a more spicy meal. Bangladeshis hailing from the Sylhet district, especially those who had worked as cooks or galley-hands on British ships, opened cafés and tea houses and, later, restaurants in major English cities. By the 1970s, the majority of Indian restaurants would be owned and run by Sylhetis from Bangladesh. At the same time, a British-based vernacular press emerged, offering daily or weekly newspapers initially in the four leading languages – Hindi (*Navin Weekly*, 1966, *Amar Deep Weekly*, 1971), Punjabi (*Desh Pardes*, 1965 and *Punjab Times*, 1965), Gujarati (*Garvi Gujarat*, 1968 and *Gujarat Samachar*, 1972) and Urdu (*Milap Weekly*, 1965, *Daily Jang*, 1971) – and later in Bengali and Sinhalese. The growth of a diversified South-Asian business sector and South-Asian media in the UK is a phenomenal success story which we shall see in the next chapter.

Transplanting Roots (2): The Struggle for Political and Education Rights

During the three decades after the Second World War, South-Asian communities began to form their own political, cultural and religious associations. Although, as previous chapters have demonstrated, South-Asian religious institutions have a long history in Britain (the Mount Vernon Street Mosque was established in Liverpool in 1887, the first purpose-built Shah Jehan Mosque was opened in Woking in 1889 and a Sikh gurdwara was established in Shepherds Bush, London in 1911), the 1960s and early 1970s saw a new phase in the development of mosques, mandirs and gurdwaras.

In the early days, given the small size of communities, the lack of suitable accommodation and the hostility of municipal planning authorities, community leaders rented out local schools or community halls. Later, as planning permission became easier to obtain, and as the communities grew in influence and affluence, they often purchased and adapted existing buildings such as unused warehouses, cinemas or churches or even terraced houses, to use as places of worship. (The construction of large, lavish religious buildings – such as the Baitul Futuh Mosque in Morden, South London, the Shri Swaminarayan Mandir in Neasden, north-west London or the Singh Sabha Gurdwara in Southall, London, was not seen before 1990.) These premises had multiple functions besides the important religious ones. They acted as a meeting place for the exchange of community news, a venue for festivals, a forum for political groups and sports clubs and a reception area for important visiting dignitaries from South Asia. Sometimes they even acted as a temporary refuge for new arrivals. Very quickly, these multi-purpose places of worship proliferated, serving a growing population and also reflecting the diversity of traditions within each of the main South-Asian religious communities. Although exact figures are not available, there are currently over 1,200 mosques, over 300 gurdwaras and around 150 mandirs in Britain.[20]

Two functions fulfilled by the religious centres were particularly important. The first was their role in the transmission of cultural heritage, especially the teaching of a community's language to younger generations. Given that the British school curriculum was geared towards 'assimilating' or 'integrating' school children, South-Asian parents expected religious centres to teach their children about their own culture. Staffed by community volunteers or visiting clerics or priests, and operating either after normal school hours or at weekends, the religious centres acted as supplementary schools (or *madrassas* in the case of Muslims). Even today, the centres provide most of the instruction in South-Asian languages. Although some local education authorities, often after considerable parental pressure, have included 'community languages' in the school curriculum, and although there is a mandatory requirement for schools to teach a second language, the onus still appears to be on South Asians to offer their own provision of language teaching.[21]

Religious sites also became places where the 'politics of the homeland' could be debated. All major South-Asian political organisations, representing very different shades of opinion, worked hard to secure representation on the management committees of the centres in order to have a forum for their views. Some organisations such as the Indian Workers Associations (IWA) used their forum to raise issues relating to the exploitation of South-Asian workers and the state of race and industrial relations in Britain or to launch their support for striking South-Asian workers at Mansfield Hosiery, Sterling Metals, Imperial Typewriters, Woolf Rubber Company or Grunwick. Other organisations such as those representing the overseas branches of the Congress Party or the Shiromani Akali Dal (a pro-Sikh political party from Punjab) publicised issues relating to self-determination for Sikhs back home or other India-related issues. Within Pakistani and Bangladeshi communities, the Kashmir issue[22] and the Bangladeshi liberation movement focused the minds of community leaders. Among Sri Lankans, a clear communal divide emerged between the Singhalese and Tamils, with some of the latter providing political and financial support to the Tamil separatist movement. Within the Sikh community, representation on gurdwara committees was highly contested, and factional fighting at election times sometimes drew the attention of the local police and the Charity Commissioners with whom many of the religious centres had registered. This trend was to intensify after Operation Bluestar in 1984 when Indian Prime Minister Indira Gandhi authorised an armed attack on the Sikh's holiest place, the Darbar Sahib (popularly known as the Golden Temple) in Amritsar, to flush out armed militants taking sanctuary there. This single act openly exposed the sectarian divide that by this time characterised the British Sikh community.[23] Highly inflammatory debates ensued in religious centres throughout the UK, though the vast majority of Sikhs, while strongly condemning the Indian government's brutal action, were not prepared to support political organisations which demanded their support for a violent struggle for a separate state for the Sikhs.

The important point here is that 'homeland politics' – whether about Kashmir, Khalistan or Tamil Nationalism – often dominated political discourses within British South-Asian communities, causing further factional divide. Furthermore, the wars in South Asia – such as that between India and Pakistan in 1965 and the 1971 Bangladesh war – caused additional rifts and divisions amongst the various British South-Asian communities.

One of the most enduring South-Asian political associations, with a history of over sixty years in Britain, is the *Bharati Mazdoor Sabha* (later also known as the IWA). It was first established in 1938 in Coventry by factory workers and peddlers, supplemented by similar associations with varying political allegiances formed in other major cities with large number of Punjabi workers. Indeed, the Punjabis – Sikhs, Hindus and some Muslims – have remained the backbone of the IWAs ever since. In the 1940s, especially after independence in 1947, its influence waned, but it was reconstituted in the 1960s by far-sighted individuals who saw a new purpose for its existence. The post-war emergence of a South-Asian working class in major industrial areas created the need for an organisation to mobilise support for industrial action, express solidarity with British workers, combat racial discrimination and safeguard working conditions and wages.

The effort by the IWA in Southall to unionise Indians working in Woolf's rubber factory is a good example of an attempt to build solidarity between South-Asian and British workers. But IWAs also had wider objectives: to win the support of the Indian High Commission in the UK in the pursuit of their objectives, to strengthen the ties of friendship with different peoples of Britain, to inform British people about political, economic and social developments in India and to promote social, cultural and welfare activities for the benefit of its members. In Southall and Coventry, for instance, IWAs ran Indian cinema halls which premiered new Indian films and also acted as important venues for political rallies and cultural shows. IWAs grew more popular steadily: according to Dewitt John,[24] in many cities more than half of the Indian-born adult Punjabi males may have joined their local IWA. In Southall, for instance, the largest area of Punjabi settlement, by 1965 IWA had recruited 3,900 members from the 10,000 to 15,000 Punjabis who lived in and around Southall.[25]

In fact, the first Punjabi Member of Parliament (MP) in Britain – Piara Singh Khabra, who has represented Ealing Southall since 1992 – was very much a product of the Southall IWA. Despite the establishment of rival organisations to represent Pakistani workers, the numbers of Indian Punjabis in West London and the West Midlands generally ensured the dominance of local IWAs as political organisations. Elections to key positions in the IWAs were always highly contested – and often highly emotional – involving the local gurdwaras. IWA leaders such as Chanan Singh (prominent in the Midlands), Ajit Singh (from Southall, London) and Lachman Singh (from Coventry) used their village, caste or locality (*ilaqa*) affiliations to mobilise support for their candidatures. A sober assessment of the IWAs' contribution to UK race relations or to UK industrial relations still remains to be written, though it is noticeable that from the late 1960s, their political power once more waned, partly due to periodic splintering along ideological lines (often mirroring events in South Asia) and partly because of the growing influence of other cultural, religious and political organisations.[26] When, in the late 1960s, around 2,000 cinema houses due for demolition were bought by South Asians, it was not to use them for political purposes, but to show the increasingly popular Bollywood films – a welcome alternative to divisive debates about 'homeland politics'. Besides, by the 1980s IWAs offered little appeal to second-generation South-Asians who were now beginning to enter the skilled labour market in greater numbers and who perceived themselves to be more integrated into British society.

South-Asian Children in British Schools

With growing numbers of South-Asian children entering the education system, local authorities sometimes faced a dilemma. For a start, white parents often protested against the very presence of South-Asian children at their local schools, claiming they would have a negative impact on the education of their own children. Under such pressure, some local authorities adopted quota restrictions on enrolment, 'bussing' surplus children to schools outside their area. As early as 1963, in Southall, white parents successfully lobbied councillors in the London Borough of Ealing to adopt a policy of 'dispersal', and in June 1965 the Department of Education and Science adopted this policy nationally.[27] South-Asian parents were unsuccessful, even with the help of their community organisations, in getting these policies reversed until the rise of multi-culturalism later. South Asians themselves had other concerns too: the attendance of their children at school assemblies with their marked Christian ethos, compulsory school uniforms which required girls to wear a skirt, school meals which ignored the dietary requirements of some faiths – even mixed-gender schools. Over time, such concerns became even more pronounced. South-Asian families continued to request multi-faith school assemblies, the relaxation of school uniform rules to allow turbans and headscarves (hijab) and the availability of halal meals or a vegetarian option in school meals. Eventually, in the 1980s, they were successful as education authorities adopted the policy of providing multicultural education.[28]

It is difficult to generalise about discrimination. Different South-Asian communities have tended to have different experiences depending on their cultural needs and their acceptance of pluralistic values. Of all the South-Asian communities, Muslims and then Sikhs have struggled hardest against perceived discriminatory cultural practices in education. Hindus or Buddhists, on the other hand, have made fewer demands, perhaps reflecting their more pluralistic and liberal historical background. For Muslims, the issues have been particularly wide ranging. As well as dietary and dress requirements, they have argued for special prayer rooms in schools, accommodation of the Ramadan (fasting) and Eid periods, special exemptions for sports and swimming classes for girls, more single sex schools (during a period when co-educational comprehensive schooling was the preferred mode), state funding for faith-based Muslim schools and extended periods out of school for family holidays 'back home'.

All these were encapsulated in a single incident which triggered a national furore in 1985: the Honeyford Affair. Ray Honeyford was Head Teacher of Drummond Middle School in Bradford and a critic of Muslim practices as they related to education. In a series of articles published during 1984 in a minor right-wing publication, the *Salisbury Review*, he voiced his concerns over disruptions to Muslim pupils' education, especially when their parents took them for extended holidays to Pakistan during school term. In this, Honeyford was very much reflecting the growing frustrations of the Bradford local education authority (and of local Bradford politicians such as Eric Pickles and many Bradford white residents) at the continual pushing of boundaries of tolerance by Muslims with their requests that the school accommodate their cultural practices. The Honeyford Affair quickly developed into a national debate on a range of subjects including the merits of multicultural education versus integration, 'bussing', racism, immigration and British identity and the meaning of British citizenship.[29] As multiculturalism was the prevailing ideology of the day, Honeyford was investigated by the government for his 'right-wing' views, vilified as a racist by the vernacular Muslim and British tabloid press and eventually suspended as head teacher for five months. Five months after his reinstatement, he took early retirement. How ironic then that in post-9/11 and -7/7

Britain, with serious questions being asked about the nature of British multiculturalism – questions very similar to those raised by Honeyford – that the government in 2006 should establish a new Commission for Integration and Cohesion with a remit to look at ways to create a more socially integrated and cohesive Britain.

Sikhs had similar experiences with schools and education authorities. Their main issues concerned dress: the right to wear a turban rather than a school cap as part of school uniform, the right to wear a small kirpan (a small symbolic wood or steel sheathed sword worn by a baptised Sikh child) and the right to wear a suitable kara (steel bangle) during normal school hours or sports activity. More recently, a minority of Sikhs have demanded more state-funded Sikh faith schools. But the main Sikh struggle for the free expression of their cultural and religious beliefs has not been in schools but in society at large, at work places and in the streets. Here, their struggle – ultimately successful – necessitated landmark changes in British legislation.

Sikh Struggles: Beards and Turbans

One of the most important outward symbols of Sikh identity is the keeping of unshorn *kesh* (hair), with a *kangha* (steel comb) and turban to keep them tidy and covered. Many early Sikh pioneer migrants working in the metal-bashing industries in the Midlands opted for the, sake of convenience, to cut their hair and shave their beards. But Sikhs pursuing other occupations such as the Bhatra Sikh pedlars or those working in public transport or catering kept the outward symbols of their Sikh identity, even at the risk of racial discrimination.

In 1959, 43-year-old Gyani Sundar Singh Sagar alleged that he was rejected for a bus conductor's job in Manchester because he wore a turban, apparently forbidden under Manchester Corporation's conditions of service. In support of management's decision, Charles Morris, Labour Chair of Manchester's Transport Committee said, 'If turbans are permitted, there is nothing to prevent the whole string of religious beliefs turning up to work with all sorts of badges and devices.'[30] But the long legal struggle which followed between Sagar and the Corporation ended with victory for Sagar. His main line of defence was that since Sikhs were allowed to wear turbans, not helmets, in the British Indian army (and 82,000 Sikhs had been killed in the two world wars fighting for the British Empire), why should they not wear them on the buses?

Some years later, a similar case occurred in Wolverhampton. Tarsem Singh Sandhu, employed on the local buses, had been clean-shaven, but returned to work after illness sporting a beard and turban, the result of a personal spiritual revival. This put him in breach of Wolverhampton Council's regulations, and he was prohibited from working unless he shaved off his beard and removed his turban. The dispute lasted for two years, involving mass marches and representations to both the British and Indian governments by the Sikh community.[31] Under pressure, with some Sikhs even threatening self-immolation, the Council finally relented. Sikhs in the transport industry could now no longer be discriminated against for having beards or wearing turbans (so long as they wore colours that closely matched those of the uniform), and the number of Sikhs subsequently working on buses and in transport generally increased markedly. Ironically, the Sikh victory prompted Enoch Powell, the local Wolverhampton MP, to make his infamous 'rivers of blood' speech, warning of the dangers of further immigration and ethnic segregation. But Sikh community leaders saw the Manchester and Wolverhampton decisions as crucial victories allowing thousands of Sikhs to keep beards and turbans as important markers of their British-Sikh identity. It is interesting to note that, in retrospect, David Beethem has argued that the Wolverhampton dispute had more to do with identity politics in the Punjab than UK race relations, because the dispute so often focused on the ideological differences between the politics of the Punjab-based Akali Party and the Wolverhampton chapter of the IWA.[32] Be that as it may, the outcome of the disputes had a permanent impact on the lives of British-Sikhs.

Turbans were also at the heart of another statutory change involving motorcycle helmets. Now that Sikh community leaders had successfully got across their view that the turban was not just a piece of fashionable headgear but an essential religious symbol, they lobbied the government for exemption from wearing motorcycle helmets.[33] After a couple of years of campaigning, the government acceded to Sikh arguments by inserting a new subsection in the Motor Cycle Crash Helmets (Religious Exemption) Act in November 1976 (later consolidated in the 1988 Road Traffic Act). Although this was undoubtedly a major concession to the Sikh community, it has not had straightforward practical consequences. The law remains unclear, especially concerning the award of compensation for or against a Sikh involved in a traffic accident. There are also obvious safety issues. We have not seen many Sikhs riding motorcycles with just turbans. It has remained, therefore, a largely symbolic victory.

Slowly, the most blatant and direct forms of racial discrimination were outlawed through legislation. However, indirect – often more insidious and challenging – forms of discrimination remained. Sikhs also challenged these, and one of the most important cases – the lengthy Mandla *v.* Dowell Lee case – returns us to the area of education.

Although the 1976 Race Relations Act (Section 17c) had made it unlawful for educational establishments to deny services to pupils on the basis of indirect discrimination, there had been no test case until July 1978, when Sewa Singh Mandla (twice migrant from Kenya and *amritdhari* Sikh) brought a case against Park Grove School, a private school in Birmingham, which had refused admission to his 13-year-old son Gurinder Singh Mandla. The school's uniform included a school cap and required boys to keep short hair, and Gurinder, who kept *kesh* and wore a turban, would clearly have infringed the rules. The Mandla family pursued the case through the British courts until finally – in 1983 – they won a landmark House of Lords ruling, at the heart of which was a formal acceptance that Sikhs constituted a 'racial group' since they could be defined by reference to their distinct ethnic origins.[34] Unfortunately, this victory was of no practical value to Gurinder himself because by then he had finished his secondary schooling, but the family and the Sikh community which supported them felt that a vital point of principle had been established and the public profile of the Sikhs enhanced. Indeed, the decision by the House of Lords which accepted that Sikhs and their turbans were covered by the protection of the 1976 Act led to further legislation to outlaw indirect discrimination. Since 1976, Sikhs have relied upon the indirect discrimination provisions of the Act in a number of other areas. They have won cases against clubs and public houses which operated a no-headgear rule, and against factories with stringent hygiene requirements where turbans are now accepted as a substitute for caps and beards can be worn if covered by face masks or nets. Finally, after extensive lobbying of Parliament, turbaned Sikhs were given exemption from wearing safety helmets on building sites in the Construction (Head Protection) regulations of 1989 which came into force in March 1990, despite opposition from some parliamentarians. Sikhs have subsequently used similar arguments to gain exemption from EU directives relating to the wearing of safety helmets on construction sites.

Taken as a whole, the three decades after the Second World War were a period of extraordinary change for the South-Asian communities in Britain. The initial reception faced by those peoples of the Empire who 'came home' in ever greater numbers was uneasy and often hostile. The general British public remained opposed to entry of more immigrants. Politicians, fearing an electoral backlash, showed ambivalence, passing laws to promote good race relations at the same time as closing doors on new immigration. The early migrants themselves (mostly, at this stage, young men) remained unsure of their long-term intentions until their hand was forced by the impending immigration legislation in 1962. For those who elected to make Britain their home, reuniting with their families and beginning to put down roots, a new struggle began: the fight for the recognition of their cultural and religious rights. Despite racist provocations, the vast majority remained law abiding and were relatively successful in improving their well-being, with some doing extremely well.

There were, however, other trends, perhaps not noticed at the time, which are worth highlighting. During this period, we witness increased spatial concentration and the development of relative economic self-sufficiency among different South-Asian communities, a trend which gathered momentum from the 1980s onwards, with two important consequences: the disconnection of some South-Asian communities from the mainstream community, and polarisation within South-Asian communities themselves, as they splintered into self-sufficient political, social, economic and cultural networks, each attempting to negotiate their own identity relations with the British State.

In the post-9/11 and -7/7 period, during the ongoing war on terror, tensions within South-Asian communities have increased. It has become common for Muslim, Hindu and Sikh groups to reject the all-embracing label 'Asian' (used in Britain to cover all South Asians). The reasons and consequences of such developments are the subject of the next chapter.

Chapter 8

The 1980s and After: From Adversity to Celebration

Shinder S. Thandi

The decade of 1980s was a difficult period for South-Asian communities as they felt the brunt of Thatcherite policies which accelerated manufacturing decline and the pain of economic restructuring that followed. Rising unemployment among South-Asian males required new strategies for survival: some tried their luck in the services sector, some re-trained, many entered self-employment and those in their 50s joined the long-term unemployed. At the same time, Asian women joined the workforce in greater numbers, both to supplement stagnant family incomes and to take advantage of the growth in new 'feminised' jobs with their more flexible work patterns. The uneven effects of these developments led to growing socio-economic polarisation amongst South-Asian communities which continues to this day; indeed, it was not until the 1990s – with a British-born, educated and more-skilled second generation entering the labour market in sizable numbers – that overall economic regeneration took place.

However, the same period also saw the emergence of a significant South-Asian middle class exercising greater leverage in the economic, civic, cultural and political arenas. The achievements of Asian enterprise and entrepreneurship, their changing employment experience and growing political engagement – all covered later in the chapter – are particularly revealing, especially when explored in relation to key debates about South-Asian identities in general and the Britishness of British-born South Asians of the second and third generations in particular.

In fact, the period since the 1980s has seen increasingly confident celebrations of Asian identities and increasingly vibrant Asian contributions to British popular culture and lifestyle, in particular in the media, performing arts, music, sport, cuisine, fashion, the wedding economy and annual *melas*. At the same time, with the revolution in global telecommunications compressing time and space, there has been a strengthening and deepening of multiple and circular forms of diaspora–homeland relations which, in turn, have influenced modes of cultural transmission and helped shape British South-Asian identities. For instance, the growing radicalism amongst Muslim youth can be explained, at least partly, by the development of a de-territorialised pan-Muslim identity that may in some circumstances supersede British identity. Other groups too have used global networks to promote and defend their cultural and religious rights, increasingly through agitation politics. What will the outcome be? In this uncertain situation, one can only speculate about the cohesive strength of multiculturalism, and the impact of future developments and major challenges that may face South-Asian communities in Britain in coming years. To engage with these issues, it is important, first, to ascertain the basic facts about South Asians in Britain, and a good starting point is the 2001 census.

A Brief Profile of the South-Asian Community

The 2001 census for the first time collected information on ethnicity and religious identity, and offered a detailed statistical profile of socio-economic conditions and lifestyles of Asians in Britain. It revealed that, without question, Britain was more culturally diverse than ever before.

It also confirmed, of course, that the overwhelming majority of the UK population was still white (92 percent). Of the 59 million people in the United Kingdom, only 4.6 million (8 percent) were non-white. Of the non-white population, Asian or Asian British accounted for around 2.3 million (50 percent). Indians accounted for just over 1 million (23 percent), Pakistanis for 0.75 million (16 percent), Bangladeshis for 283,000 (6 percent) and 'Other Asian' (which would include Sri Lankan and Nepalese as well) for 250,000 (5 percent).

In terms of religious affiliation, Christians remained the largest single group in the United Kingdom, accounting for just over 41 million (nearly 72 percent) of Britain's population. Amongst South-Asian faith groups, the largest three segments were Muslims (1.58 million or 2.8 percent of the UK population but 52 percent of non-Christian group), Hindus (558,342 or 1 percent of the UK population and 18 percent of the non-Christian group), followed by Sikhs (336,179 or 0.6 percent of the UK population and 11 percent of the non-Christian group).

In terms of ethnicity, 97 percent of Christians were white, 74 percent of Muslims were from a South-Asian ethnic background (43 percent from Pakistan, 16 percent from Bangladesh and 8 percent from India), and 84 percent of Hindus were from an Indian background, as were 91 percent of the Sikhs.

When studied in terms of their country of birth, the Indian group turned out to be religiously more diverse: 45 percent of Indians were Hindu, 29 percent Sikh and a further 13 percent Muslims. In contrast, Pakistani and Bangladeshi groups appeared to be the most homogeneous, with Muslims accounting for 92 percent of each ethnic group. (These figures do not pick up sectarian divides such as between *Sunnis*, *Shias* and *Ahmediyas* or different traditions within communities.)

Perhaps most interesting of all is the South Asians' perception of their national identity. Most non-whites identified themselves as British rather than English, Scottish or Welsh, and South Asians were no exception, identifying themselves with a strong British national identity – 80 percent of Pakistanis and Bangladeshis and 75 percent of Indians identified themselves in this way. It suggests that while most South-Asian groups affirm a strong religious identity, they affirm an equally strong British national identity, giving us the hyphenated British-Hindu, British-Sikh and British-Muslim categories, with which most British-born Asians would readily identify. This is the general picture. At an individual level, however – especially among the young – identities are more fluid and situational: research suggests that the young affirm a shifting school, home, work, local, regional or national identity, contingent on the context.

The demographic picture highlighted by the census is also extremely revealing. The majority of the South-Asian population remained concentrated in the two large urban areas of London and West Midlands. The extent of concentration, however, varied according to the South-Asian group. More than half the Bangladeshi group lived in London, compared with only 19 percent of Pakistanis who were concentrated mainly in the West Midlands (21 percent), Yorkshire and Humber (20 percent) and the North West (16 percent). Clearly, there has not been much dispersion from the concentrations of the early 1960s. It means that all South-Asian groups are over-represented among people living in the most deprived local authorities, with Bangladeshi and Pakistani groups constituting the largest over-representation.[1] The problem faced by many early migrants, who were forced to settle in run-down inner-city areas suffering from multiple deprivation (especially poor public provision of education, transport and social services), was still being faced, suggesting a cycle of economic deprivation, low business development and low employment generation. We need to remember, however, that the census statistics may conceal the possibility that some of the earlier communities of Indians and Pakistanis may have moved out of deprived areas to better, leafy suburbs within the same borough or city. Indeed, this pattern in housing mobility is probably repeated in many localities: better-off Asians move out, the relatively poor remain, and new immigrants move in. Where first-generation migrants or their children have retained ownership of their original properties or purchased more, which they rent out to poorer or new immigrant groups, a significant Asian *rentier* or landlord class has emerged.

The census also revealed that most of the South-Asian groups, especially Bangladeshis and Pakistanis, have relatively young age structures (with a high proportion of their population under the age of 16), suggesting that population growth for these groups is likely to remain relatively high in the near future. It also showed that Asians tended to live in larger households: Bangladeshis the largest, with an average household size of 4.5 people, followed by Pakistanis at 4.1 and Indians at 3.3, compared with the white British households at 2.3. The importance attached to the extended family unit is underlined by the fact that over 50 percent of all South-Asian households contained a married couple and often more than one family with dependent children.

The incidence of inter-ethnic marriages (a critical and contentious factor in debates about British identity and arguments about the relative merits of multiculturalism and assimilation/integration) was very low in the 2001 census: only 2 percent of all marriages in England and Wales. Most of those involved a white partner and/or mixed race person, and in many instances, especially in mixed marriages involving media personalities or business people, the marriages tended to be strategic alliances, allowing one of the partners access to a different social or business network. The data also showed that people from South-Asian backgrounds were least likely of all minority ethnic groups to get married to someone of a different ethnic group. Only 6 percent of Indians, 4 percent of Pakistanis and 3 percent of Bangladeshis had married outside the Asian group. This does not preclude the possibility that there may have been intra-Asian marriages – Hindus marrying Sikhs or Muslims, or vice versa – but, in reality, religious and cultural factors have tended to limit both inter-ethnic and intra-Asian marriages. As a result, even second- and third-generation Asians abide by ethnic or caste boundaries in negotiating their choice of marriage partner with their parents.

It is worth adding that anecdotal evidence suggests cohabitation rates between whites and South Asians, and between different South Asian groups, are probably higher than actual marriages.

Education is generally acknowledged to be an important vehicle in securing good jobs and upward social mobility, and evidence confirms a strong link between educational qualifications and an individual's lifetime earnings. The 2001 census revealed that 47 percent of Indians were in social class I and II (professional, managerial and technical), having moved up the social class ladder from classes V and VI (partly skilled and unskilled) over the previous couple of decades – a reflection of their educational advancement and career progression. As previously discussed, South-Asian parents commonly place a high value on education and develop proactive strategies to access quality education for their children. However, the 2002 educational qualifications of South Asians (measured by achievement of 5 GCSEs at A*–C grades) are varied, with the Indian group at the top end (at around 64 percent) and Bangladeshi and Pakistanis at the lower end (around 45 and 40 percent respectively), although recent studies show that the gap may be narrowing.[2] Studies also show that South Asians have disproportionately higher rates (almost 80 percent of 18- to 19-year-olds) of participation in higher education, compared with whites. For the high fliers, irrespective of the social class of their parents, degree courses in medicine, dentistry, pharmacy, accountancy and law remain strong favourites. However, the vast majority of South-Asian students are concentrated in the 'new' post-1992 universities, especially in the Midlands. For instance at Wolverhampton University, University of Central England, Coventry University and De Montfort University in Leicester, South-Asian students may constitute up to 40 percent of the total student body, and, on some courses, especially computer science, business studies and finance, enrolment rates can be as high as 80 percent of total course enrolment. Participation rates are also high on intermediate courses which provide access to degree courses. Unfortunately, quite a significant number of South-Asian students fail to progress on their course and eventually drop out of higher education altogether, gaining only sub-degree level qualifications.

This difference in the level of qualifications and achievement suggests there is a 'forking' path for South-Asian groups: between Indians on the one hand and Pakistanis and Bangladeshis on the other, and also *within* particular South-Asian communities as well – for example, a small number of Sikh or Muslim children may do quite well whilst the majority of them do not. Interesting gender differences also emerge from recent evidence. Girls from South-Asian background on the whole do much better than boys, both in terms of qualifications and career development, whereas boys tend to underachieve (as is the case nationally), though structural changes in the economy, with female-friendly service-oriented jobs becoming more plentiful, may be a factor. But it is true that girls often show a greater motivation to succeed. Evidence certainly suggests that in the media, arts, government employment, business and education, Asian females are becoming more visible. However, we need to keep in mind that although quite a large number of young Asians are doing well in education, and subsequently in the workplace, there remains a significant minority who simply fall out of the system. They become discouraged, demoralised and alienated and this affects their chances of employability even further. Some fall foul of the law, become victims of drug or alcohol addiction, or join fringe or extremist religious groups, especially if they promise to provide 'easy' answers to complex questions.

The Empire Strikes Back: South-Asian Achievement in Multicultural Britain

Entrepreneurship: A Shining Success?

As South-Asian communities grew in size and matured, the number of South-Asian businesses also grew, especially rapidly after the 1980s, helped by the arrival of East African Asians in the 1970s. As nearly half of the ethnic minority population was concentrated in the Greater London area, it is not surprising that Asian businesses should also be concentrated there. According to the 2004 London Annual Business Survey, there were 39,000 Asian-owned businesses that year, providing 300,000 jobs and yielding a turnover of £60 billion in 2003/2004.[3] South Asian-owned businesses were, in fact, a major component of ethnic businesses across the United Kingdom, and they flourished in all areas of South-Asian settlement, sometimes becoming familiar nationally. Many South Asians moved into niche sectors of the economy, where they established positions of great influence. Take the medical services, for example. Although South Asians only represented 4 percent of the population, they accounted for 16 percent of the general practitioners, nearly 20 percent of hospital doctors and about 12 percent of the pharmacists. But their major impact was in retailing, where they owned over 50 percent of the 'cash and carry' stores and over 55 percent of the independent (non-supermarket) retail trade. In this trade they were primarily concentrated in six areas: grocers, CTNs (confectionary, tobacco and newsagents), off-licences, pharmacists, sub-postmasters and forecourt operators. In fact, South Asians owned 30,000 out of the 46,000 CTN shops and 70 percent of the 83,200 independently-owned neighbourhood shops.[4]

The image that emerges is one of a successful, vibrant and diversified South-Asian business community contributing hugely to the economic and business success of Britain. Certainly, this is the perception that South-Asian business leaders and politicians of all major political parties would like to present, and it seems to be reinforced by the list of Britain's Richest Asians, which appears annually in *Eastern Eye*, a popular South-Asian English-language newspaper, identifying the top 200 wealthy South Asians (defined as those having wealth in excess of £5 million). The reality, however, may be somewhat different if we dig beneath the surface. Despite high-profile attempts to present a picture of 'Asian business success' across the board, there is in fact great unevenness in business success rates. An overwhelming majority of businesses, numerically at least, still remain small-scale and family run. There is a danger that well-meaning publicity, attempting to present a positive image and dispel the stereotype of the over-worked, struggling Asian corner-shopkeeper, may camouflage serious structural difficulties faced by South-Asian businesses in Britain. There is a need to address the paradox of apparent success and growing differentiation. What is the true picture? Are Asian entrepreneurs really glorified corner-shop owners, or has there been real breakout in terms of both scale and diversity?

Let us first of all take up the issue of the rise of South-Asian business. What accounts for greater self-employment among South Asians? Are they more entrepreneurial than white? Are some South-Asian groups more entrepreneurial than others? What motivates South Asians towards self-employment? These are complex questions and our current stock of knowledge does not provide any convincing answers to them. However, it seems certain that there are circumstances where certain individuals have no option but self-employment. For some, self-employment may be prompted by a negative employment experience due to racism or a perceived obstacle to career advancement or by 'exploitation' encountered in the workplace. As a result, South Asians may choose to set up their own businesses and/or do business only with co-Asians. Mainstream explanations of entrepreneurship generally fail to acknowledge these negative reasons. A better way to explain the complexity of South-Asian entrepreneurship is to explore the interplay between the opportunity structure facing prospective entrepreneurs and their ability to access or own businesses. Some opportunities are obvious – for example, the supply of ethnic foods, newspapers and other culture-specific goods imported from South Asia to local South-Asian communities: it is no surprise to see South Asians owning grocery stores selling such produce. Over time, there also emerge South Asian–owned businesses providing a range of specialist travel, legal, tax and accountancy and property services to these communities.

Typically, many food-retailing businesses also set up a supply chain link with businesses in their homeland with a view to serving a larger or niche market and moving higher up the value chain. Female ethnic clothing is another example of successful entrepreneurship. Just as food retailers such as East End Foods, Natco, Tilda and Patak all started small and expanded, diversifying into importing, packaging, distribution and domestic manufacture under their own brand label, a number of boutiques catering for female fashion clothing (supplying bespoke, designer or customised *salwaar kameez*, *lenghas* or *cholis*) and located in prime sites in major areas of South-Asian settlement have developed transnational production and distribution chains.[5] We see many of these boutiques thriving in Green Street in East London, on the Broadway in Southall or Soho Road in Birmingham.

Although existing opportunity structures are important, South Asians also create economic opportunities for themselves, drawing on their cultural and social capital. Furthermore, various types of South-Asian associations can facilitate the exchange of market information and put up finance – though such opportunities are restricted when a business suffers from the triple disadvantage of operating in deprived areas, being small and having only a limited client base. More recently, the emergence of large retail superstores has posed a direct challenge to many Asian grocery stores, as has the withdrawal of many government services from post offices. Many only continue to survive by trading for long hours and by tolerating profit margins only just sufficient to provide economic security for the family. In many cases, simple economic freedom is more important than profit growth: life on the margins preferable to the humiliation and drudgery of low-pay, dead-end jobs. It is this aspect of South-Asian business life that gets lost in the hype about South-Asian business success.

A Changing Industrial Landscape

South-Asian labour experience and prospects have been profoundly affected by changing employment patterns in Britain. The decline in manufacturing jobs in areas where the majority of South Asians have traditionally lived has led to an acute mismatch between labour-market requirements and the characteristics and location of South-Asian workers. Put simply, too many South Asians were employable only in the declining manufacturing sector – and now they happened to be living in the wrong places too. The emergence of a 'knowledge-based economy', the associated employment growth in jobs related to information and communications technology (ICT), the move in the manufacturing sector away from full-time to part-time work, and the trend of flexible work patterns in new service-oriented sectors (where female-friendly and part-time jobs predominate), all hit South-Asian male workers particularly hard, especially those over 50 years old. In many cases, the increase in newly employed South-Asian females (especially Indian women), although empowering for them personally, did not fully compensate for the fall in family income. This became quickly apparent during the Gate Gourmet strike at Heathrow in 2005 after predominantly South-Asian female workers were laid off, and their families faced acute financial hardship.[6]

All South-Asian workers, male or female, are over-represented in certain sectors, such as engineering, textiles and clothing, distribution and transport, public health and education. However, if we consider industry-level employment, variations amongst South Asians are more pronounced. For instance, 52 percent of Bangladeshi male employees and self-employees work in the restaurant industry (compared with 1 percent for white men), where a third of them are cooks or waiters. Of male Pakistanis in the labour market, one in six is a taxi driver or chauffeur (compared with the national average of one in hundred). Five percent of Indian men at work are medical practitioners – almost ten times the national average. South-Asian women have high work inactivity rates – especially Bangladeshi and Pakistani women (77 and 68 percent respectively) – compared with about 25 percent for white British women. When employed, Pakistani women are eight times more likely than white

British women to be working as packers, bottlers, canners and fillers. Similarly, Indian women are almost seven times more likely than white British women to be working as sewing machinists. All this reinforces the simple fact that South-Asian workers tend to be disproportionately concentrated in low-skill, low-pay declining sectors with high labour turnover, the sectors most at risk from forces of international competition and globalisation. This partly explains why Pakistanis and Bangladeshis have the highest unemployment rates – 18 percent and 14 percent respectively for men – compared to a rate of 5 percent for white British men.

High unemployment or low activity rates amongst South-Asian workers are also explained by demand and supply-side forces, which operate together to disadvantage them. In many cases, demand for South-Asian workers is poor because they live in inner-city neighbourhoods with low levels of business activity. For this reason, few of the 70 percent of Bangladeshis working in the catering industry are able to progress above cook or waiter status. In Oldham, where the textile industry has been in decline, many Pakistanis have turned to taxi driving.[7] The spatial mismatch – geographical concentration in areas where jobs are lost rather than created – can lead to serious social and political consequences for all communities in that neighbourhood. Higher levels of relative poverty and increased competition for private and public resources can create racial tensions – as happened in the northern towns in 2001 – which in turn create space for right-wing groups such as the British National Party to exploit the situation. The outcome, in too many cases, is fear and violence.

Since South-Asian businesses are largely restricted to areas of South-Asian settlement, they hardly expand, producing only small increases in demand for labour. Furthermore, very rarely do South-Asian businesses employ labour across ethnic lines. For example, an Indian-owned business may only employ Indian labour, a *halal* butcher is unlikely to hire a Sikh, and a Hindu, Christian or Sikh association is unlikely to hire people from other religious denominations. Such cultural and religious barriers not only reduce job opportunities but also restrict employment across ethnic lines. More recently the situation has been further complicated by the fresh wave of migration to Britain (estimated to be over half a million) associated with the arrival of a whole variety of immigrants such as asylum seekers and refugees from Somalia and Afghanistan, and economic migrants from new member states of the European Union, such as Poland. Since these groups also tend to settle in poorer, more affordable neighbourhoods and compete for similar work, this creates further barriers to employment and can lead to a backlash against these new migrants from South Asians, who fail to see the irony of having faced the same backlash themselves in the 1950s and 1960s.

Civil disorder involving mainly Muslim youth, in the summer of 2001 in some northern mill towns such as Oldham, Burnley, Bradford and Leeds, has prompted some observers to reiterate the view that 'assimilation' or 'integration' of South-Asian communities is necessary to their economic success. According to this view, minority groups of Pakistanis and Bangladeshis, who appear poorly integrated – and may in fact be living parallel lives in parallel communities in relatively homogeneous ethnic neighbourhoods[8] – are suffering economically as a result. Although the concepts of assimilation and integration are problematic, being open to many interpretations, some writers have refined this problem as a lack of 'social capital' – a concept popularised earlier by Robert D. Putnam in *Bowling Alone.*[9] Social capital measures the connectedness of individuals to their local communities and is usually divided into two broad types: *bridging* and *bonding* social capital. 'Bridging social capital' consists of various formal and informal networks that link members of a given social group with the wider society. 'Bonding social capital', on the other hand, connects members of a social group with each other. Here, the level of bridging social capital is key. A 'disconnected community' or 'ethnic enclave', such as the Bangladeshis and Pakistanis lacking bridging social capital (because, for instance, of their limited English-language skills) is not likely to benefit from employment opportunities, even if they exist. To compensate, their highly developed bonding social capital would provide the basis for a successful local ethnic economy – and indeed this is the case, reflected in the rise of Pakistani and Bangladeshi-owned businesses in Birmingham and East End of London. Some argue that it is precisely this lack of bridging social capital that is the principal cause of the growing alienation amongst some young Pakistanis and Bangladeshis and their recent tendency to engage in civil disorder or embrace militant Islam. It is interesting to note, however, that although the four British-born Muslim suicide bombers of July 2005 London bombings may have perceived themselves to be alienated from wider society they certainly did not fall into the category of unemployed and disadvantaged youth. It is also difficult to comprehend that lack of social capital can explain the transition from alienation to suicide-bombing.

Political Participation

As Commonwealth citizens, all legally settled South Asians have a right to vote and stand for seats in British local and national elections irrespective of whether they choose to hold British passports or not. Indeed, studies show that more British Asians turn out at national elections than members of the mainstream community, which may reflect their admiration of, and belief in, democratic values. Given the socio-economic background of most South Asians, they have a natural affiliation with the Labour Party (although, with the emergence of a sizable British-Asian middle class, some now feel that Conservatives or Liberal Democrats are better able to meet their aspirations). At any rate, South Asians have traditionally considered the Labour Party the major vehicle for political success, and from the 1970s onwards, many South Asians joined Labour, some with a view to serve as local councillors and a few with ambition to become MPs. Over time, many Asians have been elected as councillors and some of them have also served as Lord Mayors. However, unlike in the past, it has proved extremely difficult in the modern period for South Asians to gain selection for a constituency seat, let alone be elected as MP. The political parties themselves were at first very reluctant to allocate seats to South Asians, not considering them winnable candidates, even in safe seats.

More recently, this has changed. With the general growth of a South-Asian electorate, especially in certain inner-city wards and key marginal constituencies, the major political parties, especially Labour (having lost three consecutive elections between 1979 and 1987), began to pay attention to the strategic selection of South-Asian candidates. The breakthrough came in the 1987 General Election when Keith Vaz (representing Labour) won the seat for Leicester East, becoming the first elected Asian in Parliament since 1929. More South Asians were to follow, both in the House of Commons and House of Lords, the latter mostly as Labour peers in recognition of their contribution to different aspects of British life. Table 1 provides a summary of South Asians in British Parliament since 1987, and, as we can see, the post-1990s period – which, unsurprisingly, coincides with the rising achievement of South Asians discussed earlier – is the most important. However, we need to bear in mind that despite this apparent success in political representation, currently there are only 10 serving South-Asian MPs out of 659 (1.5 percent) and only 18 Peers out of 714 (2.5 percent) in Parliament from a South-Asian population representing 4 percent of Britain's population.

Important work has been done by South Asians in both local councils and Parliament (to take the achievements of the ex-president of the Liberal-Democrats, Lord Dholakia, as only one example), and British South Asians have also been represented in the European Parliament as MEPs. Increasingly, more and more Asians engage in British politics through different channels: business and political lobby groups[10], All-Party Parliamentary Groups, and campaigns for self-determination in their homeland and against human rights abuses in their country of origin.

Table 8.1
South Asian Representation in British Parliament, 1987 to October 2006

Date	House of Commons	Date	House of Lords
1987	Keith Vaz, Labour, Leicester East, 1987– (first Asian in Parliament in post-war period)	1978	Lord (Swaraj) Paul of Marleybone, Labour
1991	Ashok Kumar, Labour, Middlesborough South and Cleveland East, 1991–1992, 1997–	1991	Lord (Meghnad) Desai, Labour (first Asian academic in Lords)
1992	Piara Singh Khabra, Labour, Ealing Southall, 1992–	1997	Baron (Raj Kumar) Bagri of Regent's Park, Conservative, 1997
1992	Nirj (Niranjan) Deva, Labour, Brentford and Isleworth, 1992–1997 (first Sri Lankan born MP, elected to European Parliament in 1999)	1997	Baron (Navnit) Dholakia of Waltham Brooks, West Sussex. Liberal Democrat (president of Liberal Democrat Party since 1999)
1997	Marsha Singh, Labour, Bradford West, 1997–	1998	Lord (Waheed) Alli of Norbury, Labour

(continued)

Table 8.1
(continued)

Date	House of Commons	Date	House of Lords
1997	Mohammed Sarwar, Labour, Glasgow Govan and Glasgow Central, 1997–2005, 2005– (first Muslim MP)	1998	Baroness (Pola) Uddin of Bethnal Green, Labour (only Muslim female member)
2001	Khalid Mahmood, Labour, Birmingham Perry Barr, 2001–	1998	Baron (Nazir) Ahmed of Rotherham, Labour (first Pakistani and Muslim in Lords)
2001	Parmjit Singh Dhanda, Labour, Gloucester, 2001 (one of the youngest MPs)	1999	Lord King of West Bromwich, Labour (first Sikh in Lords)
2005	Shahid Malik, Labour, Dewsbury, 2005– (along with Sadiq Khan (below), the first British-born Muslim to enter Parliament)	1999	Baroness (Usha) Prasher of Runnymede, Cross bench
	Sadiq Kahn, Labour, Tooting, 2005–	1999	Bishop (Michael) Nazir-Ali of Rochester (first Asian and non-white Lord Spiritual)
	Shailesh Vara, Conservative, North West Cambridgeshire, 2005– (ex-Vice Chair of Conservative Party and Shadow Deputy Leader in the House of Commons)	1999	Baron (Narendra) Patel of Dunkeld in Perth and Kinross
		2000	Baron (Bhikhu) Parekh of Kingston upon Hull, Labour

Table 8.1
(continued)

Date	House of Commons	Date	House of Lords
		2001	Baron (Amir) Bhatia of Hampton, Cross bench (Ismaili Muslim born in East Africa and moving to United Kingdom in 1972)
		2004	Baron (Kumar) Bhattacharyya of Mosely, Labour
		2004	Baron (Daljit Singh) Rana of Malone, County Antrim, Northern Ireland. Peoples' Peer
		2006	Baron (Karan) Bilimoria of Chelsea, Labour (fourth Parsi to enter British Parliament after Dadabhai Naoroji (1892–1895), Mancherjee Bhownagree (1895–1906) and Shapurji Saklatvala (1922, 1924–1929)
		2006	Baron (Kamlesh) Patel of Bradford, West Yorkshire, Peoples' Peer
		2006	Baron (Mohamed Iltaf) of Cornhill in the City of London, Conservative

'Asian Cool': South Asians in Popular Culture

It is not only in politics that there has been a significant breakthrough in South-Asian participation. There is a new and vibrant South-Asian presence in British popular culture. The contemporary popularity of *chicken tikka masala* – officially the nation's favourite dish – is a far cry from the former denigration of curry as a smelly 'colonial' food, and the acceptance of *salwaar kameez* as authentic global ethnic wear is far removed from the days when it was a garment of derision, worn by 'peasant' migrant women. On the contrary, helped by the endorsements of the latePrincess Diana, Cherie Booth and Jemima Khan, who have all dressedin Asian ethnic wear at public occasions, South-Asian fashions are definitely chic.

Both cuisine and fashion are important aspects of thriving Asian cultural economy generating increasing employment and wealth. Another example is the South-Asian wedding economy, which incorporates a whole range of ancillary services such as music, video and photography, florists, bespoke wedding invitation cards, catering, jewellery, bridal make-up services, bridal fashion wear, dresses for bridesmaids, outfits for best man, and so on. These services are promoted nationally – and indeed globally – through bridal exhibitions such as Bride & Groom, Bridal Asia, Celebrating Vivah, Asian Wedding Exhibition and Asian Bride Show, in glossy magazines such as *Asian Bride*, *Occasions* and *Asian Woman*, in Bollywood films and on Asian satellite channels now available throughout the South-Asian diaspora. In the United Kingdom alone, over 6,000 Indian weddings take place annually, and the total South-Asian wedding industry is estimated to be worth £300 million, with the average wedding costing between £15,000 and £20,000, and average wedding outfit starting at around £2,000.[11]

From such achievements has flowed new confidence, new forms and forums for expression and a new assertion of cultural identities and identity politics. Elaborate street parades at the festivals of *Vaisakhi*, *Diwali* or *Eid*, celebrations marking important historical and political anniversaries at top venues, annual *melas* and sports tournaments in major cities, are all cultural expressions of this new confidence and re-affirmation of new hybrid British-Asian identities. Perhaps, however, the most significant achievements have been in British-Asian popular culture: in the media, the performing arts – including drama and music – cuisine and sport.

The Media

The achievement of South Asians in the media, defined here as TV, radio and newspapers, is twofold: the rise to prominence of Asians in the mainstream British media and the growth of South-Asian media. They are parallel movements and both together have had a significant impact on Asian visibility and influence.

The struggle for Asians to gain visibility in the mainstream media was a long and protracted affair, but over time, a few individuals began to break the mould and now Asians are well represented at different levels; as owners, actors, presenters, producers, directors, playwrights and journalists. Even the 'hideously white' BBC (according to its ex-Director General Greg Dyke) now uses a large pool of Asian talent on its TV and radio networks. In 1989, Lisa Aziz, of Bangladeshi origin, became the first South-Asian news presenter on mainstream British television, serving as a journalist and presenter for HTV, TV-am and then on ITV, BBC and Sky. She also emerged as the first important role model for South-Asian women, in particular Muslims. She was followed by many other, now familiar, British-Asian media stars such as George Alagiah, Reeta Chakravarti, Shiulie Ghosh, Anya Sitaram, Krishnan Gurumurthy and Nina Hossain, to name but a few. Scores of aspiring South-Asian journalists and presenters work for the regional television and radio networks of BBC and ITV.

Yasmin Alibhai-Brown, a double migrant from East Africa, became one of the first regular South-Asian columnists for a daily newspaper, the *Independent*. Currently, there are a number of high-profile journalists, such as Nina Nanner (arts correspondent, ITV), Razia Iqbal (arts correspondent, BBC), Pallab Ghosh (science and technology correspondent, BBC), Vikram Dodd (*The Guardian*), Mihir Bose (*The Daily Telegraph* and now editor of BBC Sport) and Sathnam Sanghera (*The Financial Times*), who work in the media either on a contractual or freelance basis.

Besides these more visible faces, we can also identify many other powerful Asians in the media, working mainly behind the cameras. These include the Labour peer and TV executive Waheed Alli, (chairman of *Chorian*, which owns the rights to *Noddy* and *Miss Marple*, and who was one of the creators of Channel 4's *The Big Breakfast*), writer and actress Meera Syal and her husband Sanjeev Bhasker (of *Goodness Gracious Me* and *Kumars at Number 42* fame, also responsible for debunking earlier stereotypes that 'Asians Can't be Funny' and transforming 'Comic Asians to Asian Comics'),[12] Nav Raman (Channel 4's factual entertainment commissioning editor, who recently brought *Bollywood Star* and *The Ultimate Pop Star* to screen), Aaquil Ahmed, (Channel 4's commissioning editor for religion, renowned for using innovative ways of bringing religion to TV), Anil Gupta, (executive producer of Gasp Productions and Hat Trick, companies which produced *Goodness Gracious Me*, *Kumars at Number 42* and the cult series *The Office*), Tanika Gupta (playwright, writing widely for theatre and TV, including *EastEnders, Grange Hill, Flight, A Suitable Boy, Crossroads, The Bill, London Bridge* and *All About Me*) and Bobby Friction and Nihal Arthanayake, BBC Radio 1 DJs who have championed Asian music on the nation's number 1 music station. At the beginning of the twenty-first century, the UK media industry is truly multicultural and South Asians are beginning to represent a powerful voice within it.

Paralleling the above, we see the growth in South-Asian media, supplementing the growth in vernacular press discussed in Chapter 7. This growth has come both from South-Asian communities settled here and also through the rise of South-Asian cable and satellite TV, which has virtually brought the subcontinent to people's living rooms in Britain. On channels provided by Zee TV, Sony, Star, B4U, NDTV and others, British Asians are able to watch news, film, drama and musical shows at the same time as their cousins back home. This not only sustains the nostalgic yearnings of elderly Asians, but also provides visual, albeit distorted, representations of the subcontinent to the younger generation, strengthening their subcontinental identity.

Particularly important contributions to the growth of British-Asian media were made by Sarwar Ahmad, the Bangladeshi Managing Director for Smart Asian Media Ltd and Sumerah Ahmad, co-founder and director of award-winning radio station Club Asia. In 1989, targeting second-generation Asians, Sarwar Ahmad founded *Eastern Eye*, a *Sun*-style tabloid, and it became the fastest-growing Asian newspaper in Britain. In 2001, after recognising a gap in the radio-channels market, Sumerah Ahmad and her sister Humerah, both from Barking, launched Club Asia, aiming to reach young South Asians by 'playing their music, celebrating their lifestyle, understanding their hopes and fears and speaking the same language'. In its very first year, Club Asia became the fastest growing commercial radio station in London. Other media entrepreneurs include Avtar Lit, owner of nationally popular and successful Southall-based *Sunrise* radio, along with several other radio stations, and Tommy Nagra, former head of Asian Programmes Unit at the BBC and now senior executive producer at Maverick TV.

Performing Arts and Drama

Over the years, young British Asians have made a significant contribution to performing arts, film and drama. Hanif Kureishi's 'filthy' *My Beautiful Launderette*, Ayub Khan Din's 'dirty' *East Is East*, Gurinder Chadha's 'funny' *Bhaji on the Beach*, 'feel-good' *Bend It Like Beckham* and finally Hanif Kureishi's 'alarming'[13] *My Son the Fanatic*, all gave their authors mainstream recognition as writers unafraid to tackle issues which the community itself may treat as taboo. At the same time, a thriving South-Asian theatre scene emerged, both developing and extending issues of concern to the British-Asian community, adapting Asian and British classical works with a tinge of Asian flavour for mainstream consumption. Arguably, the two best-known Asian theatrical groups in London are Tara Arts and Tamasha Theatre Company. Tara Arts, founded in 1977 by its artistic director Jatinder Verma, and now established for over thirty years, has developed a distinctive 'Binglish' style of theatre, drawing on an eclectic mix of traditional South-Asian performance techniques and applying them to the European cannon. Besides its own productions, it has undertaken a number of co-productions with the National Theatre, and, in the late 1990s, developed a trilogy of plays – *Journey to the West* (2002) – which narrated the story of migration and transformation during the twentieth century 'through the eyes of those who had lived it'.[14] Tamasha was founded by actress-turned producer Sudha Bhuchar and director Christine Landon-Smith in 1989 to adapt for stage the great Indian novel by Mulk Raj Anand, *Untouchable*. Tamasha has produced over fifteen plays, some later adapted for radio, winning many prestigious awards. In its productions, the company reflects South-Asian experience both here in Britain and on the Indian subcontinent, also producing inter-cultural material for schools and offering young artists training workshops in acting and writing skills. One of its most popular productions, involving a large cast, and cashing in on the British Bollywood boom, was an elaborate adaptation of existing British and Bollywood films, *14 Songs, Two Weddings and a Funeral*. Its recent, hugely popular show, running since 2005, *The Trouble with Asian Men*, entertainingly explores 'the hidden lives' of South-Asian men. Besides these two major theatre groups, there are many others, including community dance schools which have sprung up in emulation of 'Bollywood Dreams', a Andrew

Lloyd Webber collaboration with Bollywood musician A. R. Rahman and actor-writer Meera Syal. Finally, any assessment of British-Asian success in the performing arts needs to acknowledge the contribution of artistic director and choreographer Shobana Jeyasingh, who has, through her London-based dance company, created brilliantly innovative 'fusions' between Indian classical dance Bharatya Natyam and western ballet and dance.

Music

The spectacular rise in the popularity of Bhangra music, Punjabi in origin but with a wide following among all South-Asian communities, is now well documented.[15] Although British Bhangra originated amongst the Birmingham Sikh community, it later became popular in West London. A number of bands emerging in the 1980s – such as Apna Sangeet, Heera, Alaap, DCS and Malkit Singh of Golden Star – paved the way for others, mainly boy bands and artistes, some of whom (for example Punjabi MC and Nitin Sawhney) eventually succeeded in crossing over to the mainstream British popular music scene. Experiments with fusion, using either reggae or Bollywood music, had been made much earlier by musicians and producers such as Apache Indian and Bally Sagoo, but with mixed results. But in the middle of the 1990s, the British-Asian music scene really took off. A decade later, fusion ('*desi* beats') is well established and tremendously diverse, blending different genres of world music – from Bhangra, RnB and Hip-Hop, Asian House and UK Garage to Bollywood and Asian Underground, and reaching a large market. Like *chicken tikka masala, desi* beats is peculiarly British (Asian) and highly popular. By contrast, Indian classical music and dance now has limited appeal.

Cuisine

The British fondness for Asian spices is an old story but in the more recent period, starting with the promotion of South-Asian food by actor-turned-writer Madhur Jaffrey, it has become hugely popular in Britain, and the industry is now worth around £2.5 billion annually, directly employing 70,000 people. There is tremendous diversity in outlets and consumers – South-Asian takeaways, balti houses, 'curry' public houses, restaurants (around 10,000) and supermarkets together serve over two million meals every week. Many South-Asian entrepreneurs – such as Parween Warsi and Sir Gulam Noon – have successfully taken advantage of this upsurge to make fortunes and achieved highest recognition. The appeal of South-Asian cuisine is so strong that lobby groups fear that future demand may outstrip supply because of a lack of British-trained chefs, and they call for relaxation of immigration controls. At the same time, colleges and universities are beginning to offer courses in Asian cuisine.

Sport

The visibility of Asians in British sport has increased markedly in the last two decades. Their achievements in cricket, however, are long-standing, a colonial legacy perhaps,[16] with Pakistani, Indian and Sri Lankan cricketers representing their counties over many years. In West Yorkshire, Asians have even established their own cricket clubs in the *Quaid-i-Azam League*. Interestingly, at county level, Yorkshire held a policy of choosing their players only from those actually born in the county – a policy which many aspiring Asian child migrant cricketers in Yorkshire found to be racially discriminatory – but this rule was dissolved when Sachin Tendulkar, the Indian cricketing superstar, played for the team in the 1990s. The breakthrough at national level came when mixed-race, but Indian-born, Nasser Hussain was named captain of the England cricket team in 1999 – exactly 100 years after Ranjitsinhji was appointed first Indian-origin captain of the England cricket team. Since then, players such as Mark Ramprakash (of half-Guyanese Indian descent), subcontinent-born child-migrants Vikram Solanki and Owais Shah and, more recently, British-born Loughborough University graduates Sajid Mahmood (cousin of boxer Amir Khan) and Monty Panesar (the first Sikh to play at national level) have all played for England.

Asians have often been criticised for failing to make an impact in the higher levels of football (soccer), still the most popular sport in Britain.[17] But this has begun to change. Zesh Rehman (British born of Pakistani origin) became the first Asian player to play in the Premiership in April 2004, appearing for Fulham against Liverpool; others, such as Cardiff City's Michael Chopra have established themselves at club level. Off the field, successful Asians include Manish Bhasin (presenter of *Football Focus* on BBC), Caj Sohal (producer of *Football Focus* and *Match of the Day*), Javed Khan (the Premier League's director of finance), Abdul Jafar (the first Asian chairman of league club: Bournemouth FC), Imraan Ladak (the owner of non-league club Kettering FC) and Jarnail Singh (the only Asian Football League referee). Progress has been made though it has been slow, a fact that many have blamed on the football authorities for not tackling racism seriously on the field or off it. In other sports – hockey, kick-boxing, martial arts, boxing, and so on – Asians have achieved at the very highest levels, frequently representing the England team. Some, such as Bolton-born boxer Amir Khan, who won a silver medal at the 2004 Athens Olympics, have become national heroes.

New British Asian Identities, Multiculturalism and Rise of Identity Politics

South-Asian achievement, enthusiastically celebrated by South-Asian communities themselves and supported by the general British public, which has embraced South-Asian cuisine, music and fashion, has also been officially sanctioned with the promotion of multicultural policies encouraging and financially rewarding cultural difference at both national and municipal levels. Local authorities have sponsored multicultural events, and some have even used South-Asian localities to promote tourism. In Birmingham, Bradford, Manchester, Ealing and Tower Hamlets, South-Asian cuisine and culture has been the focus of promotions attracting tourists to 'Baltistan', 'Banglatown', 'Little Punjab' and 'Curry Mile'.

At the same time, South Asians have developed a sense of community pride, a particular kind of diasporic self-image and sensibility – which they are prepared to protect against attacks by outsiders who denigrate their faith, values and institutions. In recent years, they have asserted their cultural identities by invoking identity politics, both nationally and globally, an important change in the nature of South-Asian protest. It has had the effect of dividing South Asians along faith lines. Whereas in the 1970s and 1980s South Asians were relatively united in their fights against racism or unfair work practices (for example, the infamous Grunwick dispute[18]), mobilising through pan-Asian groups such as the Asian Youth Movement in Southall, from the 1990s agitations have often involved only specific communities, be they Muslims, Hindus or Sikhs. For example, recent high-profile agitations – the anti–Iraq War movement or protests against the abuse of anti-terrorist laws – have mainly involved Muslim communities, with only lukewarm, if any, support from other South-Asian groups. The development is very marked if we look at recent cases of protest involving each of the three main South-Asian faith groups.

Muslims

Before the late 1980s, British Muslims were not known for their public contribution to British national or ethnic issues. According to Werbner, their lives were largely 'submerged into hidden networks of kin, friends, and work or business partners. These networks were sustained by an elaborate ceremonial gift economy controlled by women, and by antagonistic rivalries for status and power by men.'[19] This perception of Muslims (assuming it was correct in the first place) was, however, to change drastically with the 'Rushdie Affair'. Ever since then – and especially since 9/11 and 7/7 – the issue of Muslim identity politics, both nationally and globally, has been passionately debated by both Muslims and non-Muslims.

The Rushdie affair started soon after the publication, in 1988, of Salman Rushdie's controversial novel *Satanic Verses*, which the majority of Pakistani and Bangladeshi Muslims found blasphemous and deeply offensive to their religion – especially as it came from a lapsed Muslim. Expressing their indignation, Muslims across Britain engaged in peaceful protests and campaigns to persuade the government to ban the book. Some of these protests, however, turned violent. At the infamous protest organised by the Bradford Council of Mosques in January 1989 and others, copies of the book were burned. Shortly afterwards, the Ayatollah Khomeini of Iran issued a *fatwa* sentencing Rushdie to death, and offering a reward for anyone carrying it out. After receiving many death threats, Rushdie, largely unrepentant and repeatedly re-affirming his strong belief in free speech, thought and expression, was forced to go into hiding under special police protection. The British public and the global literary community expressed sympathy for his right to free expression, but not until 1999, nine years later, was the fatwa finally lifted. By then Rushdie had decided to settle in the United States, where he has remained a strong critic of militant Islam and its increasingly intolerant nature.

The Rushdie affair both exposed and radicalised Muslims. With their violent protest and book-burning, they appeared intolerant of values dear to a secular society and incapable of rational debate; some even labelled them 'fifth columnists' or 'the enemy within' (as they did after the London bombings in July 2005). Muslims who remained silent appeared to be condoning both the calls to ban the book and the fatwa. In general, the Muslim community seemed alienated from popular opinion, isolated, polarised and at odds with British values. Feelings ran high. After the book-burning incident in Bradford, the local newspaper labelled the protestors 'intellectual hooligans', comparing their action with those of the Nazis.[20] Subsequent attempts by some Muslim groups to bring about an extension in blasphemy and race discrimination laws to include religion failed, largely because they could not convince other major faith communities to support them. Many Muslims began to openly question the way in which secular values of equality, fairness and justice were being applied. The relationship between the Muslim community and the British public in general had reached a new low, any possibility of civic engagement on the basis of mutual trust seriously compromised. Over time, this general 'mistrust' between British Muslims and the state was to become even more problematic.

The Rushdie affair proved to be an important turning point for Muslim identity politics in Britain. As a result of it, the Muslim community learned new mobilisation strategies, realised the importance of communicating in the right idiom and developed a tendency to explore their location in the transnational moral religious community, the *umma*. In many ways, Werbner says, 'it liberated Pakistani settler-citizens from the self-imposed burden of being a silent, well-behaved minority, whatever the provocation, and opened up the realm of activist, anti-racist and emancipatory citizenship politics'.[21]

Sikhs

Traditionally, Sikh protest has been peaceful and law-abiding. In their successful campaigns for legal protection of their cultural and religious rights, they appealed to the special Anglo-Sikh relationship, without resorting to violent protest. Demonstrating against the Indian Congress government's decision, in June 1984, to send the army into their holiest shrine, the Darbar Sahib (Golden Temple) at Amritsar, they kept their anti-India protests largely within the confines of British law. Even during many years of political and financial support by a small minority of British Sikhs for the Khalistan movement in Punjab[22], there were only few instances of violence and those remained largely contained within the community. Recently, however, this has changed. Some Sikhs have taken a more militant, agitational stance on certain cultural practices which they see as detrimental to Sikh religion. One such issue has been the alleged disrespect shown to *Shri Guru Granth Sahib*, Sikh's holiest scripture and living Guru, by allowing the scripture to be taken to weddings or religious functions held in clubs, hotels and community centres where alcohol or smoking is permitted. In a number of cases, self-styled leaders of the *Respect for Guru Granth Sahib* group have halted a ceremony by force rather than reason.[23] This growing intolerance came to national attention when Sikh protests forced the premature closure of the play *Behzti* (Dishonour),by a British-born Sikh woman, Gurpreet Kaur Bhatti, in Birmingham in 2004.

The *Behzti* affair in some ways mimics the Rushdie affair. Set within the precincts of a gurdwara (Sikh Temple), the play aimed to expose hypocrisy and pretence among the Sikh community and human failing in general. Billed as a black comedy and featuring three lead characters, two female and one male, it – rather ambitiously – attempted to explore a wide range of topical subjects, such as homosexuality, corruption, social status and acceptance, suppression, drugs, domestic violence, rape, murder, mixed-race relationships and paedophilia, using Bhatti's own Sikh community as the backdrop. Aware of the controversial nature of the play, the Birmingham Repertory Theatre held consultations with the local Sikh community before staging the play. However, negotiations broke down with the latter insisting that the play be moved from its setting inside a gurdwara to a community centre. Importantly, the Sikh community objected not to the content of the play, but to the setting, which in their view violated 'Sikh sacred space'. Taking the contrary view, that to shift the setting would be a form of censorship, the Birmingham Rep compromised by inviting the Sikh community to write a statement expressing their views, to be given to every member of the audience and also read out in the auditorium before each performance. The play opened on 9 December 2004 and was set to run till 30 December. At first, the daily protests by members of the Sikh community were peaceful. On 19 December, however, they turned violent: 400 Sikhs attempted to storm the theatre, attacking security guards, destroying a foyer door and breaking windows in a restaurant. At the height of the fracas, eighty-five police officers – thirty in riot gear – were involved. Two people were arrested and five police officers were slightly injured – and the play was indefinitely cancelled, though the Birmingham Rep was quick to emphasise that this was not because the Sikh community found the play offensive but because the Rep had 'duty of care of its audiences, staff and performers'.[24] It later emerged that many of the ring leaders of the protest on the night of 19 December were from outside the area, from as far as Coventry, Leicester, Leeds and London.

As in the Rushdie affair, the dispute became a classic conflict between the artist's right to freedom of expression in a secular society and a community's wish to have their faith treated with dignity. The incident made headlines in the global media, leading to expressions of sympathy from Sikh organisations around the world for the local Sikh community, which felt betrayed by a lack of law to protect the sensibilities of religious communities. The artistic community, on the other hand, both South Asian and non-South Asian, fully supported the Birmingham Rep and Bhatti's right to stage the play, and organised an active media campaign to publicise their cause. Leading figures from the art world were among the 700 plus signatories, who wrote an open letter to *The Guardian* supporting the freedom of expression of the Sikh playwright.[25] Bhatti also made an impassioned defence of her play in a letter to *The Guardian*, ending with: 'You can all rest assured – this warrior will not stop fighting.'[26] But, like Rushdie, Bhatti was forced to leave her family home and go into hiding because of hate mail and death threats. Nearly two years on, she has yet to make a public appearance.

As before, with the Sikhs' turbans and beards campaigns of the 1970s, the *Behzti* affair threw the British Sikh community into the limelight, and some Sikh commentators were concerned that the community's image had been tarnished by 'third-rate talent', warning that it could have 'catastrophic' effects if the British media portrayed Sikhs in the same negative light as British Muslims, or once again (as they had done during the years of the Khalistan agitation) tried to equate the turban with terrorism. However, there is no evidence to suggest that the anti-*Behzti* protests left any permanent negative image problem. If anything, the Sikh community's anxieties in the post-9/11 and post-7/7 periods have related more to the possibility of mistaken identity between Muslims and Sikhs.

Hindus

Recently, the Hindu Forum of Britain, an umbrella organisation of different Hindu groups in Britain, commissioned the Runnymede Trust to conduct research into the identity and public role of British Hindus under the Connecting British Hindus Research Programme. The results of the project, sponsored by the Cohesion and Faith Unit of the Department for Communities and Local Government, were released in the summer of 2006.[27] The report acknowledged the need for Hindus (the third largest faith group in Britain) to become more visible and active in the public realm and to contribute to the ongoing debate about the role of faith communities in relation to the state. The report also subtly attempted to differentiate Hindus from other South-Asian and Indian communities, presenting them as progressive, dynamic, tolerant and more integrated into British way of life. Like the Sikhs, who have also campaigned to have separate 'ethnic' monitoring, Hindus began to challenge the notion of a generalised British-Asian identity and to question whether it still remains a meaningful category in contemporary Britain. In a sense, they were reacting against the type of British multiculturalism and ethnic classification, which does not necessarily take into account religious identities, leading to situations in which, for instance, a policy target to recruit British Asians can be met without a single Hindu, Sikh or a Muslim being recruited.

The report indicated a new level of confidence among British Hindus aiming to give a cohesive voice to Hindu interests, a distinct change in the community's traditional image, and this has been reinforced by the way Hindu groups have recently mobilised to stop the misuse of Hindu sacred and cultural symbols. Spearheaded by the London-based Hindu Human Rights organisation, but with the global Hindu community in mind, British Hindus have increasingly used agitational politics to secure their aims. In this way, they attempted to ban the use of 'Lord Ram' on designer shoes sold by French firm Minnelli's; they got a Californian company, Fortune Dynamic, to withdraw a range of shoes with Hindu images on them; they protested against 'Café Press' for putting sacred Hindu symbols on thongs; they protested against the fashion designer Roberto Cavalli for depicting Hindu goddesses on bikinis; they campaigned to stop the abuse of the 'swastika' (a Hindu sacred symbol) and misuse of the term 'Aryan', after Prince Harry wore an outfit with Nazi insignia at a party; they protested against the film *Goddess*, in which Tina Turner plays a goddess sex symbol dancing on a tiger; and they protested against the Royal Mail for abusing Hindu imagery. The website of the Hindu Human Rights has even produced a pictorial gallery to illustrate the many worldwide misuses of Hindu imagery.[28]

Sometimes this Hindu militancy has a clearly sinister side, seen in the activities of US- and British-based Hindu groups which, acting under cover of charitable organisations, funded communalism and hate in Gujarat in India.[29] More recently, Hindus forced the closure of an exhibition of paintings by internationally renowned Indian Muslim artist Maqbool Fida Husain at Asia House (a pan-Asian organisation in

Britain promoting a greater understanding of the rich and varied Asian cultures and economies). The exhibition, inaugurated by the Indian High commissioner Kamalesh Sharma on 10 May 2006, was due to continue till 5 August. But the Hindu Forum of Britain and the Hindu Human Rights group, alleging that Husain's paintings of Hindu gods and goddesses had outraged the global Hindu community by 'showing obscene images of Hindu goddesses', called for it to be stopped, and, on 22 May, Asia House abruptly cancelled the exhibition on security grounds, apparently after two paintings had been vandalised. Surprisingly, the incident did not get much coverage in the mainstream British media. Lord Desai, in a letter to *The Guardian* on 26 May, commented: 'This is an outrageous attack on artistic freedom in the British context. Would the media have ignored such an event had the protesters been Muslims and not Hindus?'[30] He went on to point out that

> Hindu goddesses can be seen in a variety of poses which many may find erotic in the temples of Khajuraho and Tirupati and many others. Hindu society and religion are remarkably relaxed and tolerant about sexual practices of human beings as well as of their gods and goddesses. What we are witnessing is the import into the UK of a group which under the guise of Hindu human rights is practising censorship for which there is no sanction in Hindu religion.[31]

Another letter to *The Guardian* on 30 May, signed by over fifty leading scholars in South-Asian studies, reiterated the point about diverse traditions of expression in Hinduism and questioned the legitimacy of the protesters to represent all Hindus. They suggested that: 'Groups such as Hindu Human Rights and the Hindu Forum of Britain are wielding the same tactics used by organisations in India. These groups are known for repeatedly attacking the works of artists and intellectuals, undermining India's constitutional right to freedom of thought and expression.'[32]

These cases of militancy show the growing importance of identity politics in Britain, where some British Asians, aided by their global networks, engage in the increasingly high-profile conflict between 'traditional' British secular values and the public promotion of religions under the guise of multiculturalism. Paradoxically, there are other issues urgently in need of discussion, which may be overlooked, issues which challenge all South-Asian communities but which many British Asians and whites are afraid to discuss openly for fear of a backlash. These are exactly the sorts of issues sensationalised in the worst possible way in the British tabloid press – 'forced marriages', 'honour killings', 'sex selection and illegal abortion', 'alcohol and drug abuse', 'domestic violence', 'dowry harassment', 'human trafficking and illegal immigration', 'forced conversions', 'conflicting doctrinal interpretations over wearing of the veil, the *niqab*', 'child abuse, incest or paedophilia', 'homosexuality', 'prostitution and pornography', 'growing popularity of black magic and spiritual healers to exorcise the "evil eye"' and so on. Such issues are often met by British Asians with blank denial, or an attempt to blame the victim, or the claim that these problems have been 'imported' from western secular culture, or even that the problems belong to *other* Asians, not themselves. Both Hindus and Sikhs have tried to distance themselves from them by blaming Muslims for giving British Asians a bad name, a doubly unfortunate act because no community is immune to such problems, and their accusations only add to the misery of the beleaguered Muslim community, which feels the rising tide of Islamophobia from both the mainstream community as well as from non-Muslim Asians.

Not surprisingly, Islamophobia reached new heights after the tragic London bombings of 7 July 2005, which killed fifty-two London morning commuters and the four Muslim suicide bombers themselves. Three of the bombers came from Yorkshire (two from Leeds, one from Dewsbury; the fourth was born in Jamaica), where they had apparently lived totally normal lives. None had any record of previous political or terrorist involvement. The bombing came as a big shock for the British, who found it difficult to understand the circumstances which might have created 'home-grown' suicide bombers, the first ever on British soil. For Britain's 1.6 million Muslims, it formed an absolutely critical juncture.

What made these angry young Muslims take such drastic action? What right did they have to tarnish the whole community? Did they act out of frustration of seeing large numbers of their community living in poverty? Were they reacting to the persistent racism in British society, especially intolerable for young British-born Muslims? Or were the bombings a sign of an unnoticed growth in radical Islam among Muslim youth, some of whom had been influenced by the inflammatory speeches of visiting *imams* (clerics) and the activities of fundamentalist (and *jehadist*) groups such as Hizb-ut-Tahrir and Al-Muhajiroun (which have suspected links with Al Queda), not to mention the recent media coverage of global 'Muslim suffering', whether in Palestine, Kashmir, Bosnia, Chechnya, Afghanistan or Iraq?

All are likely contributory factors. But it is interesting, in this context, to read the comments of Moazzam Begg, a British Muslim detained for two years in Guantanamo Bay. Writing about the reasons which pushed him towards a greater acceptance of his Muslim identity, he reveals that he was first attracted to the idea of joining 'a gang' (that is, an anti-fascist organisation) in reaction to the collusion he witnessed between the state (particularly the police) and racist elements operating in their neighbourhoods. He further states:

> Britain has the best multicultural society in Europe, but still in most parts of the country I feel out of place. I'd like to go to an English country village, with my dark skin, my beard and my wife in her *hijab* and not be stared at or singled out ... I'd like the people to see that we generally want the same things in life, that they should not feel threatened by me. I want the English to like me, because they are accepting – not just to tolerate me, if I am trying to assimilate.[33]

Clearly, multiculturalism in Britain failed Begg, and he looked for something else. International events, such as the first Gulf War and the massacre of Bosnian Muslims, proved life-changing for him.

Whatever the motivations of the suicide bombers, the July bombings badly damaged British–Muslim relations and opened up new divisions among the largely peaceful community itself, exacerbating the general 'mistrust' developed during the earlier period. The post-bombing period has been marked by a significant increase in hate crime against Muslims, although, because perpetrators have usually been unable to distinguish between Muslims and other South Asians, many non-Muslim South Asians have suffered too. In the political domain, the July bombings sharpened the debates on the merits of the British form of multiculturalism.

Growing Backlash against Multiculturalism and Future of British South-Asian Identities

The British brand of multiculturalism, described by Trevor Phillips (Chair of Commission for Racial Equality) as 'sleep walking to segregation', has come under increasing criticism over the last decade, but especially since 9/11 and the bombings in London in July 2005.[34] The charges against multiculturalism have been numerous: that it allows the use of political patronage at local level to gain electoral advantage; that it leads to the formation of numerous 'unrepresentative' organisations in the race industry such as the CRE, local RECs and now Community Cohesion Units, and so on; that it tolerates public policy consultation through unrepresentative community organisations; that it allocates public funding, through the Lottery Fund and other funding bodies, to very marginal communities or sectarian groups (amongst all Hindu, Sikh and Muslim minorities) who want to assert their own identity against the larger faith groups; and so on. In many cases, British multiculturalism has resulted in the transplantation of subcontinental politics at local level, where community vote banks are used by incumbent and aspiring councillors and MPs to maintain political influence. Many such state policies have tended to undermine the credibility of British form of multiculturalism, and their contribution in facilitating ethnic segregation is now openly criticised.

Along with other forces, British multiculturalism has propelled most South Asians towards integration and assimilation, promoting mixed relationships, a more secular outlook, value systems based on respect for individualism and rule of law. At the same time, however, in a globalised world, counter-pressures have pulled them towards a homeland identity, albeit in a diasporic 'in-between' sense. The growth in popularity and support for Indian/Pakistani/Sri Lankan cricket teams, the huge popularity of Bollywood cinema, Indian film and pop music and South-Asian satellite TV, and the development of heritage tourism are some of the factors which directly strengthen a British-Asian diasporic identity.

Such an identity is further strengthened with the explicit assistance of outreach policies of the 'homeland' states. India, for example, has tried to inculcate an idea of Indianness among diaspora Indians by introducing favourable policies towards them – offering privileges in savings and investment facilities, holding annual celebrations (such as *Pravasi Bharatiya Divas*) for diaspora communities, granting dual nationality, fast-tracking legal redress and even promising votes in Indian elections. The influence of such policies should not be underestimated. But their impact may only work for groups who have a 'homing desire' or continuing pride in their South-Asian ancestry. Many young second- or third- generation Asians, especially those determined to better themselves in Britain, may be less affected by South-Asian cultural influences, even though they may find it difficult to totally ignore them. The rise of India as a global power, with its growing influence on global business, education, media, fashion, arts and culture also draws British Indians towards hybrid, hyphenated identities. Many South-Asian icons seem to relish making an impact on both markets – and even globally. Cultural entrepreneurs such as Gurinder Chadha and others, whilst being proud of their British identity, see themselves as having multiple identities because they themselves are multiple migrants.

In the context of ongoing debates about community cohesion, it seems very doubtful if integration (if defined as assimilation/acceptance of a Christian ethical value system and loyalty to British identity) can be achieved. Just as many Asians need to demonstrate greater cultural accommodation and re-affirm their belonging to the state, the British public too needs to accept a more re-negotiated notion of Britishness, which is not exclusivist and which does not offer equal dignity and respect for all South-Asian 'home' cultures. Resolution of this debate is likely to be the major challenge facing Britain in the next decade. Furthermore, the current historical phase, dominated by the 'war on terror', may have lasting unintended consequences, both on relations between the white majority community and South Asians and within South-Asian communities themselves. The real danger lies in throwing away or reversing the considerable achievements of multiculturalism, which have enriched the lives of most people of Britain.

List of Illustrations

Note: Although every attempt has been made to trace copyright holders, it has proved impossible in some cases. If any copyright holders acknowledged incorrectly will contact the publisher, corrections will be made in future editions.

Bibliography

Ali, N., Kalra, V.S. and Sayyid, S., *A Postcolonial People: South Asians in Britain* (London: C. Hurst & Co., 2006).

Allahabad Review.

Anand, Sushila, *Indian Sahib: Queen Victoria's Dear Abdul* (London: Duckworth, 1996).

Annual Register.

Anonymous, *Epicure's Almanack; or, Calendar of Good Living* (London: Longman, Hurst, Rees, Orme, and Brown, 1815).

Anonymous, Review of Karim Khan, 'Siyahat Namah' (1841), *Blackwood's Edinburgh Magazine*, vol. 54, no. 338, December 1843, p. 762.

Ansari, Humayun, *The Infidel Within: The History of Muslims in Britain, 1800 to the Present* (London: Hurst & Co., 2004), p. 333.

Anwar, M. and Bakhsh, Q., *British Muslims and State Policies* (Centre for Research in Ethnic Relations, University of Warwick, 2003).

Archer, Mildred, *India and British Portraiture 1770–1825* (London: Sotheby, Parke, Bernet, 1979).

Aurora, G.S., *The New Frontiersman: A Sociological Study of Indian Immigration in the United Kingdom* (Bombay, India: Popular Prakashan, 1967).

Awaaz, *In Bad Faith? British Charity and Hindu Extremism*, accessed at http://www.awaazsaw.org/ibf/ (London: South Asia Watch Ltd, 2004).

Baijnath, L., *England and India* (Bombay, India: J.B. Karani, 1893).

Balachandran, G., 'Circulation through Seafaring: Indian Seamen, 1890–1945', in Claude Markovits, Jacques Pouchepadass and Sanjay Subrahmanyam (eds), *Society and Circulation: Mobile People and Itinerant Cultures in South Asia, 1750–1950* (New Delhi, India: Permanent Black, 2003), pp. 89–130.

Baldwin, Marjorie, *Story of the Forest*, 2nd ed. (Colgate: St Savior's Church, 1985).

Ballard, R. (ed.) *Desh Pardesh: The South Asian Presence in Britain* (London: Hurst & Co., 1994).

Ballard, Roger, 'The South Asian Presence in Britain and Its Transnational Connections', in H. Singh and S. Vertovec (eds), *Culture and Economy in the Indian Diaspora* (London: Routledge, 2002).

Bance, Peter, *The Duleep Singhs: The Photographic Album of Queen Victoria's Maharajah* (Stroud: Sutton Publishing, 2004).

Banerjee, Brajendra Nath, *Rajah Rammohun Roy's Mission to England* (Calcutta, India: N.M. Raychowdhury, 1926).

Barber, Jill, *Celebrating the Black Presence*, vol. 2, *Hidden Lives* (Westminster: City of Westminster Archives Centre, 2000).

Basu, Baman Das, *Story of Satara*, ed. Ramananda Chatterjee (Calcutta, India: Modern Review Office, 1922).

Basu, Shrabani, *Spy Princess: The Life of Noor Inayat Khan* (Stroud: Sutton Publishing, 2006).

BBC Written Archives, Cavasham.

Beaconsfield Parish Church, Baptismal Records.

Beaconsfield Parish Register.

Beetham, David, *Transport and Turbans: Comparative Study of Local Politics* (London: Institute of Race Relations, 1970).

Begg, Moazzam, *Enemy Combatant: My Imprisonment at Guantanamo, Bagram, and Kandahar* (London: New Press, 2006).

Bellot, H. Hale, *University College London, 1826–1926* (London: University of London Press, 1929).

Bhachu, Parminder, *Twice Migrants* (London: Tavistock, 1985).

——, *Dangerous Designs: Asian Women Fashion the Diaspora Economies* (London: Routledge, 2004).
Bhatti, Gurpreet, 'The Warrior is Fighting On', *The Guardian* (13 January 2005).
Board Collections, The British Library, London.
Bombay Times.
Bombay, Political Diary, 1794–1807, Maharashtra State Archives, Mumbai, India.
Bombay, Public and Secret and Political Diaries 1794–1816, Maharashtra State Archives, Mumbai, India.
Booth, Robert, 'Sikh Protestors Disrupt Wedding', *The Guardian* (27 June 2005).
Borthwick, Meredith, *Keshub Chandra Sen: A Search for Cultural Synthesis* (Calcutta, India: Minerva, 1977).
Boyė, Jerome, ed., *L'Extraordinaire Aventure de Benoit de Boigne aux Indes* (Paris: Echanges Culturels et Actions de Development, 1996).
Boyle, M., *Court Guide* (London: Saunders and Otley, 1818).
Brah, Avtar, 'Inter-generational and Inter-ethnic Perceptions: A Comparative Study of South Asian and English Adolescents and Their Parents in Southall, West London', PhD thesis, University of Bristol.
——, *Cartographies of Diaspora* (London: Routledge, 1996).
Braidwood, Stephen, J., *Black Poor and White Philanthropists: London's Blacks and the Foundation of the Sierra Leone Settlement, 1786–1791* (Liverpool: Liverpool University Press, 1994).
Braningan, Tania, 'Stars Sign Letter in Support of Playwright in Hiding', *The Guardian* (23 December 2004).
The Brighton Gazette.
The Brighton Guardian.
The Brighton Herald.
Brighton, East Sussex and Sussex Poll Books 1820–1847, Institute of Historical Research, London.
Brinda, Maharani of Kapurthala (as told to Elaine Williams), *Maharani: The Story of an Indian Princess* (New York: Henry Holt and Company, 1953).
British Indian Association (Aligarh), *Supplement to the Bylaws of the British Indian Association N.W.P., Relative to the Department for Encouraging Travel to Europe* (Aligarh, India: Syed Ahmed: 1869).
Broughton Papers, MSS EUR F.213/6, The British Library, London.
Brown, F.H., 'Indian Students in Britain', *Edinburgh Review*, vol. 217, no. 443, January 1913, pp. 138–156.
Burke, Edmund, *Correspondence*, 10 vols, ed. Thomas W. Copeland (Cambridge: Cambridge University Press, 1958–1978).
Burton, Antoinette, 'Making a Spectacle of Empire: Indian Travellers in Fin-de-Siecle London', *History Workshop Journal*, vol. 42, 1996, pp. 126–146.
Burton, Antoinette, 'From Child Bride to "Hindoo Lady": Rukhmabai and the Debate on Sexual Respectability in Imperial Britain', *The American Historical Review*, vol. 103, no. 4, October 1998, pp. 1119–1146.
Burton, Antoinette, *At the Heart of the Empire* (Berkeley: University of California Press, 1998).
Burton, Antoinette, 'Tongues Untied: Lord Salisbury's "Black Man" and the Boundaries of Imperial Democracy', *Comparative Studies in Society and History*, vol. 42, no. 3, July 2000, pp. 632–661.
Burton, Antoinette, *Dwelling in the Archives: Women Writing House, Home and History in Late Colonial India* (Oxford: Oxford University Press, 2003).
Calcutta Review.
Callaghan, John, *Rajani Palme Dutt: A Study in British Stalinism* (London: Lawrence and Wishhart, 1993).

Cantle, Ted (Chair), *Community Cohesion; A Report of the Independent Review Team* (London: Home Office, 2001).
Carpenter, Mary, *Last Days in England of the Rajah Rammohun Roy* (London: Trubner, 1866).
Catalogue of the Royal Academy Exhibitions, 1819.
Chandra, Sudhir, *Enslaved Daughter: Colonialism, Law and Women's Rights* (New Delhi, India: Oxford University Press, 1998).
Chaudhuri, K.N., *English East India Company* (London: Frank Cass: 1965).
Chuckerbutty, S. Goodeve, 'Present State of the Medical Profession in Bengal', *British Medical Journal* (23, 30 July 1864), pp. 86–88, 109–112.
Clutton, Sir George, 'Cheetah and the Stag', *Burlington Magazine*, vol. 112, 1970, pp. 539–540.
Cobbett, William, *Parliamentary History of England*, 36 vols (London: Hansard, 1806–1820).
Collet, Sophia Dobson, *Life and Letters of Raja Rammohun Roy* (London: Harold Collet, 1900).
Collier, Richard, *Make Believe: The Magic of International Theatre* (New York: Dodd, Mead and Company, 1986).
Committee on Distressed Colonial and Indian Subjects, CD 5133 and 5134 (22) 1910.
Compton, Herbert, *Particular Account of the European Military Adventurers in India, from 1784 to 1803* (London: T. Fisher Unwin, 1893).
Cotton, Sir Evan, 'Begum in Sussex', *Bengal Past and Present*, vol. 46, 1933, pp. 91–94.
Court Minutes, The British Library, London.
Das, Harihar, 'Early Indian Visitors to England', *Calcutta Review*, 3rd series, vol. 13, 1924, pp. 83–114.
——, *Life and Letters of Toru Dutt* (New Delhi, India: Oxford University Press: 1920).
de Boigne, Charlotte, *Memoirs*, ed. Sylvia de Morsier-Kotthaus (London: Museum Press, 1956).
Department for Education and Skills, *Aiming High: Raising the Achievement of Minority Ethnic Pupils* (London: DfES, 2003).
Department of Education and Science, *The Education of Immigrants: Circular 7/65* (London, HMSO, 1965).
Desai, Meghnad, 'Closure Threat to Artistic Freedom', *The Guardian* (26 May 2005).
Devi, Sunity, *Autobiography of an Indian Princess* (London: John Murray, 1921).
DeWitt John, *Indian Workers' Associations in Britain* (London: OUP, 1969), p. 47.
Dixon, Conrad, 'Lascars: The Forgotten Seamen', in Rosemary Ommer and Gerald Panting (eds), *Working Men Who Got Wet: Proceedings of the Fourth Conference of the Atlantic Canada Shipping Project, July 24–July 26, 1980* (Newfoundland: Memorial University, 1980), pp. 265–281.
Docket Book (B.4.31), National Archives, London.
Dutt, R.C., *Three Years in Europe: Extracts from Letters Sent by a Hindu*, 2nd edition (London: S.K. Lahiri & Co., 1873).
Dutt, H., *Lieutenant Suresh Biswas: His Life and Adventures* (Calcutta, India: P.C. Dass, 1900).
East India Yearbook.
Economic and Overseas Department: L /E /9 series The British Library, London.
Elphinstone Papers, F.88, The British Library, London.
Elphinstone's Journal, F.88/14, The British Library, London.
Express and Star, 'Sikh in Bus Row', 9 August 1967.
Feilding, Cecilia, *Royalist Father and Roundhead Son: The Memoirs of the First and Second Earls of Denbigh, 1600–1675* (London: Methuen, 1915).
Finance and Home Committee Minutes and Papers, The British Library, London.

Fisher, Michael, H., *First Indian Author in English: Dean Mahomed (1759–1851) in India, Ireland, and England* (Delhi, India: Oxford University Press, 1996).
——, *Counterflows to Colonialism: Indian Travellers and Settlers in Britain, 1600–1857* (Delhi, India: Permanent Black, 2006).
Forbes collection Mss.Eur 341/147. Lam, M., Autumn Leaves, *Some Memories of Yesterday*. The British Library, London.
Forbes, Geraldine, *Women in Modern India* (Cambridge: Cambridge University Press, 1996).
Foreign Political Correspondence, National Archives of India, New Delhi.
Foster, William, *English Factories in India*, 13 vols (Oxford: Clarendon Press, 1906–1927).
Friend of India.
Ganashakti Online, accessed at www.ganashakti.com.
Gandhi, M.K., *An Autobiography or My Story of My Experiments with Truth* (Boston: Beacon, 1957).
Gash, Norman, *Lord Liverpool: The Life and Political Career of Robert Banks Jenkinson, Second Earl of Liverpool, 1770–1828* (Cambridge: Harvard University Press, 1984).
Gentleman's Magazine.
George III, King, *Correspondence*, 6 vols, ed. Sir John Fortescue (London: Macmillan, 1927–1928).
Gillespie, Marie, 'From Comic Asians to Asian Comics: *Goodness Gracious Me*, TV Comedy and Ethnicity', in M. Scriven and E. Roberts (eds), *Group Identities on French and British Television* (Oxford: Bergham, 2003).
Gilroy, Paul, 'There Ain't No Black in the Union Jack', *The Cultural Politics of Race and Nation* (London: Hutchinson, 1987).
GLA Economics, *The Contribution of Asian Owned Businesses to London's Economy* (Mayor of London, Greater London Authority, June, 2005).
Great Britain, Parliamentary Papers, Returns (Commons).
Great England, Public Record Office, *Calendar of State Papers, Colonial Series*, vol. 2, ed. W. Noel Sainsbury (London: Public Record Office, 1862).
Grewal, Shivdeep, 'Southall, Capital of the 1970s: Of Community Resistance and the Conjecture of April the 23rd 1979', *International Journal of Punjab Studies*, vol. 10, nos 1 and 2, January–December 2003, pp. 77–111.
Grewal, Inderpal, *Home and Harem: Nation, Gender, Empire and Cultures of Travel* (London: University of Leicester, 1996).
The Guardian, 'Playing with Fire', Leader (21 December 2004).
The Guardian, 'Reinstate Indian Art Exhibition', signed by Dr Chetan Bhatt, Goldsmiths College, London, Prof. Rajeswari Sunderrajan, Oxford University and Dr Priyamvada Gopal, Cambridge University and thirty-nine other UK academics (30 May 2006).
Gundara, Jagdish, S. and Ian Duffield, eds, *Essays on the History of Blacks in Britain: From Roman Times to the Mid-Twentieth Century* (Aldershot: Avebury, 1992).
Hahn, Daniel, *Tower Menagerie* (New York: Simon and Schuster, 2003).
Hall, Stuart, 'Old and New Identities, Old and New Ethnicities', in Anthony D. King (ed.), *Culture, Globalization and the World System: Contemporary Conditions for the Representations of Identity* (London: Minneapolis: University of Minnesota, 1991), pp. 41–68.
Halstead, Mark, *Education, Justice and Cultural Diversity: An Examination of the Honeyford Affair, 1984–85* (London: The Falmer Press, 1988).
Hansard, T.C., ed., *Parliamentary Debates* (London: Hansard, 1812–).
Hansen, R., *Citizenship and Immigration in Post-war Britain: The Institutional Origins of a Multicultural Nation* (Oxford: Oxford University Press, 2000).
Hastings, Warren, Warren Hastings Papers, Add. 39884–39885, The British Library, London.

Hawkins, William, *Hawkins' Voyages*, ed. Clements R. Markham (New York: B. Franklin, 1970).
Hedges, William, *Diary*, 3 vols, ed. Henry Yule (London: Hakluyt Society, 1887–89).
Helweg A., *Sikhs in England* (Oxford University Press, 1979).
Hickey, William, *Memoirs of William Hickey*, 4 vols, ed. Alfred Spencer, 3rd ed. (London: Hurst and Blackett, 1913–1925).
Hindu Forum of Britain, *Connecting British Hindus: An Enquiry into the Identity and Public Engagement of Hindus in Britain* (London, Runnymede Trust, 2006).
Home Miscellaneous Series, vol. 708, The British Library, London.
Hughes, Sir Edward, 'Log', L/MAR/B/354C, The British Library, London.
Hunter, William, *Essay on the Diseases Incident to Indian Seamen, or Lascars on Long Voyages* (Calcutta, India: Company's Press, 1804).
Illustrated London News.
India News.
India Today, 'Dream Merchants' (30 August 2004).
The Indian: At Home and Abroad.
The Indian: At Home and Overseas.
International Genealogical Index.
I'tisam al-Daula, Mirza, *Wonders of Vilayat*, trans. Kaiser Haq (Leeds: Peepal Tree Press, 2001).
——, *Shigrif-namah-i Wilayat*, OR 200, The British Library, London.
——, *Shigurf Namah-i Velaet*, ed. and trans. James Edward Alexander and Munshi Shumsher Khan (London: Parbury, Allen, 1827).
Jain, Ravindra, K., *Indian Communities Abroad: Themes and Literature* (New Delhi, India: Manohar, 1993).
Jayaram, N. (ed.), *The Indian Diaspora: Dynamics of Migration* (New Delhi, India: Sage, 2004).
Josephedis, Sasha, 'Organisational Splits and Political Ideology in the Indian Workers Associations', in Pnina Werbner and Mohammed Anwar (eds), *Black and Ethnic Leaderships* (London: Routledge, 1991).
Kalra, Virinder, *From Textile Mills to Taxi Ranks: Experiences of Migration, Labour and Social Change* (Aldershot: Ashgate, 2000).
Kalsi, S., *The Evolution of the Sikh Community in Britain: Religious and Social Change among the Sikhs of Leeds and Bradford* (Leeds: Department of Theology and Religious Studies, 1990).
Karim, Khan, 'Siyahat Namah', Mss Or 2163, The British Library, London.
Khan, Abu Talib, *Masir Talibi fi Bilad Afranji*, Persian reprint, ed. Hosein Khadive-Jam (Tehran: Hosein Khadive-Jam, 1983).
——, 'Masir Talibi fi Bilad Afranji', Persian Add 8145–8147, The British Library, London.
——, *Poems of Mirza Abu Talib Khan*, trans. George Swinton (London: Author: 1807).
——, *Travels of Mirza Abu Taleb Khan*, 2 vols, trans. Charles Stewart (London: Longman, Hurst, Rees, and Orme, 1810; 1814).
Khan, Gulfishan, *Indian Muslim Perceptions of the West during the Eighteenth Century* (Karachi, Pakistan: Oxford University Press, 1998).
Kling, Blair, B., *Partner in Empire: Dwarkanath Tagore and the Age of Enterprise in Eastern India* (Calcutta, India: Firma KLM, 1976).
Lahiri, S., 'Patterns of Resistance: Indian Seamen in Britain', in Anne J. Kershen (ed.), *Language, Labour and Migration* (Aldershot: Ashgate, 2000), pp. 155–178.
——, 'British Policy towards Indian Princes in Late Nineteenth and Early Twentieth-century Britain', in *Immigrants and Minorities*, vol. 15, no. 3, November 1996, pp. 214–232.

——, 'South Asians in Post-Imperial Britain: Decolonisation and Imperial Legacy', in Stuart Ward (ed.), *British Culture and the End of Empire* (Manchester: Manchester University Press, 2001), pp. 200–216.

——, 'Uncovering Britain's South Asian Past: The Case of George Edalji', in *Immigrants and Minorities*, vol. 17, no. 3, November 1998, pp. 22–33.

——, *Indians in Britain: Anglo-Indian Encounters, Race and Identity, 1880–1930* (London: Frank Cass, 2000).

Lambert, Sheila, ed., *House of Commons, Sessional Papers of the Eighteenth Century*, 147 vols (Wilmington: Scholarly Resources, 1975).

Lascar Papers, The British Library, London.

Lawrence, Sir Walter, 'Report on Indian Hospitals', WO 32/5110, National Archives, Kew.

Lindeborg, R.H., 'The "Asiatic" and the Boundaries of Victorian Englishness', in *Victorian Studies*, vol. 37, no. 3 (Spring 1994), pp. 381–404.

The Listener.

Liverpool Law Review, 'Turban or Not Turban – That is the Question' (Mandla *v.* Dowell Lee), vol. 5, no. 1, 1983.

Llewellyn-Jones, Rosie, *Engaging Scoundrels: True Tales of Old Lucknow* (New Delhi, India: Oxford University Press, 2000).

London Calling: The Overseas Journal of the British Broadcasting Corporation.

London Magazine.

Lutfullah, *Autobiography of Lutfullah, a Mohamedan Gentleman*, eds Edward B. Eastwick and S.A.I. Tirmizi (London: Smith, Elder, 1857).

Lutfullah, Syed, *Azimullah Khan Yusufzai, the Man Behind the War of Independence, 1857* (Karachi, Pakistan: Mohamedali Educational Society, 1970).

Magnus, Philip, *Edmund Burke: A Life* (London: John Murray, 1939).

Mahomed, S.D., *Shampooing, or, Benefits Resulting from the Use of the Indian Medicated Vapour Bath* (Brighton: The Author, 1822; 1826; 1838 edns).

——, 'Mahomed's Visitors' Book' (*c.* January 1827), Brighton Reference Library, Brighton.

Mahomet, Dean, *The Travels of Dean Mahomet: An Eighteenth-Century Journey through India*, ed. Michael H. Fisher (Berkeley: University of California Press, 1997).

Majeed, Javed, 'Bathos, Architecture and Knowing India: E.M. Forster's Passsage to India and Nineteenth-century British Ethnology and the Romance Quest', *Journal of Commonwealth Literature*, vol. 40, no. 1, March 2005, pp. 21–36.

Majumdar, Janaki Agnes Penelope, *Family History*. Edited and with an introduction by Antoinette Burton (New Delhi, India: Oxford University Press, 2003).

Malabari, B.M., *The Indian Eye on English Life* (Bombay, India: Apollo Printing Works: 1895).

Martindale, Louisa, *A Woman Surgeon: Louisa Martindale* (London: Victor Gollancz, 1951).

Mathur, Saloni, 'Living Exhibits: The Case of 1886', in *Cultural Anthropology*, vol. 15, no. 4, November 2000, pp. 492–524.

Mayhew, Henry, *London Labour and the London Poor* (London: C. Griffin, 1861).

Metcalf, Thomas, *Ideologies of the Raj* (Cambridge: Cambridge University Press, 1995). Minerva: 1977).

Mir Muhammad Husain, 'Risalah-i Ahwal-i Mulk-i Farang', Maulana Azad Library, Aligarh, India.

Miscellaneous Letters Received, E/1 series, The British Library, London.

Mittra, Kissory Chand, *Memoir of Dwarkanath Tagore* (Calcutta, India: Thacker, 1870).

Modern Review.

Mookerjee, G.K., *The Indian Image of Nineteenth-Century Europe* (London: Asia Publishing House, 1967).

Morning Chronicle.

Moving Here: 200 Years of Migration to England, accessed at www.movinghere.org.uk.

Mukharji, T.N., *A Visit to Europe* (Calcutta, India: W. Newman, 1889).
Murshid, Ghulam (ed.), *The Heart of a Rebel Poet: Letters of Michael Madhusudan Dutt* (New Delhi, India: Oxford University Press, 1984).
Murshid, Ghulam, *Reluctant Debutant: Response of Bengali Women to Modernisation, 1849–1905* (Rajshasi, Bangladesh: Rajshasi University, 1983).
National Archives of India, *Fort William-India House Correspondence*, 17 vols (New Delhi, India: National Archives of India, 1949–1981).
Neill, Edward, D., *Memoir of Rev. Patrick Copland* (New York: Charles Scribner, 1871).
Ommisi, David (ed.), *Indian Voices of the Great War: Soldiers' Letters, 1914–1918* (Harmondsworth: Macmillian Press, 1999).
The Oriental Post.
Ouseley, Sir Herman (Chair), *Community Pride Not Prejudice: Making Diversity Work in Bradford* (Bradford: Bradford District Race Review, Bradford Vision, 2001).
Pal, B.C., *Memories of My Life and Times, vol. 1, 1886–1900* (Calcutta, India: Yugayatr Prakashak, 1951).
Palmer, Sarah, *Politics, Shipping and the Repeal of the Navigation Laws* (Manchester: Manchester University Press, 1990).
Parasnis, D.B., 'Original Correspondence between the English and the Marathas', in *Indian Historical Record Commission, Proceedings*, vol. 5, 1923, pp. 91–99.
Parekh, Bhikhu (Parekh Report), *The Future of Multi-Cultural Britain* (London: Profile Books, 2000).
——, 'South Asians in Britain', in *History Today*, vol. 57, no. 9, September 1997, pp. 65–68.
Paul, Kathleen, *Whitewashing Britain: Race and Citizenship in the Postwar Era* (New York: Cornell University Press, 1997).
Peach, C. and Gale, R., 'Muslims, Hindus and Sikhs in the New Religious Landscape of England', in *The Geographical Review*, vol. 93, no. 4, 2003, pp. 469–490.
Penny, Frank, *The Church in Madras: Being the History of the Ecclesiastical and Missionary Action of the East India Company in the Presidency of Madras* (London: Smith, Elder, 1904).
Philips, C.H., *East India Company, 1784–1834* (Manchester: Manchester University Press, 1940).
Political and Military References Memoranda, The British Library, London.
Proceedings of the Old Bailey, Guildhall Library, London.
Public Advertiser.
Public and Judicial Department: L/PJ/6 and L/PJ/12/series. The British Library, London.
Punch.
Putnam, Robert, D., *The Collapse and Revival of American Community* (New York: Simon & Schuster, 2000).
Radice, W., 'Letters from Europe', in K. Dutta and A. Robinson (eds), *Purabi – A Miscellany in Memory of Rabindranath Tagore, 1914–1991* (London: The Tagore Centre, 1991).
Ragaviah, P.J., *Pictures of England* (Madras, India: Ganz Brothers, 1876).
Rama Rau, Dhanvanthi, *An Inheritance: The Memoirs of Dhanvanthi Rama Rau* (London: Heinemann,1978).
Ramdin, Ron, *Reimagining Britain: 500 Years of Black and Asian History* (London: Pluto, 1999).
Ray, A.K., *Impressions of England* (Calcutta, India: New Arya Mission Press, 1905).
Ray, Renuka., *My Reminiscences: Social Development During the Gandhian Era and After* (New Delhi, India: Allied Publishers, 1982).
Revenue, Judicial, and Legislative Committee Minutes and Reports, The British Library, London.
Revenue, Judicial, and Legislative Committee References L/P&J/1 series, The British Library, London.

Ritchie, David (Chair), *One Oldham, One Future: Oldham Independent Review*, Government Office for the North West (Manchester, 2001).
Roopa Lekha, Quarterly Journal of the All India Fine Arts and Crafts Society.
Roy, Rammohun, *English Works*, ed. Jogendra Ghose (New Delhi, India: Cosmo, 1906).
——, *Exposition of the Practical Operation of the Judicial and Revenue Systems of India* (London: Smith Elder, 1832).
Sabrang Communications Private Limited and The South Asia Citizens Web, *The Foreign Exchange of Hate: IDRF and the American Funding of Hindutva* (2002).
Salter, Joseph, *Asiatic in England: Sketches of Sixteen Years' Work among Orientals* (London: Seely, Jackson, and Halliday, 1873).
——, *The East in the West* (London: S.W. Patridge,1896).
Scobie, Edward, *Black Britannia: A History of Blacks in Britain* (Chicago: Johnson Publishing Company, 1972).
Scott, A. F., *Every One a Witness* (London: White Lion, 1974).
Scriven, M. and Roberts, E., eds, 'Comedy and Ethnicity', in *Group Identities on French and British Television* (Oxford: Bergham, 2003), pp. 93–108.
Sen, Satadru, *Migrant Races: Empire, Identity and K.S. Ranjitsinhji* (Manchester: Manchester University Press, 2004).
Sen, Simonti (ed.), *Krishnabhabini Daser England Banga Mahila* (Calcutta, India: Stree, 1996).
——, *Travels to Europe: Self and Other in Bengali Travel Narratives, 1870–1910* (New Delhi, India: Longman Orient, 2004).
Sengupta Chowdhury, Indira, 'The Effeminate and the Masculine: Nationalism and the Concept of Race in Colonial Bengal', in Peter G. Robb (ed.), *Concepts of Race in South Asia* (New Delhi, India: Oxford University Press: 1995), pp. 282–303.
Seth, Vikram, *Two Lives* (London: Little Brown, 2005).
Shah, A.B. (ed.), *Letters and Correspondence of Pandita Ramabai* (Bombay, India: Maharashta State Board Literature and Culture, 1977).
Sharma, S., Hutnyk, J. and Sharma, A., eds, *Dis-Orienting Rhythms: The Politics of the New Asian Dance Music* (London: Zed Books, 1996).
Shaw, A., *A Pakistani Community in Britain* (Oxford, Blackwell, 1988).
Shipping Committee Minutes, The British Library, London.
Singh, Sikander, *Udham Singh, Alias, Ram Mohamed Singh Azad: A Saga of the Freedom Movement and Jallainwala Bagh* (Amritsar, India: Chattar Singh Jiwan Singh, 1998).
St Marylebone Parish Register, Greater London Record Office.
Standing Committee on the Hindu Sea-Voyage Question, *Hindu Sea-Voyage Movement in Bengal* (Calcutta, India: S.N. Banerjee, 1894).
Subrahmanyam, Sanjay, *Explorations in Connected History*, 2 vols (New Delhi, India: Oxford University Press, 2004).
Sussex Weekly Advertizer.
Sutton Court Collection, Mss Eur F.128 series, The British Library, London.
Symons, Edward William, *Law Relating to Merchant Seamen*, 3rd ed. (London: Longman, Brown, Green and Longmans, 1844).
Tabili, Laura, 'We Ask for British Justice', *Workers and Racial Difference in Late Imperial Britain* (Ithaca: Cornell University Press, 1994).
Tate Gallery, *George Stubbs* (London: Tate Gallery, 1984).
Tatla Darshan, S., *The Sikh Diaspora: The Search for Statehood* (London: UCL Press, 1999).
Taylor, Basil, 'George Stubbs's Painting of a Cheetah with Two Indians', in Philip Wilson and Annamaria MacDonald (eds), *Art at Auction 1969–70* (New York: Viking, 1970).
Thackery, William Makepeace, *The Newcomes* (London: Harper and Brothers, 1899).
Theatre Museum Collection, London.
The Times (London).

Tinsley, Jonathan and Jacobs, Michael, 'Deprivation and Ethnicity in England: A Regional Perspective' in *Regional Trends* 39 (2006).
Vanity Fair, Kumar Shri Ranjitsinhji, issue no. 1504 (London: n.d.).
Vertovec, Steve, 'Multiculturalism, Multi-Asian, Multi-Muslim Leicester: Dimensions of Social Complexity, Ethnic Organisation and Local Interface', in *Innovations*, vol. 7, no. 3, 1994, pp. 259–276.
Visram, Rozina, *Asians in Britain: 400 Years of History* (London: Pluto, 2002).
——, *Ayahs, Lascars and Princes* (London: Pluto, 1986).
Viswanathan, Gauri, *Outside the Fold: Conversion, Modernity, and Belief* (Princeton: Princeton University Press, 1998).
Wadia, Avabai, B., *The Light is Ours: Memoirs and Movements* (London: International Planned Parenthood Federation, 2001).
Walker, Richard, *Regency Portraits*, 2 vols (London: National Portrait Gallery, 1985).
Walter Lawrence collection, MSS EUR F 143/88, The British Library, London.
Watson, J.L. (ed.), *Between Two Cultures: Migrants and Minorities in Britain* (Oxford: Blackwell, 1977).
Wecter, Dixon, *Edmund Burke and His Kinsmen, a Study of the Statesman's Financial Integrity and Private Relationships* (Boulder: University of Colorado, 1939).
Weller, P., *Multi-Faith Directory* (Derby: University of Derby, 1997).
Werbner, Pnina, *Imagined Diasporas among Manchester Muslims* (London: James Currey, 2002), pp. 62, 258.
Westminster Poll Books, Westminster Archives Centre, London.
Westminster Ratebooks, Westminster Archives Centre, London.
Willis' Current Notes.
Young, Desmond, *Fountain of the Elephants* (New York: Harper and Brothers, 1959).
Zastoupil, Lynn, 'Defining Christians, Making Britons', *Victorian Studies*, vol. 44, no. 2, January 2002, pp. 215–243.

About the Authors

Michael H. Fisher, Robert S. Danforth Professor of History, Oberlin College, USA, teaches and writes about the early history of relations between Asians and Britons in Britain and Asia. His most recent books include: *Counterflows to Colonialism: Indian Travellers and Settlers in Britain, 1600–1857* (New Delhi: Permanent Black, 2004; Paperback edition, 2006); *The Travels of Dean Mahomet: An Eighteenth Century Journey through India* (edited) (Berkeley: University of California Press, 1997); and *Visions of Mughal India: An Anthology of European Travel Writing* (London: I.B. Tauris, 2007).

Shompa Lahiri is Harry Weinrebe Research Fellow at the Centre for the Study of Migration, Queen Mary, University of London. She is the author of *Indians in Britain: Anglo-Indian Encounters, Race and Identity, 1880–1930* (London: Frank Cass, 2000) and numerous journal articles and book chapters for both the academic and general reader. Her interdisciplinary teaching and research interests encompass aspects of British Imperial and Indian colonial history, cultural, post-colonial and feminist theory and colonial and post-colonial geography. She is currently working on a book entitled *Mobilities, Performances, Embodiments: South Asians in the West, 1900–1947*.

Shinder S. Thandi is currently Head of Department of Economics, Finance and Accounting at Coventry University and has teaching interests in the areas of development economics and international political economy. He has published widely in the area of Punjabi and Sikh migration and diaspora issues in the UK, especially on financial dimensions of diaspora–homeland relations. He is the founder editor of the *Journal of Punjab Studies* and has co-edited two books: *Punjabi Identity in a Global Context* [ed. with Pritam Singh] (New Delhi: Oxford University Press, 1999) and *People on the Move: Punjabi Colonial and Post Colonial Migration* [co-edited with Ian Talbot] (Karachi: Oxford University Press, 2004). He is currently working on a book entitled *The Sikh Diaspora: From Struggles to Celebration*.

Notes

Introduction

1. Ramdin, *Reimagining Britain: 500 Years of Black and Asian History* (Pluto: 1999), p. x. See, for example, Gundara and Duffield, *Essays on the History of Blacks in Britain* (Aldershot: 1992), p. 2. Gilroy, *'There Ain't no Black in the Union Jack': The Cultural Politics of Race and Nation* (University of Chicago Press: 1991). In contrast, Scobie blames Indian seamen for degrading the status of 'Blacks' by which he means African and African-Caribbean peoples. Scobie, *Black Britannia*, p. 64. Hall, S., 'Old and New Identities', in King (ed.), *Culture, Globilization and the World System* (University of Minnesota Press: 1991), pp. 41–68.

2. Ballard, R., 'The South Asian Presence', in Singh and Vertovec (eds), *Culture and Economy* (Routledge: 2002), p. 3. www.art.man.ac.uk/CASAS/pdfpapers/southasianbritain.pdf.

Chapter 1: Earliest South-Asian Visitors and Settlers during the Pre-colonial Period, *c.*1600–1750s

1. Evidence about these earliest Indians in England comes largely from the East India Company's own records, currently held in the British Library. Many of these are reprinted in Great England, Public Record Office, *Calendar of State Papers, Colonial Series*, vol. 2, ed. Sainsbury (Public Record Office: 1862).

2. In addition to the East India Company's records, evidence about Hawkins and his Indian wife comes from his journal, published as Hawkins, *Hawkins' Voyages*, ed. Markham (B. Franklin: 1970) and the Parish register of Saint Nicholas Acons Parish Church, 21 February 1613, Greater London Record Office.

3. He took the name Peter Pope (perhaps suggesting Catholic sympathies). Court Minutes 19 August 1614, 18 July 1615; Penny, *Church in Madras* (Smith, Elder: 1904), pp. 14–15; Neill, *Memoir of Rev. Patrick Copland* (Charles Scribner: 1871), pp. 11–14, 85; Das, 'Early Indian Visitors to England', *Calcutta Review,* 3rd series, 13 (1924), pp. 83–114.

4. John Dryden portrayed Mariam as 'Ysabinda', the heroine and victim of Dutch perfidy.

5. Wages are cited in various currencies of fluctuating values, so these figures are only estimates. See Court Minutes 14 April 1757 and L/MAR/B/series, passim, The British Library and Foster, *English Factories in India*, 13 vols (Clarendon Press: 1906–1927).

6. Chaudhuri, *English East India Company* (Frank Cass: 1965), p. 105.

7. The most crucial was Act 12, Car. 2, *c.*18 (1660). Parliament periodically modified these acts until largely repealing them in 1849 and 1854.

8. Court Minutes 1–8 November 1749, 6 December 1749.

9. Chaudhuri, *English East India Company*, p. 91.

10. Court Minutes 24 November 1714.

11. *Annual Register* 12–17 September 1769, Chronicle, p. 131.

12. Act 55 Geo. 3, *c.*116 (1814–1815). Great Britain, Parliamentary Papers, *Returns (Commons)*, 1814–1815, vol. 3, paper 471, pp. 217–229.

13. See Court Minutes 19 April 1706 to 15 February 1721.

14. Court Minutes 2–21 January 1713.

15. *Times* 9 December 1814; *Morning Chronicle* 30 November 1785, 1 December 1785.

16. Court Minutes 29 March 1693. But payments varied widely, see L/MAR/B/series, passim, The British Library.

17. Public Record Office, *Calendar*, vol. 7, p. xliii. See also Feilding, *Royalist Father and Roundhead Son* (Methuen & Co.: 1915), p. 77.

18. Court Letters 4 May 1683 cited in Hedges, *Diary*, ed. Yule (Hakluyt Society: 1888), vol. 2, p. ccclvii.

19. See Barber, *Celebrating the Black Presence*, vol. 2, *Hidden Lives* (Westminster Archives Centre: 2000), pp. 25–34.

20. *Flying Post* 11–14 July 1702 cited in Scott, *Every One a Witness* (White Lion: 1974), pp. 231–232.

21. For this case, see Court Minutes 21 February 1721 to 9 February 1726.

22. See Fisher, *Counterflows to Colonialism* (Permanent Black: 2006), pp. 82–84.

Chapter 2: South-Asian Arrivals during Early Colonialism, 1750s–1790s

1. See Subrahmanyam, *Explorations in Connected History*, 2 vols (Oxford University Press: 2004).

2. Court of Directors' letter 17 March 1769, National Archives of India, *Fort William* (National Archives of India: 1949), vol. 5, p. 186.

3. *Public Advertiser* 2 December 1786. Emphasis in original.

4. *Public Advertiser* 5 December 1786.

5. Home Public Consultations 5 January 1798, no. 55, Extract Proceedings of Military Department 22 December 1797, National Archives of India.

6. *London Magazine* (November 1759), p. 603; *Annual Register* (1759), Chronicle, p. 119; Court of Directors' correspondence, E/4/42, E/4/617, The British Library. See also Hahn, *Tower Menagerie* (Simon and Schuster: 2003), p. 183.

7. Court Minutes 21 September 1763, 31 October 1764.

8. Archer, *India and British Portraiture, 1770–1825* (Sotheby Parke Bernet: 1979), p. 413; George Clutton, 'Cheetah and the Stag', *Burlington Magazine*, 112 (1970), pp. 539–540; Tate Gallery, *George Stubbs* (Tate Gallery: 1984), pp. 79–80; Taylor, 'George Stubbs's Painting of a Cheetah with Two Indians', in Wilson and MacDonald (eds) *Art at Auction* 1969–70 (Viking: 1970).

9. *Proceedings of the Old Bailey* 27 February 1765.

10. *Morning Chronicle* 30 November 1785, 1 December 1785; Court Minutes 25 February 1761, 20 June 1764.

11. *Proceedings of the Old Bailey* 14 September 1785.

12. Marine Department, L/MAR/C.902, The British Library.

13. E.g., *Public Advertiser* 16 March 1785, 6–21 December 1785.

14. *Public Advertiser* 5–12 January 1786, 3 January 1787; *Morning Chronicle* 28 January 1786.

15. Braidwood, *Black Poor and White Philanthropists* (Liverpool University Press: 1994), pp. 32 ff.

16. See Fisher, *First Indian Author in English* (Oxford University Press: 1996) and Mahomet, *Travels of Dean Mahomet*, ed. Fisher (University of California Press: 1997).

17. Khan, 'Masir Talibi fi Bilad Afranji', Persian Add. 8145–8147, 97 ff., The British Library.

18. Khan, *Masir Talibi fi Bilad Afranji*, Persian reprint ed. Khadive-Jam (Hosein Khadive-Jam: 1983); Mir Muhammad Husain, 'Risalah-i Ahwal-i Mulk-i Farang', Maulana Azad Library, Aligarh; Khan, *Indian Muslim Perceptions of the West during the Eighteenth Century* (Oxford University Press: 1998).

19. Khan, *Travels of Mirza Abu Taleb*, trans. Stewart (Longman, Hurst, Rees, and Orme: 1810).

20. Khan, *Masir*, Reprint, p. 64.

21. Khan, *Masir*, Reprint, pp. 109–110.

22. Khan, *Poems of Mirza Abu Talib Khan*, trans. Swinton (Author: 1807); Khan, *Masir*, Reprint, pp. 124, 139; Warren Hastings Papers, Add. 39884–39885, The British Library.

23. Khan, *Masir*, Reprint, pp. 253–254.

24. Gash, *Lord Liverpool: The Life and Political Career of Robert Banks Jenkinson, Second Earl of Liverpool, 1770–1828* (Harvard University Press: 1984), p. 10.

25. Khan, *Masir*, Reprint, p. 173.

26. Her name is given as Zarphanisa Khanem (1758–1822) in http://worldroots.com/brigitte/royal/crommelin/jacquescolteedesc1680.htm; see also www.starcourse.org/emd/emdwho.htm.

27. de Boigne, *Memoirs*, ed. de Morsier-Kotthaus (Museum Press: 1956); Compton, *Particular Account of the European Military Adventurers in India* (Fisher Unwin: 1893); Cotton, 'Begum in Sussex', *Bengal Past and Present*, 46 (1933), pp. 91–94; Young, *Fountain of the Elephants* (Harper Collins and Brothers: 1959).

28. Baldwin, *Story of the Forest*, 2nd edn (St Savior's Church: 1985), pp. 19–22; Boye, ed., *L'Extraordinaire Aventure de Benoit de Boigne aux Indes* (Echanges Culturels et Actions de Development: 1996), p. 149; Llewellyn-Jones, *Engaging Scoundrels* (Oxford University Press: 2000), pp. 89–90, 121–122. Family records of de Boigne, personal communication, William Dalrymple, 20 June 2001.

29. See Khan, *Travels*, trans. Stewart. See the reference to Abu Talib's 'Vindication' in anonymous review of Karim Khan, 'Siyahat Namah' (1841), *Blackwood's Edinburgh Magazine*, vol. 54, no. 338 (December 1843), p. 762.

30. Shah Alam to King of Great Britain, Sutton Court Collection, MSS EUR F.128/111, 100 ff., The British Library.

31. His Persian manuscript is OR 200, The British Library. For a partial translation, see I'tisam al-Daula, *Shigurf Namah-i Velaet*, trans. and ed. Alexander, assisted by Munshi Shumsher Khan (Parbury, Allen; 1827). For a full translation (via Bengali), see I'tisam al-Daula, *Wonders of Vilayat*, trans. Haq (Peepal Tree Press: 2001). See also Khan, *Indian Muslim*, pp. 72–78.

32. Lambert, *House of Commons* (Scholarly Resources: 1975), vol. 135, pp. 546–549; vol. 138, p. 124; Impey, *Memoirs* (Simpkin, Marshall: 1846), p. 237. He converted to Christianity as Robert Goneshamdass.

33. Lambert, *House of Commons*, vol. 138, pp. 39–40.

34. George III, *Correspondence*, ed. Fortescue (Macmillan: 1927–1928), vol. 5, pp. 260–261.

35. Burke, *Correspondence*, ed. Copeland (Cambridge University Press: 1958–1978), vol. 4, pp. 367–372.

36. After returning to India, Hanumantrao reportedly purified himself by passing through a pure gold *yoni* (symbolising rebirth). Parasnis, 'Original Correspondence between the English and the Marathas', *Indian Historical Record Commission, Proceedings*, vol. 5 (1923), pp. 94–95. See also 'Standing Committee on the Hindu Sea-Voyage Question', *Hindu Sea-Voyage Movement in Bengal* (S.N. Banerjee: 1894), pp. 36–37.

37. He himself used Odudeen as his name although some called him 'Ahid al-Din Khan'. Court Minutes 5 February 1794 to 22 April 1795; Personal Records O/6/8, 53 ff., The British Library. See also Bombay, Public and Secret and Political Diaries, 1794–1816, Maharashtra State Archives; Log of Sir Edward Hughes, L/MAR/B/354C, The British Library.

38. Khan, *Masir*, Reprint, p. 151.

Chapter 3: Widening and Deepening of the South-Asian Presence in Britain, 1790s–1830s

1. For his life, see Hickey, *Memoirs*, 3rd edn, ed. Spencer (Hurst and Blackett: 1919–1925), vol. 4.

2. Hickey, *Memoirs*, vol. 4, pp. 405–406.

3. Hickey, *Memoirs*, vol. 4, p. 467.

4. See Burke, *Correspondence*, ed. Copeland (Cambridge: Cambridge University Press, 1958–1978), vol. 9, p. 87; Magnus, *Edmund Burke* (John Murray: 1939), p. 288; William Burke, Will (13 October 1795) in Wecter, *Edmund Burke and His Kinsmen* (University of Colorado: 1939), p. 94.

5. Hickey, *Memoirs*, vol. 4, p. 473; *Beaconsfield Parish Register*, 27 February 1809.

6. Beaconsfield Parish Church, *Baptismal Records*, 27 February 1814.

7. At 19 Manchester Building, Parliament Street. Boyle, *Court Guide* (Saunders and Otley: 1818); Westminster Ratebook (1818) and Westminster Poll Book (1820), Westminster Archives Centre.

8. *Catalogue of the Royal Academy Exhibitions*, 1819, no. 245; *Times* 27 April 1820. See Walker, *Regency Portraits* (National Portrait Gallery: 1985), vol. 1, p. 249, vol. 2, p. 574.

9. William Munnew, born 10 December 1820, christened 5 January 1821, St Mary Magdaline, Richmond, Surrey, *International Genealogical Index*.

10. Burial certificate, St John Evangelist, Smith Square, 10 February 1827, Westminster Archives Centre.

11. See Fisher, *First Indian Author in English*. I thank Professor Stewart Cameron and Dr Rozina Visram for additional information about Dean Mahomed's family and descendants.

12. Charles Street has been built over, but a Japanese Restaurant, Yumi, currently stands near the site.

13. See Anonymous, *Epicure's Almanack* (Longman, Hurst, Rees, Orme, and Brown: 1815), pp. 123–124; Khan, *Travels*, trans. Stewart (1814 edn), 1:124, footnote.

14. *Times* 27 March 1811.

15. Anonymous, *Epicure's Almanack*, pp. 123–124.

16. Anonymous, *Epicure's Almanack*, pp. 123–124.

17. Docket Book B.4.31 (18 March 1812), National Archives, London.

18. Dean Mahomed later had this servant arrested for stealing a hooka and tobacco. *Proceedings of the Old Bailey* 13 May 1812.

19. *Times* 20 April 1813.

20. See *Brighton Gazette*, *Brighton Herald*, and *Sussex Weekly Advertizer*.

21. Mahomed, *Shampooing* (Author: 1822; 1826; 1838).

22. E.g., Deenshah Firamgee, probably a Parsi from Bombay, approved of the cure. Mahomed's Visitors' Book (*c.* January 1827), Brighton Reference Library. D.O. Dyce Sombre, M.P. (see Chapter IV), left a £1,000 tip in his will (but this was disallowed on grounds of insanity).

23. Brighton, East Sussex, and Sussex Poll Books 1820–1847, Institute of Historical Research, London.

24. E.g., *Brighton Gazette* 27 December 1821, 28 March 1822, 4 April 1822.

25. *Brighton Gazette* 25 September 1823.

26. Mahomed, *Shampooing* (1826), pp. viii, 17.

27. E.g., *Brighton Herald* 18 October 1845.

28. *Gentleman's Magazine* (April 1851), p. 444; *Willis' Current Notes* (March 1851), pp. 22–23; *Brighton Guardian* 26–27 February 1851.

29. *Times* 18 June 1836.

30. *Times* 27–30 March 1844.

31. *Brighton Herald* 6 July 1839; *Times* 9 April 1862.

32. *Times* 7 November 1902.

33. Court letter to Mrs Meer Hassan Ali, 14 May 1832, Miscellanious Sent, E/1/268; Court Minutes 16 November 1831. An Indian diplomat then in London critiqued her assertions about gender. Khan, *Siyahatnama*, MSS OR 2163, 277 ff., The British Library.

34. For Rammohun Roy see: HMS 708, The British Library; Banerjee, *Rajah Rammohun Roy's Mission to England* (N.M. Raychowdhury: 1926); Carpenter, *Last Days in England of the Rajah Rammohun Roy* (Trubner: 1866); Roy, *English Works*, ed. Ghose (Cosmo: 1906); Zastoupil, 'Defining Christians, Making Britons', *Victorian Studies*, vol. 44, no. 2 (January 2002), pp. 215–243.

35. Roy, *Exposition of the Practical Operation of the Judicial and Revenue Systems of India* (Smith, Elder: 1832), p. x.

36. HMS 708.

37. James Sutherland in *Indian Gazette* 18 February 1834 cited in Collet, *Life and Letters of Raja Rammohun Roy* (Harold Collet: 1900), p. 128.

38. Zastoupil, 'Defining', p. 216.

39. Roy, *Exposition*, p. x.

40. Collet, *Life*, p. 130.

41. Thackery, *Newcomes* (Harper and Brothers: 1899), pp. 78–80.

42. HMS 708; Court Minutes 21 June 1831.

43. HMS 708.

44. Roy letter to William Rathbone 31 July 1832 in Carpenter, *Last Days*, p. 54.

45. Miscellaneous Letters Received E/1/181–183; Court Minutes; HMS 708. See Philips, *East India Company* (Manchester University Press: 1940), especially pp. 276 ff.

46. *Times* 30 September 1833; Strachey letter 12 October 1833, Elphinstone Papers F.88/85; [unnamed newspaper clipping] 12 October 1833, MSS EUR B.399, The British Library.

47. Miscellaneous Letters Received E/1/182, vol. 4; Correspondence Committee Minutes 3 October 1832, The British Library. Collet misidentifies him as Roy's 'cook'. Collet, *Life*, p. 116.

48. Hunter, *Essay on the Diseases Incident to Indian Seamen, or Lascars* (Company's Press: 1804); Lascar Papers, vol. 1, 90 ff., The British Library.

49. Not all of these lascars were Indian, although they tended collectively to be regarded as such. Lascar Papers and Parliamentary Papers, *Returns* (Commons), 1823, vol. 17, paper 491, pp. 149–156.

50. Court Minutes 31 October 1798; Commons debate (25 November 1801), Cobbett, *Parliamentary History of England* (Hansard: 1820), vol. 36, pp. 288–302.

51. Shipping Committee Minutes 29 October 1813 to 14 March 1821, The British Library.

52. *Annual Register* (1784–1785), Chronicle, pp. 242–243.

53. Lascar Papers, vol. 1, 120–121.

54. Lascar Papers, vol. 1, 76 ff., 104–111, 122.

55. Lascar Papers, vol. 1, 76 ff., 95–102.

56. For these incidents, see *Times* 6 October 1803, 15 October 1805, 26 November 1805, 7 October 1806; *Annual Register* (1806), Chronicle, pp. 450–451 and (1808), Chronicle, p. 13; Shipping Committee Minutes 14 July 1813, 31 August 1813.

57. Shipping Committee Minutes 8 December 1813.

58. Shipping Committee Minutes 15 December 1813.

59. *Annual Register* (1805), Chronicle, p. 376.

60. Correspondence Committee Minutes 15 June 1814.

61. 55 George 3 (1815), *c.*116, section 8.

62. 4 George 4 (1823), *c.*80, section 31.

Chapter 4: South-Asian Settlers and Transient Networks and Communities in Britain, 1830s–1857

1. Lutfullah, *Autobiography*, eds. Eastwick and Tirmizi (International Writer's Emporium: 1987 reprint), pp. 387, 398, 413, 421.

2. See Metcalf, *Ideologies of the Raj* (Cambridge University Press: 1995).

3. Sources on Jamh ood-Deen include: Board Collections F/4/1523, 1531, The British Library; Court Minutes; *Times* 29 April 1843.

4. Hobhouse letter 29 March 1837, Broughton Papers, MSS EUR F.213/6, The British Library.

5. Hobhouse letter 30 August 1837, Broughton Papers, MSS EUR F.213/6, The British Library.

6. Hobhouse to Auckland 4 November 1839, Broughton Papers, MSS EUR F.213/7, The British Library.

7. Khan, *Siyahatnama*.

8. See my forthcoming biography of D.O. Dyce Sombre.

9. Several wrote books about their experiences including Mohan Lal, Mir Shahamat Ali and Mirza Ali Ackbar Khan Bahadur. See Fisher, *Counterflows to Colonialism* (Permanent Black: 2004), Chapters 8–9.

10. Syed Abdoollah letter 26 November 1851, L/F/2/147, The British Library.

11. Revenue, Judicial and Legislative Committee References L/P&J/1/64, no. 235a, The British Library.

12. Bishop of London, Marriage Allegations 13 December 1852, Guildhall Library, London.

13. Syed Abdoollah letter 28 June 1853, L/P&J/1/64, no. 235a, The British Library.

14. Court Minutes 28 June 1853.

15. Syed Abdoollah letter 5 September 1855, Miscellaneous Letters Received, E/1/192, 296–297, The British Library.

16. Foreign Political Correspondence 11 March 1859, nos 862–867, National Archives of India, New Delhi.

17. Syed Abdoollah letter 27 August 1856 and reply 28 August 1856, Elphinstone Papers, F.88/175, The British Library. See also Journal of Elphinstone, F.88/14, The British Library.

18. Bellot, *University College London* (University of London Press: 1929), Chart 2.

19. Sources on the Palowkars include: 'Petition of Aboo Syed' 17 February 1834, Miscellaneous Letters Received, E/1/186, fol. 60 ff.; Board Collections F/4/1371; Court Minutes; Revenue, Judicial, and Legislative Committee Minutes and Reports, The British Library.

20. Court Minutes 23 April 1834, 14 May 1834.

21. Court Minutes 11 June 1834.

22. St Leonard's Shoreditch Parish marriage records 10 February 1835, Guildhall Library, London.

23. *East India Yearbook* has Sumsoodeen Pallowkar as a merchant in Bombay at least from 1845 to 1866. Personal communication from a descendant, David Wilson, 2 May 2002.

24. Although he declared bankruptcy in 1834, he apparently recovered, dying as a master tobacconist. *Times* 4–8 November 1843. However, two sons, William John Fox Palowkar (*b.*1836), a clerk, and Mohamed Frederick Palowkar (1848–*c.*1914), a hatter, both declared bankruptcy, the latter emigrating to Australia. *Times* 21 January 1865, 15 November 1880, 20 July 1881, 13 June 1881. See also Visram, *Asians*, pp. 85, 172 and personal communication 18 September 2002.

25. Jeanne Shirley Palowkar explains '... the family now is fair skinned and blue eyed'. http://familytreemaker.genealogy.com/users/p/a/l/Jeanne-Shirley-Palowkar/ index.html.

26. Lutfullah, *Autobiography*, p. 423, cf. p. 415; Court Minutes 12 August 1857.

27. See Brown, 'Indian Students in Britain', *Edinburgh Review*, vol. 217, no. 443 (January 1913), pp. 138–156; Lahiri, *Indians in Britain* (Frank Cass: 2000), p. 3; Court Minutes; Revenue, Judicial and Legislative Committee References L/P&J1/39–52, 68; Political and Military References Memoranda, The British Library; *Times* 2 May 1845.

28. Chuckerbutty letter 26 February 1850, Miscellaneous Letters Received E/1/190, 110–111, The British Library. Chuckerbutty, 'Present State of the Medical Profession in Bengal', *British Medical Journal* (23, 30 July 1864), pp. 86–88, 109–112.

29. Goodeve letter 31 December 1846, Revenue, Judicial and Legislative Committee, L/P&J1/45, The British Library.

30. Mozoomdar letter 16 August 1847, Finance and Home Committee Papers, L/F/2/111, The British Library.

31. See Lahiri, *Indians in Britain* (Frank Cass: 2000); Viswanathan, *Outside the Fold* (Princeton University Press: 1998); Burton, *At the Heart of the Empire* (University of California Press: 1998).

32. See *Bombay Times* 2 October 1841, 19 January 1842, 17 December 1842; *Friend of India* 6 January 1841; *India News* 10 October 1842; *Times* 1 August 1842; Kling, *Partner in Empire* (Firma KLM: 1976), especially pp. 168–175; Mittra, *Memoir of Dwarkanath Tagore* (Thacker: 1870); Carpenter, *Last Days* (Trubner: 1866), pp. 130–131.

33. Commons debate (3 March 1842), *Parliamentary Debates*, ed. Hansard (Hansard: 1812–), series 3, vol. 60, p. 1377. For treatment of lascars, see, e.g., *Times* 20 November 1843.

34. Act 7 and 8 Victoria, *c*.112. See also Act 17 and 18 Victoria, c. 120. Symons, *Law Relating to Merchant Seamen*, 3rd edn (Longman, Brown, Green, and Longmans: 1844), p. 153; Hansard, *Parliamentary Debates*, series 3, vol. 76, passim; *Times* 10 June 1852.

35. Lords debate (8 April 1853), Hansard, *Parliamentary Debates*, series 3, vol. 125, pp. 791–802; Palmer, *Politics, Shipping and the Repeal of the Navigation Laws* (Manchester University Press: 1990); Shipping Committee Minutes 1 June 1821. The opposition of British seamen to Indians would continue. See Balachandran, 'Circulation through Seafaring: Indian Seamen, 1890–1945', in Markovits, Jacques Pouchepadass, and Subrahmanyam (eds), *Society and Circulation* (Permanent Black: 2003), pp. 89–130; Dixon, 'Lascars: The Forgotten Seamen', in Ommer and Panting (eds), *Working Men Who Got Wet* (Memorial University: 1980), pp. 265–281; Tabili, *We Ask for British Justice* (Cornell University Press: 1994).

36. In 1855, Colonel Hughes estimated 10,000–12,000 lascars served the British merchant fleet, with 5,000–6,000 reaching Britain annually, of whom 3,000–3,600 were Indians. Cited in Visram, *Ayahs* (Pluto: 1986), p. 52.

37. *Times* 7 June 1852, 23 June 1852.

38. *Times* 10 June 1852.

39. *Times* 21 June 1852.

40. Hughes Letter 24 January 1879, Political Department Home Correspondence, L/P&J/2/59; Foreign Political Correspondence 1 May 1857, National Archives of India; *Illustrated London News*, vol. 56 (1870), pp. 253–254; Court Minutes 14 November 1855 to 10 March 1858; Salter, *Asiatic in England* (Seely, Jackson, and Halliday: 1873), pp. 6–7, 66 ff.; *Times* 20 November 1855. The Home continued until 1927. See Act 18 and 19 Victoria, *c*.91.

41. Ali Morad letter to Court 6 July 1857 and reply 19 August 1857, Political Department Home Correspondence, L/PS/3/108, The British Library.

42. Parliamentary Papers, *Returns* (Commons) 1859(I) vol. 18, paper 125, pp. 73 ff.

43. Ali Ackbar letter to Court 9 September 1857, Political Department Home Correspondence, L/PS/3/108, The British Library; Lutfullah, *Azimullah Khan Yusufzai* (Mohamedali Educational Society: 1970), pp. 6, 31; Basu, *Story of Satara*, ed. Chatterjee (Modern Review Office: 1922), p. 142.

Chapter 5: Indian Victorians, 1857–1901

1. J. Salter, *The East in the West* (S.W. Patridge: 1896), p. 52.

2. Salter (1896), p. 20.

3. *Illustrated London News* 28 February 1857.

4. Visram, Rozina, *Asians in Britain: 400 Years of History* (Pluto: 2002), p. 60.

5. P.J. Ragaviah, *Pictures of England* (Ganz Brothers: 1876), p. 61.

6. J. Salter, *The Asiatic in England: Sketches of Sixteen Years Work among Orientals* (S.W. Partridge: 1873), p. 161.

7. J. Majeed, 'Bathos, Architecture and Knowing India: E.M. Forster's *A Passage to India* and Nineteenth-Century British Ethnology and the Romance Quest', *Journal of Commonwealth Literature*, vol. 40, no. 1, p. 29.

8. R.H. Lindeborg, 'The "Asiatic" and the Boundaries of Victorian Englishness', *Victorian Studies*, Spring 1994, p. 391.

9. H. Mayhew, *London Labour and the London Poor* (C.Griffin: 1861), p. 440.

10. Lindeborg (1994), p. 402.

11. Salter (1873), p. 260.

12. See S. Lahiri, 'Patterns of Resistance: Indian Seamen in Britain', in Kershen (ed.), *Language, Labour and Migration* (Ashgate: 2000), pp.155–178.

13. Salter (1873), p.29.

14. H. Ansari, *The Infidel Within: Muslims in Britain since* 1800 (C. Hurst and Co.: 2004), p. 126.

15. See H. Das, 'Early Indian Visitors to England', *The Calcutta Review*, vol. 13, October 1924, pp. 83–114.

16. H. Das, *Life and Letters of Toru Dutt* (Oxford University Press: 1920), p. 41.

17. A. Burton, *At the Heart of Empire: Indians and the Colonial Encounter in Late Victorian Britain* (University of California Press: 1998), p. 144.

18. A.B. Shah (ed.), *Letters and Correspondence of Pandita Ramabai* (Maharashta State Board Literature and Culture: 1977), p. 59.

19. Burton (1998), pp. 50–51.

20. The British Library: R/1/1/221.

21. S. Devi, *Autobiography of an Indian Princess* (John Murray: 1921), p. 108.

22. See S. Lahiri, 'British Policy towards Indian Princes in Late-Nineteenth and Early Twentieth-Century Britain', *Immigrants and Minorities*, vol. 15, no. 3, November 1996, pp. 214–232.

23. See S. Sen, *Migrant Races: Empire, Identity and K.S. Ranjitsinhji* (Manchester University Press: 2004).

24. Salter (1896), p. 14.

25. Salter (1896), p. 24.

26. Salter (1873), p. 51.

27. Salter (1873), p. 69.

28. Salter (1896), p. 115.

29. Visram (2002), pp. 50–51.

30. The British Library: L/P&J/6/395, 608–609, 16 April 1895.

31. Salter (1873), pp. 66–67. See also Abdoolah's letters to *The Times* 28/6/1859 9f, 25/10/1859 6e, 17/1/1860 9a, 15/11/1860 7f, 15/8/1862 4c, 28/2/1865 12f.

32. Syed Abdoollah letter 17/1/1869 and replies 27/1/1869, 16/2/1869, L/P&J/2/49, The British Library.

33. Mayhew (1861), p. 424.

34. Mayhew (1861), vol. 3, p. 189.

35. See I. Sengupta Chowdhury, 'The Effeminate and the Masculine: Nationalism and the Concept of Race in Colonial Bengal', in Robb (ed.), *Concepts of Race in South Asia* (Oxford University Press: 1995), pp. 282–303; Dutt, H., *Lieutenant Suresh Biswas: His Life and Adventures* (P.C. Dass: 1900).

36. See S. Lahiri, *Indians in Britian: Anglo-Indian Encounters, Race and Identity,* 1880–1930 (Frank Cass: 2000), pp. 65–71 and G. Murshid (ed.), *The Heart of a Rebel Poet: Letters of Michael Madhusudan Dutt* (Oxford University Press: 2004), pp. 185–275.

37. S. Mathur, 'Living Exhibits: The Case of 1886', *Cultural Anthropology*, vol. 15, no. 4, November 2000, pp. 492–524.

38. The British Library: L/P&J/6/417, 15 March 1886.

39. The British Library: L/PJ/6/271.

40. Mayhew (1861), vol. 3, p. 189.

41. S. Anand, *Indian Sahib: Queen Victoria's Dear Abdul* (Duckwoth: 1996), p. 8.

42. The British Library: L/P&S/8/61, October 1896, Minute by the Munshi.

43. British Indian Association (Aligarh) *Supplement to the Bylaws of British Indian Association N.W.P, Relative to the Department for Encouraging Travel to Europe* (Syed Ahmed: 1869).

44. *Allahabad Review* April 1890, vol. 1, no. 1.

45. Mathur (2000), p. 512.

46. S. Sen, (ed.), *Krishnabhabini Daser Englande Banga Mahila* (Stree: 1996), pp. 39–40. See also Sen, S. *Travels to Europe: Self and Other in Bengali Travel Narratives, 1870–1910* (Longman Orient: 2004).

47. A. Burton, 'Making a Spectacle of Empire: Indian Travellers in Fin-de-Siecle London', *History Workshop Journal*, 42, 1996, p. 11.

48. T.N. Mukharji, *A Visit to Europe* (W. Newman: 1889), p. 60.

49. R.C. Dutt, *Three Years in Europe: Extracts from Letters Sent by a Hindu*, 2nd edn (S.K. Lahiri & Co.: 1873), pp. 13–15.

50. G. Murshid, *Reluctant Debutant: Responses of Bengali Women to Modernisation, 1849–1905* (Rajshasi University: 1983), p. 86.

51. Das (1920), p. 63.

52. I. Grewal, *Home and Harem, Nation, Gender, Empire and Cultures of Travel* (University of Leicester: 1996), p. 173.

53. G.K. Mookerjee, *The Indian Image of Nineteenth Century Europe* (Asia publishing House: 1967), p. 42.

54. B.M. Malabari, *The Indian Eye on English Life* (Apollo Printing works: 1895), p. 85.

55. L. Baijnath, *England and India* (J.B. Karani: 1893), p. 107.

56. Mukharji (1889), p. 154.

57. B.C. Pal, *Memories of My Life and Times*, vol. 1, 1886–1900 (Yugayatri Prakashak: 1951), p. 237.

58. *Calcutta Review*, vol. 32, January, 1888, p. xxiv.

59. *Calcutta Review*, pp. xxii–xxiii.

60. Mukharji (1889), p. 175.

61. *Calcutta Review*, vol. 32, January, 1888, p. xxiv.

62. W. Radice, 'Letters from Europe', in Dutta and Robinson (eds), *Purabi – A Miscellany in Memory of Rabindranath Tagore, 1914–1991* (The Tagore Centre: 1991), p. 45.

63. Ragaviah (1876), p. 113.

64. A.K. Ray, *Impressions of England* (New Arya Mission Press: 1905), pp. 160–161.

65. Mathur (2000), pp. 501–504.

66. Mukharji (1889), pp. 103–104.

67. Burton (1996), p. 142.

68. A. Burton, 'From Child Bride to "Hindoo Lady" Rukhmabai and the Debate on Sexual Respectability in Imperial Britain' *The American Historical Review*, vol. 103, no. 4, October 1998, pp. 1119–1146.

69. See Lahiri (2000), pp. 92–95.

70. *Punch* (16 April 1870), p. 155.

71. M. Borthwick, *Keshub Chandra Sen: A Search for Cultural Synthesis* (Minerva: 1777), p. 100.

72. See Chandra Sudhir, *Enslaved Daughter: Colonialism, Law and Women's Rights* (Oxford University Press: 1998).

73. L. Martindale, *A Woman Surgeon: Louisa Martindale* (Victor Gollancz: 1951), p. 33.

74. He also lectured at University College, London. See Chapter 4.

75. For a discussion of the issues raised by the 'Black man debate' see A. Burton, 'Tongues Untied: Lord Salisbury's "Black Man" and the Boundaries of Imperial Democracy', *Comparative Studies in Society and History*, vol. 42, no. 3, July 2000, pp. 632–661.

76. Janaki Agnes Penelope Majumdar (edited and with an introduction by Antoinette Burton), *Family History* (Oxford University Press: 2003), p. 45.

77. Majumdar (2003), pp. 73–74.

78. The Bonnerjee women were prohibited from wearing saris by Womesh Chandra Bonnerjee, as they were viewed in some quarters as disreputable. Majumdar (2003), p. 130.

79. Majumdar (2003), p. 79.

80. A. Burton, *Dwelling in the Archives: Women Writing House, Home and History in Late Colonial India* (Oxford University Press: 2003), p. 53.

81. Majumdar (2003), p. 53.

Chapter 6: From Empire to Decolonisation, 1901–1947

1. Visram, Rozina, *Asians in Britain: 400 Years of History* (Pluto: 2002), p. 44.

2. S. Lahiri, *Indians in Britain: Anglo-Indian Encounters, Race and Identity, 1880–1930* (Frank Cass: 2000), p. 14.

3. See Lahiri (2000), pp. 123–132.

4. *Committee on Distressed Colonial and Indian Subjects*, CD 5133 and 5134 (22) 1910.

5. National Archives, Kew: WO 32/5110 Report of Sir Walter Lawrence on Indian Hospitals 21/7/1915.

6. D. Ommisi (ed.), *Indian Voices of the Great War. Soldiers Letters, 1914–18* (Macmillan Press: 1999), p. 13.

7. Visram (2002), p. 182.

8. M.K. Gandhi, *An Autobiography or My Story of My Experiments with Truth* (Penguin books: 1982), p. 318.

9. See Theatre Museum Collection, London, for programmes of performances.

10. S. Basu, *Spy Princess: The Life of Noor Inayat Khan* (Sutton Publishing: 2006), p. 8.

11. National Archives, Kew WO 32/5110 Report of Sir Walter Lawrence on Indian Hospitals. 15/2/1915.

12. Ibid.

13. The British Library: MSS EUR F 143/88.

14. L. Tabili, *We Ask for British Justice: Workers and Racial Difference in Late imperial Britain* (Cornell University Press: 1994), p. 29.

15. Ibid., p. 122.

16. The British Library: L/PJ/12/373, p. 38.

17. http://www.movinghere.org.uk.

18. The British Library: L/E/9/962.

19. Ibid.

20. J. Callaghan, *Rajani Palme Dutt: A Study in British Stalinism* (Lawrence and Wishhart: 1993).

21. http://www.ganashakti.com.

22. IOR: L/PJ/12/160.

23. Visram (2002), pp. 164–168. P. Bance, *The Duleep Singhs: The Photographic Album of Queen Victoria's Maharaja* (Sutton: 2004).

24. G. Forbes, *Women in Modern India* (Cambridge University Press, 1996), p. 97.

25. The British Library: Mss.Eur 341/147. M. Lam, *Autumn Leaves, Some Memories of Yesterday*. Unpublished manuscript.

26. R. Ray, *My Reminiscences: Social Development During the Gandhian Era and After* (Allied Publishers: 1982), p. 9.

27. A.B. Wadia, *The Light is Ours: Memoirs and Movements* (International Planned Parenthood Federation: 2001), p. 32.

28. Ibid., p. 30.
29. Ibid., p. 59.
30. Ibid., p. 32.
31. D. Rama Rau, *An Inheritance: The Memoirs of Dhanvanthi Rama Rau* (Heinemann: 1978).
32. Ibid., p. 169.
33. Ibid., pp. 31–32.
34. *Roopa Lekha*, Quarterly Journal of the All India Fine Arts and Crafts Society, vol. 4, no. 13, 1934.
35. See Theatre Museum Collection, London for programme of performance.
36. Brinda, Maharani of Kapurthala (As told to Elaine Williams) *Maharani: The Story of an Indian Princess* (Henry Holt and Company: 1953), p. 245.
37. R. Collier, *Make Believe: The Magic of International Theatre* (Dodd, Mead and Company: 1986).
38. *The Indian: At home and Abroad*, vol. 1, no. 1, October 1934, p. 8.
39. The British Library: L/PJ/12//256.
40. S. Lahiri, 'Uncovering Britain's South Asian Past: The Case of George Edalji', *Immigrants and Minorities*, vol. 17, no. 3, November 1998.
41. *Modern Review*, vol. 27, no. 5, May 1920.
42. Majumdar Janaki, Agnes Penelope (edited and with an introduction by Antoinette Burton) *Family History* (Oxford University Press: 2003), p. 132.
43. http://www.movinghere.org.uk.
44. *The Oriental Post*, 15th November 1938.
45. The British Library: L/PJ/12/497.
46. *The Indian: At Home and Overseas*, vol. 2, no. 3, March 1951.
47. Visram (2002), p. 348.
48. Seth, V., *Two Lives* (Little Brown: 2005).
49. The British Library: L/P&J/12/645, File on IWA, p. 29, 14-4-42.
50. Rama Rau (1978), p. 184.
51. Bance (2004), pp. 124–125.
52. The British Library: L/P&J/12/478.
53. Ibid.
54. S. Singh, *Udham Singh, Alias, Ram Mohamed Singh Azad: A Saga of the Freedom Movement and Jallianwala Bagh* (Chattar Singh Jiwan Singh: 1998).
55. The British Library: L/I/E/1/785, p. 66.
56. The British Library: L/I/1/785.
57. Email from Vijaya Deo 23/3/2006.
58. *The Listener* vol. 30, 12 January 1941, p. 174.
59. The British Library: L/I/1/785.
60. *London Calling: The Overseas Journal of the British Broadcasting Corporation*, no. 176, 21 February 1943.
61. BBC Written Archives, Cavasham, R13/153/1.
62. The script for this production is available in Theatre Museum Collections, London.
63. Lahiri, S., 'South Asians in Post-Imperial Britain: Decolonisation and Imperial Legacy', in Ward (ed.), *British Culture and the End of Empire* (Manchester University Press: 2001), pp. 201–202.

Chapter 7: Migrating to the 'Mother Country', 1947–1980

1. There is quite an extensive literature which examines the South-Asian experience and pattern of post-war migration to Britain. Some of this literature covers South Asians in general and others look at the experience of different communities. For good examples of earlier writings, see Watson (ed.), *Between Two Cultures: Migrants and Minorities in*

Britain (Oxford: Blackwell, 1977) and R. Ballard (ed.), *Desh Pardesh: The South Asian Presence in Britain* (London: Hurst, 1994). For a most recent survey, see N. Ali, Kalra, V.S. and Sayyid, S., *A Postcolonial People: South Asians in Britain* (London: C. Hurst & Co., 2006). For single community studies, see A. Shaw, *A Pakistani Community in Britain* (Oxford: Blackwell 1988), A.W. Helweg, *Sikhs in England* (Delhi: Oxford University Press, 1980), S. Kalsi, *The Evolution of the Sikh Community in Britain: Religious and Social Change among the Sikhs of Leeds and Bradford* (Leeds: Department of Theology and Religious Studies, 1990) and V.S. Kalra, *From Textile Mills to Taxi Ranks: Experiences of Migration, Labour and Social Change* (Aldershot: Ashgate, 2000).

2. The evolution of early policies towards immigration and migration policies are discussed in great detail in R. Hansen, *Citizenship and Immigration in Post-War Britain: The Institutional Origins of a Multicultural Nation* (Oxford: Oxford University Press, 2000). For a contrasting approach, especially focusing on the 1948 British Nationality Act, see Paul, Kathleen, *Whitewashing Britain: Race and Citizenship in the Postwar Era* (New York: Cornell University Press, 1997).

3. For details see, C. Peach and Gale, R. (2003) Muslims, Hindus and Sikhs in the New Religious Landscape of England. *The Geographical Review*, 93(4): 469–490. (But, actually published in 2005).

4. Labour vouchers fell into different categories. These were issued by the Ministry of Labour under the Commonwealth Immigrants Act 1962 and 1969. The vouchers were issued in three categories: *Category A* for applications by employers in this country who have a specific job to offer to a particular Commonwealth citizen; *Category B* for applications by Commonwealth citizens without a specific job to come to, but with certain special qualifications (such as nurses, teachers, medical doctors) and *Category C* for all others.

5. Ballard, for instance, has pointed out that Jalandhar and Mirpur districts of India and Pakistan, respectively, provided the greatest numbers.

6. G.S. Aurora, *The New Frontiersmen: A Sociological Study of Indian Immigrants in the United Kingdom* (Bombay: Popular Prakashan, 1967) provides some fascinating details of lifestyles of earlier migrants.

7. This issue is discussed in more detail in the next chapter, but it may suffice to note here that Pakistani and Bangladeshi children were later arrivals relative to Indian children, and this may partially explain differential experience in outcomes.

8. This led to the emergence of the 'old' Indian diaspora. For details on this emergence, see, K. Jain, Ravindra, *Indian Communities Abroad: Themes and Literature* (New Delhi: Manohar, 1993) and N. Jayaram (ed.), *The Indian Diaspora: Dynamics of Migration* (New Delhi: Sage, 2004).

9. The academic work of Parminder Bhachu, *Twice Migrants* (London: Tavistock, 1985) and Avtar Brah, *Cartographies of Diaspora* (London: Routledge, 1996) poignantly capture the experiences of these 'twice migrants'.

10. Hansen (2000) provides a very comprehensive overview of the major debates in the framing of immigration legislation and changing meaning of British citizenship starting with the British Nationality Act of 1948 to the British Nationality Act, 1981.

11. Cabinet papers released by the Public Records Office on 1 January 2003 under the 30-year rule revealed that there was 'deep sense of alarm' over the expulsion of around 70,000 East African Asian-British passport holders. In September 1972, the airlift of 27,000 Ugandan Asians to Britain triggered a campaign by Enoch Powell, the right-wing Monday Club and the National Front to keep them out. Fearing a second wave of expulsion, by November serious consideration was being given to passing a bill in Parliament to strip East African Asians of their British nationality. The cabinet also instructed the Foreign Secretary at the time, Sir Alec Douglas-Home to deal 'with the threat of a substantial new influx by instituting some scheme of comprehensive resettlement on British territory other than the United Kingdom'. The Foreign Office began to look for a suitable island among

the remaining British possessions and considered Bermuda, Solomon Islands, Virgin Islands, Cayman Islands, Seychelles and even Falklands so that 'it can serve as a place of settlement for UK passport holders long enough to make it possible to admit them to Britain over a period of time under a voucher system'.

12. This word is used as in Margaret Thatcher's assertion in 1978 that Britain 'might be rather swamped by people of a different culture'.

13. The city of Leicester was one of the largest settlement areas for East African Asians and over time developed one of the largest ethnic minority populations at 35 percent and which is expected to exceed 50 percent by 2010. The city is often portrayed a model of civic multiculturalism by academic writers. For example see Steve Vertovec (1994) 'Multiculturalism, Multi-Asian, Multi-Muslim Leicester: Dimensions of Social Complexity, Ethnic Organisation and Local Interface', *Innovation: European Journal of Social Sciences*, 7(3): 259–276.

14. Vivid details of white perceptions are given by Avtar Brah (1979) 'Inter-generational and Inter-ethnic Perceptions: A Comparative Study of South Asian and English Adolescents and Their Parents in Southall, West London', PhD thesis, University of Bristol.

15. For dramatic details of the day's events, see Shivdeep Grewal (2003) 'Southall, Capital of the 1970s: Of Community Resistance and the Conjecture of April the 23rd, 1979', *International Journal of Punjab Studies*, 10(1, 2), January–December, pp. 77–111.

16. One of the earliest organisations, funded publicly as an independent educational charity in 1958, was the Institute of Race Relations (IRR). It began to carry out research, collect resources and publish widely on race relations not only in Britain but throughout the world and it has remained one of the most progressive and radical anti-racist bodies. Since 1991, IRR also keeps a record of racially (known or suspected) motivated murders.

17. Enoch Powell made his infamous speech in Birmingham in April 1968 where, towards the end of his speech he stated: 'As I look ahead, I am filled with foreboding; like the Roman, I seem to see the River Tiber foaming with much blood.' Many workers, especially in the London docklands, came out on strike in support but some also in opposition. This speech was seized upon by the National Front and other right-wing organisations to spread racist propaganda. Enoch Powell himself was sacked as Shadow Cabinet Minister by the Shadow Leader of the Opposition, Edward Heath. Following the 'race riots' in Brixton, Toxteth and Handsworth in the early 1980s, Powell is reported to have stated that his prediction had come true.

18. The front page of the *Coventry Evening Telegraph* of 11 February 1959 reported that 680 men had staged a walk-out strike at the Sterling Metals works in Nuneaton bringing the iron foundry to a standstill. Harry Urwin, Secretary of the Transport and General Worker's Union, blaming management style for the dispute, explained, 'At present there are many problems arising from up-grading and down-grading of workers, not only in relation to their nationality. The problem is aggravated by the fact that there is growing unemployment and that there has actually been redundancy in this department recently.' Spokesman for the management, however, emphasised the role of white worker hostility, arguing that the dispute started when, 'some core shop workers refused to operate core block machinery with Indian workers in the gang' after the Indian workers had been transferred there from another site.

19. A trend started by the annual Times Rich List, Asian newspapers such as *Eastern Eye* and *Asian Times* produce their own glossy annual Asian Rich Lists.

20. Details of religious places and organisations in Britain are given in P. Weller, *Religions in the UK: A Multi-faith Directory* (University of Derby: 1997).

21. The British School curriculum specifies the teaching of one foreign language in addition to English and traditionally the choice was always from a European language, in effect French or German. As Urdu, Bengali or Punjabi were labelled 'community languages', in fact inferior to European languages which were 'modern', there was no statutory

obligation on local education authorities to teach them during school hours. However, some authorities accommodated the request of parents and taught them, albeit only after school hours. South-Asian communities objected to the lack of choice of an Asian language on the mandatory curriculum because to them learning French or German did not make sense. This was a particular issue in schools where the overwhelming percentage of pupils may be of Pakistani or Bangladeshi origin. Inevitably, this forced many parents to send their children to supplementary night or weekend schools, although that was not necessarily their preferred choice.

22. The intractable Kashmir issue has its origins in the partition of India in 1947. This princely state – Jammu and Kashmir – had been ruled by a Hindu Dogra Maharajah despite the fact that the majority of the population was Muslim. Following some discontent at the time of partition and then after a popular uprising in the current Azad Kashmir region, the Maharajah signed a treaty of accession with India despite opposition from Muslims. Historians debate the circumstances and the legality of the accession. This accession was followed by a strong Indian military offensive which led to conflict with Pakistan. The UN Security Council intervened and passed a number of resolutions which left open the possibility of a UN-supervised plebiscite for Kashmiris to decide their own future. The state is now divided into two areas separated by the Line of Control. Pakistan controls what is currently known as Azad (Free) Kashmir and the Northern Area and India controlling the remaining area, including the region of Ladakh. Needless to say, there is continuing dispute about territorial boundaries, lack of plebiscite on self-determination and accusations and counter-accusations of cross-border terrorism. The Kashmir issue remains one of the long-running territorial disputes in UN history.

23. Darshan S. Tatla in his *The Sikh Diaspora: The Search for Statehood* (London: UCL Press, 1999) provides an excellent overview of the debates in the Punjabi vernacular press on the issue of Sikh militancy and the demand for Khalistan.

24. DeWitt John, *Indian Workers' Associations in Britain* (London: OUP, 1969), p. 47.

25. Ibid., p. 48.

26. Sasha Josephedis, 'Organisational Splits and Political Ideology in the Indian Workers Associations', in Werbner and Anwar (eds), *Black and Ethnic Leaderships* (London: Routledge, 1991).

27. Department of Education and Science, *Circular* 7/65 (London: HMSO, 1965).

28. M. Anwar and Bakhsh, Q. *British Muslims and State Policies* (Centre for Research in Ethnic Relations: University of Warwick, 2003).

29. For an evaluation, see Mark Halstead, *Education, Justice and Cultural Diversity: Examination of the Honeyford Affair,* 1984–85 (London: The Falmer Press, 1988).

30. Quoted in *Turban Trouble*, a Time magazine article of 29 August 1960 archived at http://www.sikhtimes.com/news_082960a.html (accessed 2 February 2007).

31. 'Sikh in Bus Row', *Express and Star*, 9 August 1967.

32. David Beetham, *Transport and Turbans: Comparative Study of Local Politics* (Institute of Race Relations: 1970).

33. Baldev Singh Chahal of High Wycome was a tireless campaigner and he enlisted the parliamentary support of Sydney Bidwell (MP for Ealing Southall) in lobbying for this Sikh cause. Bidwell reminded Parliament of the Anglo-Sikh military tradition where Sikhs were exempted from wearing normal headgear and the fact that Sikhs would lose access to employment opportunities as policemen, motorcycle couriers, Automobile Association or Royal Automobile Club engineers or other occupations where a helmet was a requirement if no exemption was granted.

34. For a discussion of this from a legal perspective, see 'Turban or Not Turban – That is the Question (Mandla *v.* Dowell Lee)', *Liverpool Law Review*, 5(1), 1983. The full

judgement is available at http://www.hrcr.org/safrica/equality/Mandla_DowellLee.htm (accessed 2 February 2007).

Chapter 8: The 1980s and After: From Adversity to Celebration

1. Jonathan Tinsley and Michael Jacobs (2006), 'Deprivation and Ethnicity in England: A Regional Perspective', *Regional Trends* 39.

2. Department for Education and Skills (2003), *Aiming High: Raising the Achievement of Minority Ethnic Pupils*, London: DfES.

3. GLA Economics (2005), *The Contribution of Asian-Owned Businesses to London's Economy*, Mayor of London, Greater London Authority, June. The term 'Asian' in this report is as used by United Nations, that is, it also includes business people from East Asia as well as West Asia.

4. Data taken from Bhikhu Parekh (1997), 'South Asians in Britain', *History Today* 47, September.

5. For an account of these global chains involving British Punjabi fashion entrepreneurs see Parminder Bhachu (2004), *Dangerous Designs: Asian Women Fashion the Diaspora Economies*, London: Routledge.

6. Gate Gourmet, a catering company that supplies in-flight meals to British Airways, dismissed 670 workers most of whom were Asian women, via a megaphone at Heathrow airport on 10 August 2005. The subsequent wildcat strike action and spontaneous show of solidarity by mostly Asian baggage handlers brought the airport to a standstill but the dispute could not be resolved quickly and led to financial hardship for some laid-off female workers with some having to seek help from the local gurdwara.

7. For details of economic change in Oldham see Virinder Kalra (2000), *From Textile Mills to Taxi Ranks: Experiences of Migration, Labour and Social Change*, Aldershot: Ashgate.

8. In the wake of the riots in some northern towns the government initiated a number of enquiries to identify their causes. Some of the most important ones, having a subsequent impact on government legislation included *Community Cohesion: A Report of the Independent Review Team*, chaired by Ted Cantle, London: Home Office, 2001; *One Oldham, One Future: Oldham Independent Review*, chaired by David Ritchie, 2001; *Community Pride Not Prejudice: Bradford Race Review Report*, chaired by Sir Herman Ouseley, 2001.

9. See Robert D. Putnam (2001), *The Collapse and Revival of American Community*, New York: Simon Schuster.

10. The three most important ones at the moment include the Council of Muslims, Hindu Forum of Britain and the Sikh Federation.

11. *India Today* (2004), 'Dream Merchants', an advertising feature on UK weddings, 30 August.

12. Marie Gillespie (2003), 'From Comic Asians to Asian Comics: *Goodness Gracious Me*, TV Comedy and Ethnicity', in Scriven and Roberts eds., *Group Identities on French and British Television*, Oxford: Bergham, pp. 93–108.

13. The adjectives used in describing the films are taken from various film critics.

14. Taken from Tara Arts website at www.tara-arts.com.

15. A large number of articles and book have appeared on this aspect of South-Asian culture, for example see, S. Sharma, Hutnyk, J. and Sharma, A. (eds) (1996), *Dis-Orienting Rhythms: The Politics of the New Asian Dance Music*, London: Zed Books. In 2002 we also saw the launch of the first dedicated academic journal, *South Asian Popular Culture* (Taylor Francis), which explores uses of popular cultures in South Asian diasporas and development of hybrid forms of traditional cultural practices.

16. For example during the colonial era, Kumar Shri Ranjisinhji, a Rajput prince, cricketer and statesman, made his debut for Sussex in 1895, went on in 1899 to captain the

English team on a tour of America playing fifteen test matches between 1896 and 1902 and achieving phenomenal popularity in Britain and abroad. For details see *Vanity Fair*, Issue No. 1504.

17. Many popular jokes circulate about the inability of Asians to play football. One went 'Why can't Asians play football? Because every time they get a corner, they open up a corner shop!'

18. The infamous Grunwick strike, involving a predominately 'twice migrant' South-Asian female workforce erupted during the summer of 1976 and lasted for nearly two years. This dispute, led by popular leader Mrs Jayaben Desai, brought into public eye the harsh working conditions of Asian women at the film-processing plant in Willesden, North West London, and challenged the British popular stereotypes of South-Asian women as 'docile, submissive, difficult to unionise and as exploitable cheap labour'.

19. Pnina Werbner (2002), *Imagined Diasporas among Manchester Muslims*, London: James Currey, p. 62.

20. *Yorkshire Post* 18 January 1989, quoted in Humayun Ansari (2004), *The Infidel Within: The History of Muslims in Britain*, 1800 *to the Present*, London: C. Hurst & Co., p. 233.

21. Werbner, p. 258.

22. The Khalistan movement, to fight for a separate homeland for the Sikhs in Punjab, started in the late 1970s but gained momentum after the army Operation Bluestar of June 1984. By the early 1990s it was largely crushed through a combined police-army operation.

23. Robert Booth (2005), 'Sikh Protestors Disrupt Wedding', *The Guardian*, 27 June.

24. *The Guardian* (2004), 'Playing with Fire', Leader, 21 December.

25. Tania Branigan (2004), 'Stars Sign Letter in Support of Playwright in Hiding', *The Guardian*, 23 December.

26. In a direct challenge to her opponents, Bhatti stated 'The Sikh heritage is one of valour and victory over adversity. Our ancestors were warriors with the finest minds who championed principles of equality and selflessness. I am proud to come from this remarkable people and do not fear the disdain of some, because I know my work is rooted in honesty and passion. I hope bridges can be built, but whether this prodigal daughter can ever return home remains to be seen.' Quoted from *The Guardian*, 'The Warrior is Fighting On', 13 January 2005.

27. Hindu Forum of Britain (2006), *Connecting British Hindus: An Enquiry into the Identity and Public Engagement of Hindus in Britain*, with foreword by Ruth Kelly, Secretary of State for Communities and Local Government, London.

28. This gallery can be accessed at www.hinduhumanrights.org/Gallery/Gallery2.html

29. The two major reports which exposed these organisations were: (i) Sabrang Communications Private Limited and The South Asia Citizens Web (2002), *The Foreign Exchange of Hate: IDRF and the American Funding of Hindutva*, 20 November. Accessed at stopfundinghate.org/sacw/index.html, October 2006, (ii) *In Bad Faith: British Charity and Hindu Extremism*, Awaaz – South Asia Watch Ltd, 2004. Accessed at http://www.awaazsaw.org/ibf/, November 2006.

30. Meghnad Desai (2005), 'Closure Threat to Artistic Freedom', *The Guardian*, 26 May.

31. Ibid.

32. *The Guardian* (2006), 'Re-instate Indian Art Exhibition', signed by Dr Chetan Bhatt, Goldsmiths College, London, Prof. Rajeswari Sunderrajan, Oxford University and Dr Priyamvada Gopal, Cambridge University, *Letters*, 30 May.

33. Moazzam Begg was picked up as a suspected Al Queda terrorist on the border between Afghanistan and Pakistan and imprisoned in Kandahar, Bagram and Guantanamo without charge for over three years. He was freed after a great deal of public pressure

on both the Blair and Bush governments to release him. His autobiography was published under the title *Enemy Combatant: My Imprisonment at Guantanamo, Bagram and Kandahar* (Free Press, London and The New Press, New York: 2006).

34. The media and right-wing reaction to the Parekh Report on *The Future of Multi-Cultural Britain* was indicative of hostility towards any workable solutions towards an effectively managed British multiculturalism.

Index